IMMIGRATION AND ILLEGAL ALIENS

BLESSING OR BURDEN?

IMMIGRATION AND ILLEGAL ALIENS

BLESSING OR BURDEN?

Mei Ling Rein

INFORMATION PLUS® REFERENCE SERIES
Formerly published by Information Plus, Wylie, Texas

GALE GROUP

THOMSON LEARNING

Detroit • New York • San Diego • San Francisco
Boston • New Haven, Conn. • Waterville, Maine
London • Munich

IMMIGRATION AND ILLEGAL ALIENS: BURDEN OR BLESSING?

Mei Ling Rein, *Author*

The Gale Group Staff:
Editorial: Ellice Engdahl, *Series Editor*; John F. McCoy, *Series Editor*; Charles B. Montney, *Series Editor*; Andrew Claps, *Series Associate Editor*; Jason M. Everett, *Series Associate Editor*; Michael T. Reade, *Series Associate Editor*; Heather Price, *Series Assistant Editor*; Teresa Elsey, *Editorial Assistant*; Debra M. Kirby, *Managing Editor*; Rita Runchock, *Managing Editor*

Image and Multimedia Content: Barbara J. Yarrow, *Manager, Imaging and Multimedia Content*; Robyn Young, *Project Manager, Imaging and Multimedia Content*

Indexing: Lynne Maday, *Indexing Specialist*

Permissions: Julie Juengling, *Permissions Specialist*; Maria Franklin, *Permissions Manager*

Product Design: Michelle DiMercurio, *Senior Art Director and Product Design Manager*; Michael Logusz, *Cover Art Designer*

Production: Evi Seoud, *Assistant Manager, Composition Purchasing and Electronic Prepress*; NeKita McKee, *Buyer*; Dorothy Maki, *Manufacturing Manager*

Cover photo © Digital Stock.

ISBN 0-7876-5103-6 (set)
ISBN 0-7876-5400-0 (this volume)
ISSN 1536-5263 (this volume)
Printed in the United States of America
10 9 8 7 6 5 4 3 2 1

TABLE OF CONTENTS

PREFACE

Immigration and Illegal Aliens: Burden or Blessing? is one of the latest volumes in the Information Plus Reference Series. Previously published by the Information Plus company of Wylie, Texas, the Information Plus Reference Series (and its companion set, the Information Plus Compact Series) became a Gale Group product when Gale and Information Plus merged in early 2000. Those of you familiar with the series as published by Information Plus will notice a few changes from the 1999 edition. Gale has adopted a new layout and style that we hope you will find easy to use. Other improvements include greatly expanded indexes in each book, and more descriptive tables of contents.

While some changes have been made to the design, the purpose of the Information Plus Reference Series remains the same. Each volume of the series presents the latest facts on a topic of pressing concern in modern American life. These topics include today's most controversial and most studied social issues: abortion, capital punishment, care for the elderly, crime, health care, the environment, immigration, minorities, social welfare, women, youth, and many more. Although written especially for the high school and undergraduate student, this series is an excellent resource for anyone in need of factual information on current affairs.

By presenting the facts, it is Gale's intention to provide its readers with everything they need to reach an informed opinion on current issues. To that end, there is a particular emphasis in this series on the presentation of scientific studies, surveys, and statistics. These data are generally presented in the form of tables, charts, and other graphics placed within the text of each book. Every graphic is directly referred to and carefully explained in the text. The source of each graphic is presented within the graphic itself. The data used in these graphics is drawn from the most reputable and reliable sources, in particular the various branches of the U.S. government and major independent polling organizations. Every effort has been made to secure the most recent information available. The reader should bear in mind that many major studies take years to conduct, and that additional years often pass before the data from these studies is made available to the public. Therefore, in many cases the most recent information available in 2001 is dated from 1998 or 1999. Older statistics are sometimes presented as well, if they are of particular interest and no more recent information exists.

Although statistics are a major focus of the Information Plus Reference Series, they are by no means its only content. Each book also presents the widely held positions and important ideas that shape how the book's subject is discussed in the United States. These positions are explained in detail and, where possible, in the words of their proponents. Some of the other material to be found in these books includes: historical background; descriptions of major events related to the subject; relevant laws and court cases; and examples of how these issues play out in American life. Some books also feature primary documents, or have pro and con debate sections giving the words and opinions of prominent Americans on both sides of a controversial topic. All material is presented in an even-handed and unbiased manner; the reader will never be encouraged to accept one view of an issue over another.

HOW TO USE THIS BOOK

America is known as a melting pot, a place where people of different nationalities, cultures, ethnicities, and races come have come together to form one nation. This process has been shaped by the influx of both legal immigrants and illegal aliens, and American attitudes toward both groups have varied over time. Legal immigrants have faced discrimination based on prevailing social and political trends; illegal aliens have been seen by some as undesirable, but may perform labor that many Americans are unwilling to do. This book discusses these and other legal, social, and political aspects of immigration and illegal aliens.

Immigration and Illegal Aliens: Burden or Blessing? consists of eight chapters and four appendices. Each of the first six chapters is devoted to a particular aspect of immigration and/or illegal aliens in the United States, while the last two chapters provide a pro and con debate of one particular visa issue. For a summary of the information covered in each chapter, please see the synopses provided in the Table of Contents at the front of the book. Chapters generally begin with an overview of the basic facts and background information on the chapter's topic, then proceed to examine sub-topics of particular interest. For example, Chapter 3: Current Immigration Statistics begins with a discussion of exactly how America defines an "immigrant." It then examines the different countries of origin of twentieth-century immigrants, the various types of immigration status and visas granted, the states and cities where most immigrants settle, and the naturalization process for immigrants desirous of permanent residence. Also covered are the different types of nonimmigrants (aliens admitted to the U.S. on a temporary basis) and aliens turned away. Readers can find their way through a chapter by looking for the section and sub-section headings, which are clearly set off from the text. Or, they can refer to the book's extensive index if they already know what they are looking for.

Statistical Information

The tables and figures featured throughout *Immigration and Illegal Aliens: Burden or Blessing?* will be of particular use to the reader in learning about this issue. These tables and figures represent an extensive collection of the most recent and important statistics on immigration and illegal aliens and related issues—for example, the amount of government benefits received by naturalized immigrants, the number of immigrants to the United States over various periods of time, the average education level of immigrants, and public opinion on the growth in the numbers of foreign-born U.S. residents. Gale believes that making this information available to the reader is the most important way in which we fulfill the goal of this book: to help readers understand the issues and controversies surrounding immigration and illegal aliens in the United States and reach their own conclusions.

Each table or figure has a unique identifier appearing above it, for ease of identification and reference. Titles for the tables and figures explain their purpose. At the end of each table or figure, the original source of the data is provided.

In order to help readers understand these often complicated statistics, all tables and figures are explained in the text. References in the text direct the reader to the relevant statistics. Furthermore, the contents of all tables and figures are fully indexed. Please see the opening section of the index at the back of this volume for a description of how to find tables and figures within it.

In addition to the main body text and images, *Immigration and Illegal Aliens: Burden or Blessing?* has four appendices. The first is a series of maps of different parts of the world. They are intended to help the reader identify the many places where immigrants to the United States come from. The Important Names and Addresses directory is the next appendix. Here the reader will find contact information for a number of government and private organizations that can provide information on immigration and illegal aliens. The second appendix is the Resources section, which can also assist the reader in conducting his or her own research. In this section, the author and editors of *Immigration and Illegal Aliens: Burden or Blessing?* describe some of the sources that were most useful during the compilation of this book. The final appendix is the index. It has been greatly expanded from previous editions, and should make it even easier to find specific topics in this book.

COMMENTS AND SUGGESTIONS

The editors of the Information Plus Reference Series welcome your feedback on *Immigration and Illegal Aliens: Burden or Blessing?* Please direct all correspondence to:

Editor
Information Plus Reference Series
27500 Drake Rd.
Farmington Hills, MI, 48331-3535

ACKNOWLEDGEMENTS

Photographs and illustrations appearing in Immigration and Illegal Aliens 2001 *were received from the following sources:*

Center for Immigration Studies. Illustration from *Measuring the Fallout: The Cost of the IRCA Amnesty after 10 Years* (1996). Reproduced by permission.

Congressional Research Service, The Library of Congress. Illustration from *Immigration of Agricultural Guest Workers: Policy, Trends, and Legislative Issues* (Washington, D.C., 2001).

Gallup Organization. Illustrations from *Americans Ambivalent About Immigrants and Gallup Poll Topics: A-Z: Immigration* (2001). Copyright © 2000 and 2001 by The Gallup Organization. All reproduced by the permission of The Gallup Organization.

The National Immigration Forum. Illustrations from *A Fiscal Portrait of the Newest Americans* (1996). Reproduced by permission.

Rand. Illustrations from *Immigration in a Changing Economy: California's Experience* (1990). Reproduced by permission.

Social Security Administration, Office of Research, Evaluation, and Statistics. Illustrations from *SSI Annual Statistical Report, 1999* (Baltimore, 2000).

University of Arizona, Institute for Local Government. Illustrations from *Illegal Immigrants in U.S.–Mexico Border Counties: The Costs of Law Enforcement, Criminal Justice, and Emergency Medical Services* (Tucson, 2001).

U.S. Bureau of the Census. Illustrations from *The Foreign-Born Population in the United States, March 2000. Current Population Reports, Series P20-534 (2001)*. Illustration titled "Foreign-born population and percent of total population, 1850–2000." Illustration adapted from Population Division, Population Projections Program data, accessed on April 6, 2001 at http://www. census.gov/population/projections/nation/ summary, from the files np-t5-b.pdf, np-t5-f. pdf, np-t5-g.pdf, and np-t5-h.pdf.

U.S. Department of Agriculture, Food and Nutrition Service. Illustration titled "State-Funded Food Programs For Legal Immigrants" (last modified February 26, 2001), accessed April 1, 2001 at http://www.fns. usda.gov/fsp/MENU/APPS/ELGIBILITY/ WorkandAliens/Statesprogram.htm.

U.S. Department of Health and Human Services, Administration for Children and Families, Office of Planning, Research and Evaluation. Illustrations from *Temporary Assistance for Needy Families (TANF) Program: Third Annual Report to Congress (2000)*.

U.S. Department of Health and Human Services, Office of Refugee Resettlement. Illustrations from *Making a Difference: FY 1998 Annual Report to the Congress* (2000).

U.S. Department of Justice, Immigration and Naturalization Service. Illustrations from *1998 Statistical Yearbook of the Immigration and Naturalization Service* (2000), *Border Patrol FY 2000 Recruiting and Hiring Report* (2000), *Estimates of the Unauthorized Immigrant Population residing in the United States: October 1996* (1996), and *Legal Immigration, Fiscal Year 1998* (1999). Illustrations titled "Border Patrol Sectors" and "Illegal Alien Resident Population" (1996). Illustration titled "Lists of Acceptable Documents" and I-9 form, accessed on April 6, 2001 at http://www.ins.usdoj.gov/ graphics/formsfee/forms/files/i-9.pdf. Illustration titled "Temporary Protected Status," accessed on April 6, 2001 at http://www.ins. usdoj.gov/graphics/services/tps_inter.htm. All reproduced by permission.

U.S. Department of Labor. Illustrations from *Developments in International Migration to the United States: 1999* (1999) and *Effects of the Immigration Reform and Control Act: Characteristics and Labor Market Behavior of the Legalized Population Five Years Following Legislation* (1992). All reproduced by permission.

U.S. Department of State, Bureau of Consular Affairs. Illustration from *Report of the Visa Office 1998* (2000).

U.S. Department of State, Bureau of Population, Refugees, and Migration. Illustrations titled "Refugee Admissions, FY 1975 to date" and "Refugee Admissions Ceilings, FY 2001" (last modified February 2001), accessed on April 2, 2001 at http://www. usinfo.state.gov/topical/global/refugees/ adover.html.

U.S. Departments of State, Justice, and Health and Human Services. Illustrations from *Proposed Refugee Admissions for Fiscal Year 2001: Report to Congress* (2000) and *U.S. Refugee Admissions for Fiscal Year 2000: Report to Congress* (1999).

U.S. General Accounting Office. Illustrations from *Alien Smuggling: Management and Operational Improvements Needed to Address Growing Problem* (2000), *H-1B Foreign Workers: Better Controls Needed to Help Employers and Protect Workers* (2000), *Illegal Aliens: Opportunities Exist to Improve the Expedited Removal Process* (2000), *Illegal Aliens: Significant Obstacles to Reducing Unauthorized Alien Employment Exist* (1998), *Illegal Immigration: Status of Southwest Border Strategy Implementation* (1999), *Welfare Reform: Many States Continued Some Federal or State Benefits for Immigrants,* and *Welfare Reform: Public Assistance Benefits Provided to Recently Naturalized Citizens* (1999). All reproduced by permission.

CHAPTER 1

IMMIGRATION—ALMOST 400 YEARS OF AMERICAN HISTORY

The New Colossus
Not like the brazen giant of Greek fame,
With conquering limbs astride from land to land;
Here at our sea-washed, sunset gates shall stand
A mighty woman with a torch, whose flame
Is the imprisoned lightning, and her name
Mother of Exiles. From her beacon-hand
Glows world-wide welcome; her mild eyes command
Th' air-bridged harbor that twin cities frame,
"Keep, ancient lands, your storied pomp," cries she
With silent lips. "Give me your tired, your poor,
Your huddled masses yearning to breathe free,
The wretched refuse of your teeming shore.
Send these, the homeless, tempest-tost to me,
I lift my lamp beside the golden door!"

— Sonnet by Emma Lazarus (1883) on a plaque on the pedestal of the Statue of Liberty

Since the founding of Jamestown, Virginia, in 1607, immigrants have been coming to America. Some have sought freedom to worship; others have come to be part of the "New World" with its promise of a classless, democratic form of government. Many came seeking fortune in the land of opportunity, while others were brought in chains to be slaves.

During the colonial period, many immigrants came as indentured servants, required to work for four to seven years to earn back the cost of their passage. Outside of New England, which was settled mainly by religious refugees, up to two-thirds of the population was made up of indentured servants, convicts from British jails, and slaves.

The continual ebb and flow of immigrants provided settlers along the Atlantic coast, pioneers to push the United States westward, builders for the Erie Canal and the transcontinental railways, pickers for cotton in the South and vegetables in the Southwest, laborers for American industrialization, and intellectuals in all fields. Together, these immigrants have built, in many Americans' opinions, the most diverse and exciting nation in the world.

In 1790, when the first census was taken, the United States had a Caucasian (white) population of 3,277,000—all immigrants or descendants of earlier seventeenth- and eighteenth-century arrivals. The population was estimated to be 75 percent British of Protestant origin (including Scottish immigrants), 8 percent German, 4 percent Irish Catholic, and the rest mainly of Dutch, French, or Spanish descent. In addition, approximately 500,000 black slaves and perhaps an equal number of Native Americans lived within the borders of the young country.

SEND ME YOUR TIRED, YOUR POOR

The predominant sentiment toward immigration in the country's first century was generally positive. Nevertheless, indications of a more negative attitude were beginning to appear in the already settled white population. In 1753 Benjamin Franklin warned about the Germans coming to Pennsylvania.

Those who came hither are generally the most stupid of their own nation, and as ignorance is often attended with great credulity, when knavery [dishonest dealing] would mislead it, and with suspicion, when honesty would set it right; and, few of the English understand the German language, and so cannot address them either from the press or pulpit, it is almost impossible to remove any prejudices they may entertain. Not being used to liberty they know not how to make modest use of it.

Officially, with the major exception of the 1798 Alien and Sedition Acts, the United States encouraged immigration. The Articles of Confederation (1778) made citizens of each state citizens of every other state. The U.S. Constitution (1788) makes only one direct reference to immigration (Article I, Section 9, Clause I), which provides that the "immigration or importation of such persons as any of the states now existing shall think proper to admit shall not be prohibited by Congress prior to the Year (1808), but a tax or duty may be imposed on such importation, not exceeding ten dollars for each person." Article I also notes, "Congress shall have power to establish a uniform rule of naturalization [granting of U.S. citizenship to a person after birth]...."

Alien and Sedition Acts of 1798

Early federal legislation established basic criteria for naturalization—residence for five years in the United States, good moral character, and loyalty to the U.S. Constitution. These requirements were based on state naturalization laws. In 1798, in anticipation of war with France, Congress enacted four laws collectively called the Alien and Sedition Acts. The first three laws, specifically aimed at French and Irish immigrants, lengthened the residence requirement for naturalization to 14 years, authorized the president to arrest and/or expel allegedly dangerous aliens, and allowed the imprisonment or deportation of alien enemy males age 14 and over in case of declared war or invasion.

The alien laws were also a political move by the Federalists intended to weaken the opposition Republican party, then the more liberal of the political parties and the party of most immigrants. These laws met much public opposition. After the Republican Thomas Jefferson won the election in 1800, the laws were allowed to lapse.

EFFECTS OF THE FIRST CENTURY OF IMMIGRATION

Since 1820, when immigration records were first kept, about 64.6 million people have come to America. In 1820 only 8,385 immigrants entered the United States. During the 1820s the number began to rise slowly, an increase that would generally continue, with ups and downs, for more than a century, until the Great Depression in 1929. (See Table 1.1.)

Immigration is generally caused by "push-pull factors"—influences that force people to leave their native countries and elements that attract them to the United States. Immigration in the mid-nineteenth century (the 1830s to the 1860s) originated mainly from Germany, Great Britain, and the Scandinavian countries.

As land in Europe became more and more scarce, tenant farmers were pushed off their farms into poverty. Many were driven from their native lands by unemployment caused by developing technology and famine. The potato famine was especially severe in Ireland in the 1840s. It forced the Irish to choose between starving to death or leaving their country. Many Germans were impelled to emigrate by the failure of the liberal German revolutions of the 1840s. They consequently looked to the New World, which desperately needed laborers and had cheap land. Moreover, they viewed America as a land of opportunity, freedom, and social mobility.

Immigrants from Germany and Ireland came in great numbers. Indeed, between 1851 and 1860 nearly a million each of German and Irish immigrants poured into the United States at an annual rate of well over 186,000 people. (See Table 1.2.) The poorer Irish tended to stay in the cities where they first arrived, usually Boston and New York, while the more well-to-do Germans moved on to the Midwest to settle in such cities as Cincinnati, Milwaukee, St. Louis, and Chicago.

This immigration led to intense anti-Irish and anti-German feelings, compounded by an aversion toward Roman Catholicism, a religion practiced by virtually all Irish and many Germans. It also triggered the creation of many secret nativist societies (groups supposedly intended to protect the interests of the native-born against immigrants) and the formation of a new political party, the Know-Nothings (the Order of the Star Spangled Banner).

For a brief time (1854 to 1855), the Know-Nothings were politically successful, electing several governors and controlling many legislatures. With the growing concern over slavery, these groups lost power, and virtually no immigration laws were passed during their brief tenure. In contrast the 1864 Republican party platform, written in part by Abraham Lincoln, stated, "Foreign immigration which in the past has added so much to the wealth, resources, and increase of power to this nation—the asylum of the oppressed of all nations—should be fostered and encouraged by a liberal and just policy."

Post-Civil War America was characterized by the rapid expansion of the Industrial Revolution, causing the nation's flourishing factories to need workers. At the same time, America's belief in its "Manifest Destiny" (the "right" of the United States to expand throughout the North American continent) pushed settlement westward. The number of arriving immigrants grew during the 1870s and 1880s, dominated by people from Germany, Great Britain, Ireland, Sweden, and Norway. (See Table 1.2.)

A DEVELOPING FEDERAL ROLE

The increasing numbers of immigrants prompted a belief that there should be some type of administrative order to this ever-growing influx. In 1864 Congress created a Commission of Immigration under the U.S. Department of State. A one-man office was set up in New York City to oversee immigration.

The 1870s witnessed a national interest in the importation of contract labor and the limiting of such immigration. In 1875, following a presidential message that focused on immigration and considerable congressional debate, Congress passed the first major piece of legislation restricting immigration by prohibiting convicts and prostitutes from entering the country (18 Stat. 477).

With the creation of the Commission of Immigration, the federal government began to play a central role in

TABLE 1.1

Immigration to the United States: Fiscal years 1820–1998

Year	Number	Year	Number	Year	Number	Year	Number
1820 - 1998	**64,599,082**						
1820	8,385						
1821-30	**143,439**	**1871-80**	**2,812,191**	**1921-30**	**4,107,209**	**1971-80**	**4,493,314**
1821	9,127	1871	321,350	1921	805,228	1971	370,478
1822	6,911	1872	404,806	1922	309,556	1972	384,685
1823	6,354	1873	459,803	1923	522,919	1973	400,063
1824	7,912	1874	313,339	1924	706,896	1974	394,861
1825	10,199	1875	227,498	1925	294,314	1975	386,194
1826	10,837	1876	169,986	1926	304,488	1976	398,613
						1976, TQ [1]	103,676
1827	18,875	1877	141,857	1927	335,175	1977	462,315
1828	27,382	1878	138,469	1928	307,255	1978	601,442
1829	22,520	1879	177,826	1929	279,678	1979	460,348
1830	23,322	1880	457,257	1930	241,700	1980	530,639
1831-40	**599,125**	**1881-90**	**5,246,613**	**1931-40**	**528,431**	**1981-90**	**7,338,062**
1831	22,633	1881	669,431	1931	97,139	1981	596,600
1832	60,482	1882	788,992	1932	35,576	1982	594,131
1833	58,640	1883	603,322	1933	23,068	1983	559,763
1834	65,365	1884	518,592	1934	29,470	1984	543,903
1835	45,374	1885	395,346	1935	34,956	1985	570,009
1836	76,242	1886	334,203	1936	36,329	1986	601,708
1837	79,340	1887	490,109	1937	50,244	1987	601,516
1838	38,914	1888	546,889	1938	67,895	1988	643,025
1839	68,069	1889	444,427	1939	82,998	1989	1,090,924
1840	84,066	1890	455,302	1940	70,756	1990	1,536,483
1841-50	**1,713,251**	**1891-1900**	**3,687,564**	**1941-50**	**1,035,039**	**1991-98**	**7,605,068**
1841	80,289	1891	560,319	1941	51,776	1991	1,827,167
1842	104,565	1892	579,663	1942	28,781	1992	973,977
1843	52,496	1893	439,730	1943	23,725	1993	904,292
1844	78,615	1894	285,631	1944	28,551	1994	804,416
1845	114,371	1895	258,536	1945	38,119	1995	720,461
1846	154,416	1896	343,267	1946	108,721	1996	915,900
1847	234,968	1897	230,832	1947	147,292	1997	798,378
1848	226,527	1898	229,299	1948	170,570	1998	660,477
1849	297,024	1899	311,715	1949	188,317		
1850	369,980	1900	448,572	1950	249,187		
1851-60	**2,598,214**	**1901-10**	**8,795,386**	**1951-60**	**2,515,479**		
1851	379,466	1901	487,918	1951	205,717		
1852	371,603	1902	648,743	1952	265,520		
1853	368,645	1903	857,046	1953	170,434		
1854	427,833	1904	812,870	1954	208,177		
1855	200,877	1905	1,026,499	1955	237,790		
1856	200,436	1906	1,100,735	1956	321,625		
1857	251,306	1907	1,285,349	1957	326,867		
1858	123,126	1908	782,870	1958	253,265		
1859	121,282	1909	751,786	1959	260,686		
1860	153,640	1910	1,041,570	1960	265,398		
1861-70	**2,314,824**	**1911-20**	**5,735,811**	**1961-70**	**3,321,677**		
1861	91,918	1911	878,587	1961	271,344		
1862	91,985	1912	838,172	1962	283,763		
1863	176,282	1913	1,197,892	1963	306,260		
1864	193,418	1914	1,218,480	1964	292,248		
1865	248,120	1915	326,700	1965	296,697		
1866	318,568	1916	298,826	1966	323,040		
1867	315,722	1917	295,403	1967	361,972		
1868	138,840	1918	110,618	1968	454,448		
1869	352,768	1919	141,132	1969	358,579		
1870	387,203	1920	430,001	1970	373,326		

[1]Transition quarter, July 1 through September 30, 1976.

NOTE: The numbers shown are as follows: from 1820-67, figures represent alien passengers arrived at seaports; from 1868-92 and 1895-97, immigrant aliens arrived; from 1892-94 and 1898-1998, immigrant aliens admitted for permanent residence. From 1892-1903, aliens entering by cabin class were not counted as immigrants. Land arrivals were not completely enumerated until 1908.

SOURCE: "Table 1. Immigration to the United States: Fiscal Years 1820–1998," in *1998 Statistical Yearbook of the Immigration and Naturalization Service.* U.S. Department of Justice, Immigration and Naturalization Service: Washington, D.C., November 2000

TABLE 1.2

Immigration by region and selected country of last residence, 1820–1998

Region and country of last residence[1]	1820	1821–30	1831–40	1841–50	1851–60	1861–70	1871–80	1881–90
All countries	8,385	143,439	599,125	1,713,251	2,598,214	2,314,824	2,812,191	5,246,613
Europe	7,690	98,797	495,681	1,597,442	2,452,577	2,065,141	2,271,925	4,735,484
Austria-Hungary	[2]	[2]	[2]	[2]	[2]	7,800	72,969	353,719
Austria	[2]	[2]	[2]	[2]	[2]	7,124[3]	63,009	226,038
Hungary	[2]	[2]	[2]	[2]	[2]	484[3]	9,960	127,681
Belgium	1	27	22	5,074	4,738	6,734	7,221	20,177
Czechoslovakia	[4]	[4]	[4]	[4]	[4]	[4]	[4]	[4]
Denmark	20	169	1,063	539	3,749	17,094	31,771	88,132
France	371	8,497	45,575	77,262	76,358	35,986	72,206	50,464
Germany	968	6,761	152,454	434,626	951,667	787,468	718,182	1,452,970
Greece	—	20	49	16	31	72	210	2,308
Ireland[5]	3,614	50,724	207,381	780,719	914,119	435,778	436,871	655,482
Italy	30	409	2,253	1,870	9,231	11,725	55,759	307,309
Netherlands	49	1,078	1,412	8,251	10,789	9,102	16,541	53,701
Norway-Sweden	3	91	1,201	13,903	20,931	109,298	211,245	568,362
Norway	[6]	[6]	[6]	[6]	[6]	[6]	95,323	176,586
Sweden	[6]	[6]	[6]	[6]	[6]	[6]	115,922	391,776
Poland	5	16	369	105	1,164	2,027	12,970	51,806
Portugal	35	145	829	550	1,055	2,658	14,082	16,978
Romania	[7]	[7]	[7]	[7]	[7]	[7]	11[7]	6,348
Soviet Union	14	75	277	551	457	2,512	39,284	213,282
Spain	139	2,477	2,125	2,209	9,298	6,697	5,266	4,419
Switzerland	31	3,226	4,821	4,644	25,011	23,286	28,293	81,988
United Kingdom[5][8]	2,410	25,079	75,810	267,044	423,974	606,896	548,043	807,357
Yugoslavia	[9]	[9]	[9]	[9]	[9]	[9]	[9]	[9]
Other Europe	—	3	40	79	5	8	1,001	682
Asia	6	30	55	141	41,538	64,759	124,160	69,942
China[10]	1	2	8	35	41,397	64,301	123,201	61,711
Hong Kong	[11]	[11]	[11]	[11]	[11]	[11]	[11]	[11]
India	1	8	39	36	43	69	163	269
Iran	[12]	[12]	[12]	[12]	[12]	[12]	[12]	[12]
Israel	[13]	[13]	[13]	[13]	[13]	[13]	[13]	[13]
Japan	[14]	[14]	[14]	[14]	[14]	186	149	2,270
Korea	[15]	[15]	[15]	[15]	[15]	[15]	[15]	[15]
Philippines	[16]	[16]	[16]	[16]	[16]	[16]	[16]	[16]
Turkey	1	20	7	59	83	131	404	3,782
Vietnam	[11]	[11]	[11]	[11]	[11]	[11]	[11]	[11]
Other Asia	3	—	1	11	15	72	243	1,910
America	387	11,564	33,424	62,469	74,720	166,607	404,044	426,967
Canada & Newfoundland[17][18]	209	2,277	13,624	41,723	59,309	153,878	383,640	393,304
Mexico[18]	1	4,817	6,599	3,271	3,078	2,191	5,162	1,913[19]
Caribbean	164	3,834	12,301	13,528	10,660	9,046	13,957	29,042
Cuba	[12]	[12]	[12]	[12]	[12]	[12]	[12]	[12]
Dominican Republic	[20]	[20]	[20]	[20]	[20]	[20]	[20]	[20]
Haiti	[20]	[20]	[20]	[20]	[20]	[20]	[20]	[20]
Jamaica	[21]	[21]	[21]	[21]	[21]	[21]	[21]	[21]
Other Caribbean	164	3,834	12,301	13,528	10,660	9,046	13,957	29,042
Central America	2	105	44	368	449	95	157	404
El Salvador	[20]	[20]	[20]	[20]	[20]	[20]	[20]	[20]
Other Central America	2	105	44	368	449	95	157	404
South America	11	531	856	3,579	1,224	1,397	1,128	2,304
Argentina	[20]	[20]	[20]	[20]	[20]	[20]	[20]	[20]
Colombia	[20]	[20]	[20]	[20]	[20]	[20]	[20]	[20]
Ecuador	[20]	[20]	[20]	[20]	[20]	[20]	[20]	[20]
Other South America	11	531	856	3,579	1,224	1,397	1,128	2,304
Other America	[22]	[22]	[22]	[22]	[22]	[22]	[22]	[22]
Africa	1	16	54	55	210	312	358	857
Oceania	1	2	9	29	158	214	10,914	12,574
Not specified[22]	300	33,030	69,902	53,115	29,011	17,791	790	789

immigration, which had been traditionally handled by the states. Court decisions beginning in 1849 strengthened the federal government's role, limiting the states' role in regulating immigration. Finally, in 1876 the Supreme Court, in *Henderson v. Mayor of the City of New York* (92 U.S. 259), ruled that the immigration laws of New York, California, and Louisiana were unconstitutional. This ended the states' right to regulate immigration and exclude undesirable aliens. From then on Congress and the federal government would have complete responsibility for immigration.

In 1882 Congress passed the first general immigration law (22 Stat. 214), establishing a centralized immigration administration under the Secretary of the

TABLE 1.2

Immigration by region and selected country of last residence, 1820–1998 [CONTINUED]

Region and country of last residence [1]	1891 – 1900	1901 – 10	1911 – 20	1921 – 30	1931 – 40	1941 – 50	1951 – 60	1961 – 70
All countries	3,687,564	8,795,386	5,735,811	4,107,209	528,431	1,035,039	2,515,479	3,321,677
Europe	3,555,352	8,056,040	4,321,887	2,463,194	347,566	621,147	1,325,727	1,123,492
Austria-Hungary	592,707[23]	2,145,266[23]	896,342[23]	63,548	11,424	28,329	103,743	26,022
Austria	234,081[3]	668,209[3]	453,649	32,868	3,563[24]	24,860[24]	67,106	20,621
Hungary	181,288[3]	808,511[3]	442,693	30,680	7,861	3,469	36,637	5,401
Belgium	18,167	41,635	33,746	15,846	4,817	12,189	18,575	9,192
Czechoslovakia	[4]	[4]	3,426[4]	102,194	14,393	8,347	918	3,273
Denmark	50,231	65,285	41,983	32,430	2,559	5,393	10,984	9,201
France	30,770	73,379	61,897	49,610	12,623	38,809	51,121	45,237
Germany	505,152[23]	341,498[23]	143,945[23]	412,202	114,058[24]	226,578[24]	477,765	190,796
Greece	15,979	167,519	184,201	51,084	9,119	8,973	47,608	85,969
Ireland [5]	388,416	339,065	146,181	211,234	10,973	19,789	48,362	32,966
Italy	651,893	2,045,877	1,109,524	455,315	68,028	57,661	185,491	214,111
Netherlands	26,758	48,262	43,718	26,948	7,150	14,860	52,277	30,606
Norway-Sweden	321,281	440,039	161,469	165,780	8,700	20,765	44,632	32,600
Norway	95,015	190,505	66,395	68,531	4,740	10,100	22,935	15,484
Sweden	226,266	249,534	95,074	97,249	3,960	10,665	21,697	17,116
Poland	96,720[23]	[23]	4,813[23]	227,734	17,026	7,571	9,985	53,539
Portugal	27,508	69,149	89,732	29,994	3,329	7,423	19,588	76,065
Romania	12,750	53,008	13,311	67,646	3,871	1,076	1,039	2,531
Soviet Union	505,290[23]	1,597,306[23]	921,201[23]	61,742	1,370	571	671	2,465
Spain	8,731	27,935	68,611	28,958	3,258	2,898	7,894	44,659
Switzerland	31,179	34,922	23,091	29,676	5,512	10,547	17,675	18,453
United Kingdom [5][8]	271,538	525,950	341,408	339,570	31,572	139,306	202,824	213,822
Yugoslavia	[9]	[9]	1,888[9]	49,064	5,835	1,576	8,225	20,381
Other Europe	282	39,945	31,400	42,619	11,949	8,486	16,350	11,604
Asia	74,862	323,543	247,236	112,059	16,595	37,028	153,249	427,642
China [10]	14,799	20,605	21,278	29,907	4,928	16,709	9,657	34,764
Hong Kong	[11]	[11]	[11]	[11]	[11]	[11]	15,541[11]	75,007
India	68	4,713	2,082	1,886	496	1,761	1,973	27,189
Iran	[12]	[12]	[12]	241[12]	195	1,380	3,388	10,339
Israel	[13]	[13]	[13]	[13]	[13]	476[13]	25,476	29,602
Japan	25,942	129,797	83,837	33,462	1,948	1,555	46,250	39,988
Korea	[15]	[15]	[15]	[15]		107[15]	6,231	34,526
Philippines	[16]	[16]	[16]	[16]	528[16]	4,691	19,307	98,376
Turkey	30,425	157,369	134,066	33,824	1,065	798	3,519	10,142
Vietnam	[11]	[11]	[11]	[11]	[11]	[11]	335[11]	4,340
Other Asia	3,628	11,059	5,973	12,739	7,435	9,551	21,572	63,369
America	38,972	361,888	1,143,671	1,516,716	160,037	354,804	996,944	1,716,374
Canada & Newfoundland [17][18]	3,311	179,226	742,185	924,515	108,527	171,718	377,952	413,310
Mexico [18]	971[19]	49,642	219,004	459,287	22,319	60,589	299,811	453,937
Caribbean	33,066	107,548	123,424	74,899	15,502	49,725	123,091	470,213
Cuba	[12]	[12]	[12]	15,901[12]	9,571	26,313	78,948	208,536
Dominican Republic	[20]	[20]	[20]	[20]	1,150[20]	5,627	9,897	93,292
Haiti	[20]	[20]	[20]	[20]	191[20]	911	4,442	34,499
Jamaica	[21]	[21]	[21]	[21]	[21]	[21]	8,869[21]	74,906
Other Caribbean	33,066	107,548	123,424	58,998	4,590	16,874	20,935[21]	58,980
Central America	549	8,192	17,159	15,769	5,861	21,665	44,751	101,330
El Salvador	[20]	[20]	[20]	[20]	673[20]	5,132	5,895	14,992
Other Central America	549	8,192	17,159	15,769	5,188	16,533	38,856	86,338
South America	1,075	17,280	41,899	42,215	7,803	21,831	91,628	257,940
Argentina	[20]	[20]	[20]	[20]	1,349[20]	3,338	19,486	49,721
Colombia	[20]	[20]	[20]	[20]	1,223[20]	3,858	18,048	72,028
Ecuador	[20]	[20]	[20]	[20]	337[20]	2,417	9,841	36,780
Other South America	1,075	17,280	41,899	42,215	4,894	12,218	44,253	99,411
Other America	[22]	[22]	[22]	31[22]	25	29,276	59,711	19,644
Africa	350	7,368	8,443	6,286	1,750	7,367	14,092	28,954
Oceania	3,965	13,024	13,427	8,726	2,483	14,551	12,976	25,122
Not specified [22]	14,063	33,523[25]	1,147	228	—	142	12,491	93

Treasury. The law also allowed the exclusion of immigrants convicted of political offenses, the mentally retarded, and persons thought likely to end up on welfare.

Asian Exclusion

Before the discovery of gold in California in 1849, very few Asians (fewer than 200, including Asian Indians) came to the United States. Between 1849 and 1852 large numbers of Asian immigrants began arriving in the United States. These early arrivals came mostly from south China, spurred on by economic depression, famine, war, and flooding, in addition to the lure of making fortunes by panning for gold in the California hills. Thousands were brought over to work on the railroads and in the mines, in construction and manufacturing, or on the farms. Many became domestic servants or opened laundries or restaurants. Between 1851

TABLE 1.2

Immigration by region and selected country of last residence, 1820–1998 [CONTINUED]

Region and country of last residence [1]	1971 — 80	1981 — 90	1991 — 94	1995	1996	1997	1998	Total 179 years, 1820-1998
All countries	**4,493,314**	**7,338,062**	**4,509,852**	**720,461**	**915,900**	**798,378**	**660,477**	**64,599,082**
Europe	**800,368**	**761,550**	**631,921**	**132,914**	**151,898**	**122,358**	**92,911**	**38,233,062**
Austria-Hungary	16,028	24,885	13,426	2,190	2,325	1,964	1,435	4,364,122
Austria	9,478	18,340	9,600	1,340	1,182	1,044	610	1,842,722[3]
Hungary	6,550	6,545	3,826	850	1,143	920	825	1,675,324[3]
Belgium	5,329	7,066	3,055	694	802	633	557	216,297
Czechoslovakia	6,023	7,227	3,050	1,057	1,299	1,169	931	153,307
Denmark	4,439	5,370	2,799	588	795	507	447	375,548
France	25,069	32,353	16,021	3,178	3,896	3,007	2,961	816,650
Germany	74,414	91,961	42,667	7,896	8,365	6,941	6,923	7,156,257
Greece	92,369	38,377	10,096	2,404	2,394	1,483	1,183	721,464
Ireland [5]	11,490	31,969	46,564	4,851	1,611	932	907	4,779,998
Italy	129,368	67,254	48,841	2,594	2,755	2,190	1,966	5,431,454
Netherlands	10,492	12,238	5,891	1,284	1,553	1,197	1,036	385,193
Norway-Sweden	10,472	15,182	8,149	1,607	2,015	1,517	1,344	2,160,586
Norway	3,941	4,164	2,572	465	552	391	327	758,026[6]
Sweden	6,531	11,018	5,577	1,142	1,463	1,126	1,017	1,257,133[6]
Poland	37,234	83,252	96,482	13,570	15,504	11,729	8,202	751,823
Portugal	101,710	40,431	11,588	2,611	3,024	1,690	1,523	521,697
Romania	12,393	30,857	19,142	4,565	5,449	5,276	4,833	244,106
Soviet Union	38,961	57,677	193,077	54,133	61,895	48,238	28,984	3,830,033
Spain	39,141	20,433	8,251	1,664	1,970	1,607	1,185	299,825
Switzerland	8,235	8,849	4,752	1,119	1,344	1,302	1,090	369,046
United Kingdom [5][8]	137,374	159,173	76,780	14,207	15,564	11,950	10,170	5,247,821
Yugoslavia	30,540	18,762	11,507	7,828	10,755	9,913	7,264	183,538
Other Europe	9,287	8,234	9,783	4,874	8,583	9,113	9,970	224,297
Asia	**1,588,178**	**2,738,157**	**1,314,833**	**259,984**	**300,574**	**258,561**	**212,799**	**8,365,931**
China [10]	124,326	346,747	170,191	41,112	50,981	44,356	41,034	1,262,050
Hong Kong	113,467	98,215	58,676	10,699	11,319	7,974	7,379	398,277[11]
India	164,134	250,786	149,374	33,060	42,819	36,092	34,288	751,349
Iran	45,136	116,172	32,828	5,646	7,299	6,291	4,945	233,860[12]
Israel	37,713	44,273	20,252	3,188	4,029	2,951	2,546	170,506[13]
Japan	49,775	47,085	31,982	5,556	6,617	5,640	5,647	517,686[14]
Korea	267,638	333,746	76,901	15,053	17,380	13,626	13,691	778,899[15]
Philippines	354,987	548,764	248,466	49,696	54,588	47,842	33,176	1,460,421[16]
Turkey	13,399	23,233	14,036	4,806	5,573	4,596	4,016	445,354
Vietnam	172,820	280,782	110,300	37,764	39,922	37,121	16,534	699,918[11]
Other Asia	244,783	648,354	401,827	53,404	60,047	52,072	49,543	1,647,611
America	**1,982,735**	**3,615,225**	**2,429,423**	**282,270**	**407,813**	**359,619**	**298,156**	**16,844,829**
Canada & Newfoundland [17][18]	169,939	156,938	87,613	18,117	21,751	15,788	14,295	4,453,149
Mexico [18]	640,294	1,655,843	1,400,108	90,045	163,743	146,680	130,661	5,819,966
Caribbean	**741,126**	**872,051**	**436,471**	**96,021**	**115,991**	**101,095**	**72,948**	**3,525,703**
Cuba	264,863	144,578	47,556	17,661	26,166	29,913	15,415	885,421[12]
Dominican Republic	148,135	252,035	180,055	38,493	36,284	24,966	20,267	810,201[20]
Haiti	56,335	138,379	80,867	13,872	18,185	14,941	13,316	375,938[20]
Jamaica	137,577	208,148	71,927	16,061	18,732	17,585	14,819	568,624[21]
Other Caribbean	134,216	128,911	56,066	9,934	16,624	13,690	9,131	885,519
Central America	**134,640**	**468,088**	**267,591**	**32,020**	**44,336**	**43,451**	**35,368**	**1,242,394**
El Salvador	34,436	213,539	117,463	11,670	17,847	17,741	14,329	453,717[20]
Other Central America	100,204	254,549	150,128	20,350	26,489	25,710	21,039	788,677
South America	**295,741**	**461,847**	**237,615**	**46,063**	**61,990**	**52,600**	**44,884**	**1,693,441**
Argentina	29,897	27,327	13,760	2,239	2,878	2,055	1,649	153,699[20]
Colombia	77,347	122,849	55,407	10,641	14,078	12,795	11,618	399,892[20]
Ecuador	50,077	56,315	30,627	6,453	8,348	7,763	6,840	215,798[20]
Other South America	138,420	255,356	137,821	26,730	36,686	29,987	24,777	924,052
Other America	995	458	25	4	2	5	—	110,176
Africa	**80,779**	**176,893**	**108,645**	**39,818**	**49,605**	**44,668**	**37,494**	**614,375**
Oceania	**41,242**	**45,205**	**24,846**	**5,472**	**6,008**	**4,855**	**4,403**	**250,206**
Not specified [22]	12	1,032	184	3	2	8,317	14,714	290,679

and 1880 nearly a quarter of a million immigrants arrived from China, while only a few thousand arrived from other Asian countries. (See Table 1.2.)

Some people became alarmed by this increase in Chinese immigration. Fueled by a combination of racism and fears among American-born workers that employers were bringing over foreign workers to replace them and keep unskilled wages low, public opinion began to call for restrictions on Chinese immigration.

In 1882 Congress passed the Chinese Exclusion Act (22 Stat. 58), which prohibited further immigration of Chinese laborers to the United States for ten years.

1 Data for years prior to 1906 relate to country whence alien came; data from 1906-79 and 1984-98 are for country of last permanent residence; and data for 1980-83 refer to country of birth. Because of changes in boundaries, changes in lists of countries, and lack of data for specified countries for various periods, data for certain countries, especially for the total period 1820-1998, are not comparable throughout. Data for specified countries are included with countries to which they belonged prior to World War I.
2 Data for Austria and Hungary not reported until 1861.
3 Data for Austria and Hungary not reported separately for all years during the period.
4 No data available for Czechoslovakia until 1920.
5 Prior to 1926, data for Northern Ireland included in Ireland.
6 Data for Norway and Sweden not reported separately until 1871.
7 No data available for Romania until 1880.
8 Since 1925, data for United Kingdom refer to England, Scotland, Wales, and Northern Ireland.
9 In 1920, a separate enumeration was made for the Kingdom of Serbs, Croats, and Slovenes. Since 1922, the Serb, Croat, and Slovene Kingdom recorded as Yugoslavia.
10 Beginning in 1957, China includes Taiwan. As of January 1, 1979, the United States has recognized the People's Republic of China.
11 Data not reported separately until 1952.
12 Data not reported separately until 1925.
13 Data not reported separately until 1949.
14 No data available for Japan until 1861.
15 Data not reported separately until 1948.
16 Prior to 1934, Philippines recorded as insular travel.
17 Prior to 1920, Canada and Newfoundland recorded as British North America. From 1820-98, figures include all British North America possessions.
18 Land arrivals not completely enumerated until 1908.
19 No data available for Mexico from 1886-94.
20 Data not reported separately until 1932.
21 Data for Jamaica not collected until 1953. In prior years, consolidated under British West Indies, which is included in "Other Caribbean."
22 Included in countries "Not specified" until 1925.
23 From 1899-1919, data for Poland included in Austria-Hungary, Germany, and the Soviet Union.
24 From 1938-45, data for Austria included in Germany.
25 Includes 32,897 persons returning in 1906 to their homes in the United States.
NOTE: From 1820-67, figures represent alien passengers arrived at seaports; from 1868-91 and 1895-97, immigrant aliens arrived; from 1892-94 and 1898-1998, immigrant aliens admitted for permanent residence. From 1892-1903, aliens entering by cabin class were not counted as immigrants. Land arrivals were not completely enumerated until 1908. For this table, fiscal year 1843 covers 9 months ending September 1843; fiscal years 1832 and 1850 cover 15 months ending December 31 of the respective years; and fiscal year 1868 covers 6 months ending June 30, 1868.
— Represents zero.

SOURCE: "Table 2. Immigration by region and selected country of last residence, fiscal years 1820–1998," in *1998 Statistical Yearbook of the Immigration and Naturalization Service*. U.S. Department of Justice, Immigration and Naturalization Service: Washington, D.C., November 2000

Exceptions included teachers, diplomats, students, merchants, and tourists. The Chinese Exclusion Act was the first time the United States barred immigration of a national group. The law also prohibited Chinese immigrants in the United States from becoming naturalized American citizens. Fewer than 15,000 arrived during the last decade of the nineteenth century.

Four other laws that prohibited the immigration of Chinese laborers followed the Chinese Exclusion Act. The 1892 Geary Act (27 Stat. 25) extended the Chinese Exclusion Act for 10 more years. In cases brought before the U.S. Supreme Court, the Court upheld the constitutionality of these two laws. The Immigration Act of 1904 (33 Stat. 428) made the Chinese exclusion laws permanent. Under the Immigration Act of 1917 (39 Stat. 874), the United States suspended the immigration of laborers from almost all Asian countries. The Chinese exclusion laws remained in effect until 1943. During World War II, the United States and China became allies against the Japanese in Asia. As a gesture of goodwill, on December 13, 1943, President Franklin D. Roosevelt signed the Act to Repeal the Chinese Exclusion Acts, to Establish Quotas, and for Other Purposes (57 Stat. 600-1). The law lifted the ban on naturalization of Chinese nationals.

Congress established a yearly quota of 105 Chinese immigrants to be admitted to the United States.

Until the passage of the Chinese Exclusion Act, Japanese immigration was hardly noticeable, with the total flow at 335 between 1861 and 1880. Japanese immigration was not included in the Chinese Exclusion Act; and, consequently, Japanese laborers were brought in to replace Chinese workers. Japanese immigration increased from 2,270 in the 1880s to almost 130,000 during the first decade of the twentieth century. (See Table 1.2.) Japanese workers labored in the rapidly expanding sugarcane plantations in Hawaii and the fruit and vegetable farms of California.

The same anti-Asian attitudes that had led to the Chinese Exclusion Act culminated in President Theodore Roosevelt's "Gentleman's Agreement" of 1907, which cut the flow of Japanese immigration to a trickle. This anti-Asian attitude resurfaced a generation later in the National Origins Act (Immigration Act of 1924). Although aimed primarily against immigrants from southern and eastern Europe, the law included severe restrictions on Asian immigration, cutting the quotas from 19,245 in 1924 to only 3,527 in 1925. Asian immigration would not be permitted to increase until after World War II.

Greater Government Control

With the exception of Asian immigration, the federal government's main concern was not to restrict but to gain administrative control of immigration. The United States was economically booming and needed more workers to continue growing. In 1890 the federal government took over administration of immigration in the port of New York from the state authorities.

The following year (1891) the federal government assumed total control of immigration through the creation of the Office of Immigration under the Superintendent of Immigration. The 1891 act (26 Stat. 1084) also authorized the establishment of the U.S. Bureau of Immigration under the Treasury Department. This first comprehensive immigration law added to the list of inadmissible persons those suffering from certain contagious diseases, polygamists, and aliens convicted of minor crimes. The law also prohibited using advertisements to encourage immigration. On January 2, 1892, a new federal immigration station began operating on Ellis Island in New York. In 1895 the Office of Immigration became the Bureau of Immigration under the Commissioner-General of Immigration.

In 1903 the Bureau of Immigration was transferred to the newly created Department of Commerce and Labor. The Naturalization Act of 1906 (34 Stat. 596) consolidated the immigration and naturalization functions of the federal government, renaming the bureau as the Bureau of Immigration and Naturalization. When the Department of Labor and Commerce was separated into two cabinet departments in 1913, two bureaus were formed—the Bureau of Immigration and the Bureau of Naturalization. In 1933 the two bureaus were reunited as the Immigration and Naturalization Service.

A MILLION A YEAR

In the 1890s the origins of those arriving in America began to change. Fewer immigrants came from northern Europe, and the "new immigration" from southern and eastern Europe began. Of the 8.1 million European immigrants who arrived between 1901 and 1910, 72 percent came from Italy, the Soviet Union, and Austria-Hungary. (See Table 1.2.) Between 1880 and 1914, two million eastern European Jews came to the United States. They generally were not agricultural laborers but skilled artisans and tradespeople.

At the turn of the century the nation's already high immigration rate increased dramatically, doubling between 1902 and 1907. Immigration reached a million per year in 1905, 1906, 1907, 1910, 1913, and 1914 but declined during World War I (1914–1918). (See Table 1.1.) Many Americans were worried about the growing influx of immigrants, whose customs were unfamiliar to the majority of the native population. Anti-Catholic, anti-

political radicalism (usually expressed as socialism), and racist movements became more prevalent.

In 1907 Congress passed legislation (34 Stat. 898) barring the immigration of "imbeciles," feeble-minded persons, those with physical or mental defects that might prevent them from earning a living, persons with tuberculosis, children unaccompanied by their parents, persons convicted of crimes involving moral turpitude (depravity), and women coming to the United States for immoral purposes (prostitution). These restrictions, however, excluded only 1 percent of arrivals.

The 1907 law also officially classified the arriving aliens as immigrants and nonimmigrants, requiring arrivals to declare their intention of permanent or temporary stay in the United States. The law further authorized the president to refuse admission to persons he considered harmful to the labor conditions in the nation. This legislation was specifically aimed at the immigration of Japanese laborers.

THE "NEW IMMIGRANTS"

The "New Immigrants" crowded into the nation's cities in, most notably, five states—New York, Pennsylvania, Massachusetts, Illinois, and New Jersey. By the time World War I began, one-fourth of all Philadelphians and one-third of all Bostonians and Chicagoans were persons who had been born in another country. In New York four of five residents were of foreign birth or parentage. Municipal services often failed to meet the immigrants' increasing needs, enabling corrupt political bosses to build empires by offering minimal assistance to needy newcomers. The "New Immigrants" did not actually create these problems but magnified those that already existed.

The terrible conditions of the overcrowded cities, heavily populated with new immigrants, only added to already existing perceptions of racial differences. At this time race generally included what we now consider ethnic groups. Italians, Irish, and Jews, for example, were looked upon as races and were not considered "white" by most Anglo-Americans. Racism even gained "scientific" justification as respected journals published articles claiming to "scientifically" prove the racial superiority of some groups and the inferiority of others.

This attitude was reflected in the 1910 *Annual Report* of the Bureau of Immigration. The bureau observed that "thoughtful people are more and more feeling that the immigration problem, which has been growing in importance, ... take[s] on additional seriousness from the fact that too many of the aliens [who] entered in recent years belong to races differing radically from the Teutonic and Celtic stocks and that the overstraining of our powers of assimilation is a real menace."

Such concerns continued to be expressed in Bureau of Immigration annual reports through 1916. These reports proposed that the immigrants should be more widely dispersed throughout the rest of the country, instead of being concentrated mostly in the northeastern urban areas. Not only would such a distribution of aliens help relieve the nation's urban problems, but the bureau thought it might promote greater racial and cultural assimilation.

The mounting negative feelings toward immigrants resulted in the Immigration Act of 1917 (39 Stat. 874), which was passed despite President Woodrow Wilson's veto. In addition to codifying (compiling into a complete system of written law) previous immigration legislation, the 1917 act added the following groups to the inadmissible classes of immigrants: "illiterates, persons of constitutional psychopathic inferiority, men and women entering for immoral reasons, chronic alcoholics, stowaways, vagrants, persons who had suffered a previous attack of insanity," and those coming from the designated Asiatic "barred zone," comprising mostly Asia and the Pacific Islands. This provision was a continuation of the Chinese Exclusion Act and the "Gentleman's Agreement" of 1907, in which the Japanese government had agreed to stop the flow of workers to the United States by withholding passports.

Denied Entry

Despite the restrictive immigration legislation, only a small percentage of those attempting to immigrate to the United States were turned away. Between 1892 and 1970, 622,038 persons were denied entry. Between 1901 and 1930, 190,531 immigrants (or 31 percent of the total denied entry over the entire period) were turned away because they were "likely to become public charges" (the peak for this charge). Between 1892 and 1970, 82,559 were denied entry because they were considered "mental or physical defectives." In 1917 illiterate immigrants were banned, leading to 13,679 aliens being excluded over the next 50 years. Few were denied entry on political, criminal, or moral grounds.

CLOSING THE DOORS

World War I stopped the huge influx of immigrants into the United States. In 1914, 1.2 million immigrants came to the United States. A year later the number had dropped to barely 32,700. By 1918, the final year of the war, just over 110,000 immigrants came. However, the heavy flow started again after the war as people fled the war-ravaged European continent. More than 800,000 immigrants arrived in 1921. (See Table 1.1.)

Concern over whether America could continue to absorb such huge numbers of immigrants led Congress to introduce a major change in American immigration policy. Other factors influencing Congress included racial fears of the alleged effects southern and eastern Europeans would have on the nation's basically northern European stock and apprehension over many of the immigrants' politically radical ideas.

Previous immigration qualifications were based on qualities of character. In other words immigrants could enter as long as they could meet the moral and character criteria established by law. With the passing of the first quantitative immigration law, the Quota Law of 1921 (42 Stat. 5), Congress limited the number of aliens of any nationality who could enter the United States to 3 percent of the number of foreign-born persons of that nationality who lived in the United States in 1910. By 1910, however, many southern and eastern Europeans had already entered the country, a fact many legislators had overlooked.

Consequently, in order to restructure the makeup of the immigrant population, Congress approved the Immigration Act of 1924 (43 Stat. 153), also known as the National Origins Act. This act set the first permanent limitation on immigration, or the "national origins quota system." The law, using the 1890 census as the base, further restricted immigration by limiting the number of persons of each nationality to 2 percent of the population of that nationality already residing in the United States. The law, therefore, served to limit immigration from southern and eastern Europe. (See Table 1.2.) The 1924 law further required that all aliens arriving in the United States present visas obtained from a U.S. consulate abroad. (Visas are government authorizations permitting entry into a country.)

After 1929 total immigration was restricted to 150,000 persons per year, with the proportions from each country based on the number of immigrants from the different parts of the world living in the United States in 1920. The quota limitation exempted Canada, Newfoundland (which was then separate from Canada), Mexico, Haiti, the Dominican Republic, the Canal Zone in Panama, and the independent countries of Central and South America. The 1917 and 1924 acts remained the American immigration law until 1952.

The law also barred all Asian immigration, which soon led to a shortage of farm and sugar-plantation workers. Filipinos filled the gap, as they did not come under the immigration quota laws because the Philippines was an American territory. In addition, large numbers of immigrants arrived from the Caribbean, peaking during the 1911–1920 period, when more than 123,000 Caribbean immigrants entered the United States. (See Table 1.2.)

Prior to World War I Caribbean workers had moved among the islands and to parts of South and Central America, but with World War I many went north in search of work. Similarly, after World War II (1939–1945), when agricultural changes in the Caribbean forced many people off the farms and into the cities, many continued on to the United States and the United Kingdom in search of jobs.

BETWEEN THE WARS

With the new quota laws, the problem of illegal aliens arose for the first time. Previously, only a few of the small number of immigrants who had failed the immigration standards tried to sneak in, usually across the U.S.-Mexico border. With the new laws, the number of illegal aliens began increasing. Subsequently, Congress created the Border Patrol in 1924 (under 43 Stat. 240) to oversee the nation's borders and prevent illegal aliens from coming into the United States.

Immigration dropped well below 100,000 during the Great Depression of the 1930s, since America offered no escape from the unemployment rampant throughout most of the world. It did increase, however, in the latter half of the 1930s, when many people persecuted by the Nazis, mostly Jews, fled Germany. A growing concern about an increase in refugees that might result from the war led Congress to pass the Alien Registration Act of 1940 (54 Stat. 670), which required all aliens to register and those over 14 years old to be fingerprinted.

In 1940 the Immigration and Naturalization Service (INS) was transferred from the Department of Labor to the Department of Justice. This move reflected the growing fear of war, making surveillance of aliens a question of national security rather than a question of how many to admit. The job of the INS had shifted from the exclusion of aliens during the 1920s and 1930s to combating alien criminal and subversive elements, which required closer cooperation with the U.S. attorney general's office and the Federal Bureau of Investigation (FBI). The conclusion of World War II (1945) ended the INS's emphasis on hunting for enemy aliens.

IMMIGRATION AND NATIONALITY ACT OF 1952 (MCCARRAN-WALTER ACT)

A growing fear of "communist infiltration" arose during the post-World War II period. One result was the passage of the Internal Security Act of 1950 (Public Law 81-831), which made membership in communist or totalitarian organizations cause for exclusion (denial of an alien's entry into the United States), deportation, or denial of naturalization. The law also required resident aliens to report their addresses annually and made reading, writing, and speaking English prerequisites for naturalization.

This law was soon followed by the Immigration and Nationality Act of 1952 (Public Law 82-414), also known as the McCarran-Walter Act after its sponsors. Although this legislation kept the basic structure of a national origins plan and a quota system, it added preferences for relatives and skilled aliens, gave immigrants and aliens certain legal protections, made all races eligible for immigration and naturalization, and absorbed most of the Internal Security Act of 1950. The act changed the national origin quotas to only one-sixth of 1 percent of the number of people in the United States in 1920 whose ancestry or national origin was attributable to a specific area of the

world. It also excluded aliens on ideological grounds, homosexuality, health restrictions, criminal records, narcotics addiction, and involvement in terrorism.

Once again, Western Hemisphere countries were not included in the quota system. President Harry Truman vetoed the legislation, declaring,

> Today we are "protecting" ourselves as we were in 1924, against being flooded by immigrants from Eastern Europe. This is fantastic. The countries of Eastern Europe have fallen under the Communist yoke—they are silenced, fenced off by barbed wire and minefields—no one passes their borders but at the risk of his life. We do not need to be protected against immigrants from these countries—on the contrary, we want to stretch out a helping hand, to save those who have managed to flee into Western Europe, to succor those who are brave enough to escape from barbarism, to welcome and restore them against the day when their countries will, as we hope, be free again. These are only a few examples of the absurdity, the cruelty of carrying over into this year of 1952 the isolationist limitation of our 1924 law.

Congress overrode Truman's veto. Although there have been major amendments, the Immigration and Nationality Act still remains the basic statute governing who can be denied entry into the country.

During the 1950s a half dozen special laws allowed the entrance of additional refugees. Many of the laws resulted from World War II, but some stemmed from more recent developments. An example is the law affecting Hungarian refugees who fled after their 1956 revolution was crushed.

A TWO-HEMISPHERE SYSTEM

In 1963 President John F. Kennedy submitted a plan to change the quota system. Two years later Congress passed the Immigration and Nationality Act Amendments of 1965 (Public Law 89-236) in response to changes in the country sources of immigration since 1924. Most immigration-visa applications now came from Asia and Central and South America rather than from Europe. The 1965 legislation dropped the national origins quota system. Visa allocations would be on a first-come, first-serve basis, subject to a seven-category preference system for families of U.S. citizens and permanent resident aliens for the purpose of family reunification. In addition, the law set visa allocations for persons with special occupational skills, abilities, or training needed in the United States. It also established an annual ceiling of 170,000 Eastern Hemisphere immigrants with a 20,000 per-country limit, and an annual limit of 120,000 for the Western Hemisphere without a per-country limit or preference system.

The Immigration and Nationality Act Amendments of 1976 (Public Law 94-571) extended the 20,000 per-country limit and a slightly modified version of the seven-category preference system equally to the Western Hemisphere. Some legislators were concerned that the limit for Mexico (20,000 persons) was inadequate, but their objections were overruled. The Immigration and Nationality Act Amendments of 1978 (Public Law 95-412) combined the separate ceilings for the Eastern and Western Hemispheres into a single worldwide ceiling of 290,000.

REFUGEE PROGRAMS AFTER WORLD WAR II

Official American refugee programs began in response to the devastation of World War II, which created millions of refugees and displaced persons (DPs). (A displaced person is a person living in a foreign country as a result of having been driven from his or her home country due to war or political unrest.) This was the first time the United States formulated policy to admit persons fleeing persecution. The Presidential Directive of December 22, 1945, gave priority in issuing visas to about 40,000 DPs. The directive was followed by the Displaced Persons Act of 1948 (Public Law 80-744) and the Refugee Relief Act of 1953 (Public Law 83-203), which together permitted over 600,000 European refugees to enter the United States between 1948 and 1957. The Displaced Persons Act counted the refugees in the existing immigration quotas, while the Refugee Relief Act admitted them outside the quota system.

In 1956 the U.S. attorney general used the parole authority (temporary admission) under Section 212(d)(15) of the Immigration and Nationality Act of 1952 for the first time on a large scale. This section authorized the attorney general to temporarily admit any alien to the United States. While parole is not admission for permanent residence, it can lead to permanent resident or immigrant status. Aliens already in the United States on a temporary basis may apply for asylum in the United States on the grounds they are likely to suffer persecution upon return to their native lands. The attorney general is authorized to withhold deportation on the same grounds.

This parole authority was used to admit approximately 32,000 of the 38,000 Hungarians who fled to this country after the failure of the Hungarian Revolution in 1956. The other 6,000 entered under the Refugee Relief Act of 1953 and were automatically admitted as permanent residents. This parole provision was also used in 1962 to admit 15,000 refugees from Hong Kong to the United States.

In 1965, under the Immigration and Nationality Act Amendments, Congress added Section 203(a)(7) to the Immigration and Nationality Act of 1952, creating a group of "conditional entrant" refugees from communist or Middle Eastern countries, with status similar to the refugee parolees. Sections 203(a)(7) and 212(d)(15) were used to admit thousands of refugees, including Czecho-

TABLE 1.3

Foreign-born population and percent of total population, 1850–2000

Year	Number (in millions)	Percent of total
2000	28.4	10.4
1990	19.8	7.9
1970	9.6	4.7
1950	10.3	6.9
1930	14.2	11.6
1910	13.5	14.7
1890	9.2	14.8
1850	2.2	9.7

SOURCE: U.S. Bureau of the Census, Washington, D.C., 2001

slovakians escaping their failed revolution in 1968, Ugandans fleeing their dictatorship in the 1970s, and Lebanese avoiding the civil war in their country in the 1980s.

Although Congress did not intend Section 203(a)(7) for group admission of refugees, Congress consented to the granting of parole status to those leaving Cuba following the fall of Fulgencio Batista (the president overthrown by Fidel Castro in 1959). Nearly 420,000 Cuban refugees entered the United States under this parole program.

Not until the Refugee Act of 1980 did the United States have a general policy governing the admission of refugees. The Refugee Act of 1980 (Public Law 96-212) eliminated refugees as a category in the preference system and set a worldwide ceiling on immigration of 270,000, not counting refugees. It also removed the requirement that refugees had to originate from a communist or Middle Eastern nation.

FOREIGN-BORN POPULATION

The 1850 decennial census was the first census to collect data on the nativity (place of birth) of the total U.S. population. In 1850 the 2.2 million foreign-born population made up 9.7 percent of the total population. The foreign-born population (9.2 million) quadrupled by 1890, representing 14.8 percent of the total population. The huge influx of immigrants from Europe accounted for the rising number of foreign-born persons through 1930. Between 1930 and 1950, the foreign-born population declined from 14.2 million to 10.3 million, dropping to 9.6 million in 1970, a record low 4.7 percent of the total population. (See Table 1.3.)

The number of foreign-born persons has risen since 1970 due to increased immigration, especially from Asia and Latin America. Between 1970 and 1990 the foreign-born population increased more than twofold, from 9.6 million to 19.8 million. In 2000, 28.4 million foreign-born persons lived in the United States, a 43 percent increase

FIGURE 1.1

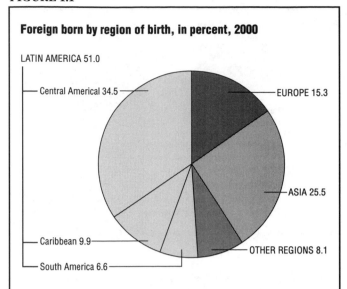

Foreign born by region of birth, in percent, 2000

LATIN AMERICA 51.0

- Central America 34.5
- EUROPE 15.3
- ASIA 25.5
- OTHER REGIONS 8.1
- Caribbean 9.9
- South America 6.6

SOURCE: Lisa Lollock, "Figure 1: Foreign Born by Region of Birth: 2000," in *The Foreign-Born Population in the United States, March 2000. Current Population Reports, Series P20-534*, U.S. Bureau of the Census, Washington D.C., January 2001.

since 1990. The proportion of foreign-born persons in 2000 (10.4 percent of the total population, or 1 of 10 U.S. residents) was lower than their proportion of the total population between 1860 and 1930 (approximately 13 percent). (See Table 1.3.)

Region of Birth

In 2000 about half (51 percent) of the foreign-born population were born in Latin America—34.5 percent from Central America, 9.9 percent from the Caribbean, and 6.6 percent from South America. About one-quarter (25.5 percent) were born in Asia, 15.3 percent were born in Europe, and another 8.1 percent were born in other regions of the world. (See Figure 1.1.)

Comparison of the Foreign Born and Natives by Age

In 2000 foreign-born persons were more likely than natives to be ages 18 to 64 (4 out of 5 persons, or 79 percent, compared to 3 out of 5 native persons, or 59.7 percent). (The Census Bureau defines natives as persons who "were born in the United States or a U.S. Island Area such as Puerto Rico, or born abroad of at least one parent who

FIGURE 1.2

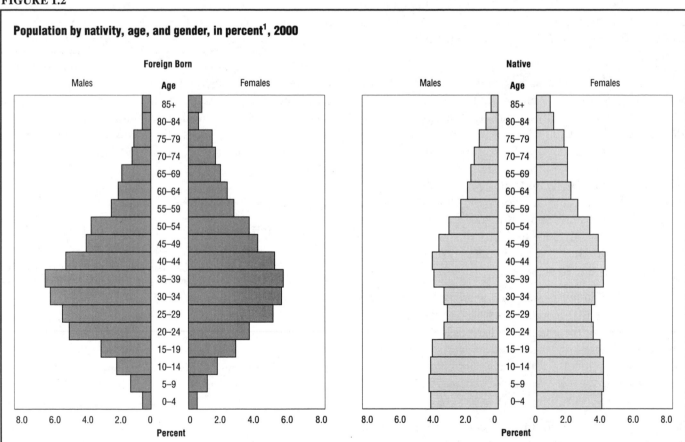

Population by nativity, age, and gender, in percent[1], 2000

[1]Each bar represents the percent of the foreign-born (native) population who were within the specified age group and of the specified sex.

SOURCE: Lisa Lollock, "Figure 4. Population by Nativity, Age, and Sex: 2000," in *The Foreign-Born Population in the United States, March 2000. Current Population Reports, Series P20-534*, U.S. Bureau of the Census, Washington D.C., January 2001.

was a U.S. citizen.") More foreign-born persons (43.6 percent) than natives (28.6 percent) were 25 to 44 years of age. Nearly one-quarter (24.3 percent) of the foreign born were ages 45 to 64, compared to 21.7 percent of natives. (See Figure 1.2.)

Whereas the proportions of persons age 65 and over were about the same for the foreign-born and native population (11 percent and 12 percent, respectively), almost three times as many natives (28.3 percent) as foreign-born people (10 percent) were younger than 18 years old. (Since most of younger children of foreign-born parents were U.S. citizens, the percentage of foreign born in this younger-age group was very small.) (See Figure 1.2.)

States and Immigrant Populations

In 2000 California had the largest foreign-born population (8.8 million), followed by New York (3.6 million), Florida (2.8 million), Texas (2.4 million), New Jersey (1.2 million), and Illinois (1.1 million). Although these six states made up just over one-third (39 percent) of the total U.S. population, they accounted for 70.4 percent of the nation's foreign-born population—California (30.9 percent), New York (12.8 percent), Florida (9.7 percent), Texas (8.6 percent), New Jersey (4.3 percent), and Illinois (4.1 percent).

Foreign-Born Persons Who Are Naturalized Citizens as of 2000

Of the 28.4 million foreign-born persons counted by the Census Bureau in 2000, 39.5 percent were admitted to the United States in the 1990s, 28.3 percent were admitted in the 1980s, 16.2 percent entered in the 1970s, and 16 percent came before 1970. By 2000 more than 4 of 5 (80.4 percent) of those who arrived before 1970 had become naturalized citizens. Among those who arrived in the 1970s, more than 3 of 5 (61.9 percent) were naturalized. Recent immigrants had lower proportions of naturalizations—38.9 percent for the 1980s arrivals and just 8.9 percent for those admitted in the 1990s. (See Figure 1.3.) European (52 percent) and Asian (47.1 percent) foreign-born persons were more likely to be naturalized citizens than those from Latin America (28.3 percent). Overall, over one-third (37 percent) of the nation's foreign-born residents were naturalized citizens in 2000.

IMMIGRATION AND POPULATION PROJECTIONS

For the first time the Census Bureau in 2000 projected the U.S. population to the year 2100. The nation's projected population of 278 million as of July 1, 2001 (middle-series projection) was estimated to double to 571 million by July 1, 2100. However, it should be noted that, as of May 30, 2001, the U.S. population had reached 284,317,739, already exceeding the Census Bureau's middle-series projection for July 1, 2001. The Census Bureau

FIGURE 1.3

U.S. citizenship of the foreign-born population by year of entry, in percent, 2000

Before 1970	80.4
1970–79	61.9
1980–89	38.9
After 1990	8.9

SOURCE: Lisa Lollock, "Figure 5. U.S. Citizenship of the Foreign-Born Population by Year of Entry: 2000," in *The Foreign-Born Population in the United States, March 2000. Current Population Reports, Series P20-534*, U.S. Bureau of the Census, Washington D.C., January 2001.

also published its lowest- and highest-series alternative projections. The lowest series projected a population increase to 314 million in 2050, declining to 283 million in 2100. The highest series projected population growth to 1.2 billion by 2100. Census Bureau analyst Frederick W. Hollmann observed, "Even though childbearing levels in the United States remain quite close to the level needed only to replace the population, the increasing number of potential parents and continued migration from abroad would be sufficient to add nearly 300 million people during the next century."

Also for the first time, the bureau included data on the foreign-born population. According to the middle-series projections, the overall foreign-born population could grow from 9.9 percent of the total population in 2001 to 13.3 percent in 2050 and then drop to 10.9 percent in 2100. The foreign-born, Hispanic population could decline from 35.5 percent of the total Hispanic population in 2001 to 20 percent in 2050 and 9.3 percent in 2100. In comparison, the foreign-born, non-Hispanic white population, 3.4 percent of the non-Hispanic whites in 2001, was projected to remain stable at 5.2 percent of this racial group in 2050 and 5.3 percent in 2100. (See Table 1.4.)

The foreign-born, non-Hispanic black population, representing 5.9 percent of the total non-Hispanic black population in 2001, was projected to almost double to 11.3 percent of this racial group in 2050 and remain steady at 11.8 percent in 2100. In 2001 foreign-born, non-Hispanic Asians and Pacific Islanders (APIs) made up 61.9 percent of the overall API population in the United States. This proportion was projected to decline to 47.5 percent by 2050, further decreasing to 32.7 percent by 2100. On the other hand, the foreign-born, non-Hispanic Native American population, at 2.3 percent of the total Native American

TABLE 1.4

Population Projections, 2001 to 2100

Number in thousands	July 1, 2001	July 1, 2005	July 1, 2025	July 1, 2050	July 1, 2075	July 1, 2100
TOTAL						
Population	277,802	287,715	337,814	403,686	480,504	570,954
Percent of Total	100	100	100	100	100	100
Native Population	250,230	257,140	296,999	349,890	420,957	508,694
Percent of Racial Group	90.1	89.4	87.9	86.7	87.6	89.1
Foreign-born Population	27,572	30,575	40,814	53,796	59,546	62,259
Percent of Racial Group	9.9	10.6	12.1	13.3	12.4	10.9
WHITE, NON-HISPANIC						
Population	197,248	199,413	209,339	212,990	218,923	230,236
Percent of Total	71	69.3	62	52.8	45.6	40.3
Native Population	190,449	192,216	200,833	201,988	206,904	218,143
Percent of Racial Group	96.6	96.4	95.9	94.8	94.5	94.7
Foreign-born Population	6,799	7,197	8,505	11,002	12,018	12,092
Percent of Racial Group	3.4	3.6	4.1	5.2	5.5	5.3
BLACK, NON-HISPANIC						
Population	33,876	35,445	43,527	53,466	63,348	74,360
Percent of Total	12.2	12.3	12.9	13.2	13.2	13
Native Population	31,888	33,125	39,732	47,399	55,716	65,585
Percent of Racial Group	94.1	93.5	91.3	88.7	88	88.2
Foreign-born Population	1,988	2,320	3,794	6,066	7,631	8,775
Percent of Racial Group	5.9	6.5	8.7	11.3	12	11.8
AMERICAN INDIAN, NON-HISPANIC						
Population	2,071	2,170	2,668	3,241	3,753	4,237
Percent of Total	0.7	0.8	0.8	0.8	0.8	0.7
Native Population	2,024	2,116	2,585	3,120	3,607	4,077
Percent of Racial Group	97.7	97.5	96.9	96.3	96.1	96.2
Foreign-born Population	47	54	82	120	145	160
Percent of Racial Group	2.3	2.5	3.1	3.7	3.9	3.8
ASIAN AND PACIFIC ISLANDER, NON-HISPANIC						
Population	10,989	12,497	20,846	35,759	52,759	71,789
Percent of Total	4	4.3	6.2	8.9	11	12.6
Native Population	4,189	4,889	9,452	18,783	32,052	48,303
Percent of Racial Group	38.1	39.1	45.3	52.5	60.8	67.3
Foreign-born Population	6,800	7,607	11,393	16,976	20,707	23,485
Percent of Racial Group	61.9	60.9	54.7	47.5	39.2	32.7
HISPANIC						
Population	33,615	38,188	61,433	98,228	141,719	190,330
Percent of Total	12.1	13.3	18.2	24.3	29.5	33.3
Native Population	21,679	24,792	44,394	78,598	122,676	172,584
Percent of Racial Group	64.5	64.9	72.3	80	86.6	90.7
Foreign-born Population	11,936	13,395	17,038	19,629	19,042	17,746
Percent of Racial Group	35.5	35.1	27.7	20	13.4	9.3

SOURCE: U.S. Bureau of the Census, Population Division, Population Projections Program: Washington, D.C. [Online] http://www.census.gov/population/projections/nation/summary Files: np-t5-b.pdf, np-t5-f.pdf, np-t5-g.pdf, np-t5-h.pdf [accessed April 6, 2001]

population in 2001, was projected to rise to 3.7 in 2050 and stay at 3.8 percent in 2100. (See Table 1.4.)

Projected Race and Hispanic-origin Distribution of the U.S. Population

It should be noted that foreign-born persons who become naturalized U.S. citizens are eventually added to the race and Hispanic-origin count of the Census Bureau. According to the bureau's projections, the Hispanic share of the U.S. population would double from 12.1 percent in 2001 to 24.3 percent in 2050, increasing to 33.3 percent in 2100, one-third of the total U.S. population. In comparison, the non-Hispanic white population, 71 percent of the population in 2001, was projected to decline to 52.8 percent of the population in 2050 and 45.6 percent in 2100. (See Table 1.4.)

The non-Hispanic black population, representing 12.2 percent of the U.S. population in 2001, was projected to rise slightly to 13.2 percent of the population in 2050 and remain at 13 percent in 2100. In 2001 non-Hispanic APIs made up 4 percent of the U.S. population. According to the Census Bureau, APIs could more than double to 8.9 percent of the population by 2050, growing threefold to 12.6 percent by 2100. On the other hand, non-Hispanic Native Americans, at 0.7 percent of the total population in 2001, were projected to remain at about the same proportion (0.8 percent of the population in 2050 and 0.7 percent in 2100). (See Table 1.4.)

CHAPTER 2

RECENT IMMIGRATION LAWS

THE IMMIGRATION REFORM AND CONTROL ACT OF 1986 (IRCA)

On November 6, 1986, after 34 years with no new major immigration legislation and a six-year effort to send an acceptable bill through both houses of Congress, the Immigration Reform and Control Act of 1986 (IRCA; Public Law 99-603) was signed into law by President Ronald Reagan. Combined with the Immigration Act of 1990, IRCA marked a decade of major change in the nation's approach to immigration and illegal aliens. IRCA tried to resolve the following problems:

• Jobs lost by citizens and taken by illegal aliens, with the resulting lower wages that were paid to illegal aliens.

• Costs of services and welfare for undocumented workers and their low tax payments.

• Exploitation of undocumented workers.

• Social fragmentation of local communities.

• The need to re-establish the power of law and the principle of U.S. sovereignty.

To control illegal immigration IRCA adopted three major strategies:

• Legalization of a portion of the undocumented population (aliens in the country without legal papers), thereby reducing the number of aliens illegally resident in the United States.

• Sanctions against employers who knowingly hired undocumented aliens.

• Additional border enforcement to impede further unlawful entries.

The "Pre-1982 Cohort"

The largest group of aliens to become eligible to apply for legalization under Section 245A of IRCA was those who had continuously resided in the United States without authorization since January 1, 1982. These aliens had entered the United States in one of two ways:

• As illegal aliens before January 1, 1982.

• As temporary visitors before January 1, 1982, with their authorized stay expiring before that date or with the government's knowledge of their unlawful status before that date. This category would include those who arrived legally on a tourist visa and then stayed to work and live in the United States.

Legalization for Section 245A aliens consisted of two phases—temporary and then permanent resident status. The one-year application period for temporary residence began on May 5, 1987, and ended on May 4, 1988. Applicants approved during Phase I were granted temporary residence for up to 42 months, during which time they were permitted to work legally while applying for permanent residence. The application period for permanent residence ran from December 5, 1988, through December 4, 1990. Those granted temporary residence had to apply for permanent residence within a one-year period beginning in the nineteenth month after their initial application for temporary residence.

To adjust to permanent resident status, aliens must have lived continuously in the United States, been admissible as immigrants (had no serious criminal record and had not tested positive for HIV, the virus that causes AIDS), and demonstrated minimal understanding and knowledge of the English language and U.S. history and government. They could apply for citizenship five years from the date permanent resident status was granted. Illegal aliens who did not apply for residence were no longer able to remain in the United States and adjust to permanent resident status unless they were immediate relatives of U.S. citizens.

HOW MANY WERE LEGALIZED? An estimated 3 million to 6 million illegal aliens were living in the United

TABLE 2.1

Total applications by Immigration Reform and Control Act program and outcome, August 1992

Status as of August 1992	Total	Section 245A (Pre-1982)	Section 210 (SAW)
Total applications[a]	3,040,948	1,763,434	1,277,514
Percent	100	58	42
Resolution			
Acceptance	2,634,662	1,558,102	1,076,560
Phase I (TRA)	[b]	1,660,157[c]	[b]
Phase II (LPR)	[b]	1,558,102	[b]
Case Pending	123,936	111,261	18,370
Phase I	[b]	5,695	[b]
Phase II	[b]	105,566	[b]
Denied	282,350	99,766	182,584
Phase I	[b]	97,582	[b]
Phase II	[b]	2,184	[b]
Percent of Applications			
Total	100	100	100
Accepted	87	88	84
Case Pending	4	6	2
Denied	9	6	14

[a]Applicants of all ages.
[b]Only the section 245A program involved two phases.
[c]Provisional acceptance.

SOURCE: *Effects of the Immigration Reform and Control Act: Characteristics and Labor Market Behavior of the Legalized Population Five Years Following Legislation,* U.S. Department of Labor, Division of Immigration Policy and Research, Washington, D.C., 1996

TABLE 2.2

Weighted distribution of Section 245A legalized adults by gender, place of origin, and age at arrival, 1992

Characteristic	Legalized Adults (percent)
Legalized adults (number)	
Unweighted	4,012
Weighted	1,294,562
Sex	
Total	100
Male	56
Female	44
Region of Origin	
Total	100
Mexico	69
Central America	15
Canada	1
Other Western Hemisphere	7
Other	8
Period of Arrival	
Total	100
Before 1975	22
1975–1979	39
1980 or later	39
Median year of arrival	1979
Age at Arrival	
Total	100
17 or less	31
18 to 24	38
25 to 34	21
35 or more	10
Median age at arrival	22
Method of Entry by Country of Origin	
Total	100
Entered without documents	75
Nonimmigrant overstay	25
Mexico	100
Entered without documents	85
Nonimmigrant overstay	15
Central America	100
Entered without documents	86
Nonimmigrant overstay	14
All Other Countries	100
Entered without documents	27
Nonimmigrant overstay	73

Note: Some percentages may not add to 100 due to rounding.

SOURCE: *Effects of the Immigration Reform and Control Act: Characteristics and Labor Market Behavior of the Legalized Population Five Years Following Legislation,* U.S. Department of Labor, Division of Immigration Policy and Research, Washington, D.C., 1996

States in 1986. By August 1992 the Immigration and Naturalization Service (INS) had processed a little over 3 million applications for legalization of both Section 245A and Section 210 aliens. (See Table 2.1.)

During Phase I of the Section 245A legalization program, nearly 1.8 million illegal aliens applied. About 1.7 million were granted temporary resident alien (TRA) status; of these, about 1.6 million received lawful permanent resident (LPR) status. By 1992 most (88 percent) aliens eligible for status adjustment under Section 245A had been admitted as permanent residents. (See Table 2.1.)

PROFILE OF THE LEGALIZED POPULATION. The U.S. Department of Labor (DOL), as mandated by IRCA, conducted the Legalized Population Follow-up Survey (LPS2) to update the profile of the pre-1982 cohort (group) legalized under Section 245A of IRCA. The DOL gathered information from 4,012 legalized aliens who had initially participated in an INS Legalized Population Survey (LPS1) during their application process. In *Effects of the Immigration Reform and Control Act: Characteristics and Labor Market Behavior of the Legalized Population Five Years Following Legalization* (Washington, D.C., 1996), the DOL described the changes in the social and economic status of these immigrants during their first five years of legal residence.

LPS2 found that 56 percent of the pre-1982 LPRs were male and 44 percent were female. Most came from

Mexico (69 percent) and Central America (15 percent, primarily from El Salvador and Guatemala). Nearly 8 in 10 (78 percent) entered the United States after 1975, and nearly 7 in 10 (69 percent) arrived when they were 24 years old or younger. (See Table 2.2.)

Overall, most (75 percent) Section 245A LPRs had entered the United States without documents. The rest (25 percent) had entered using temporary nonimmigrant visas that had since expired. About 85 percent of Mexicans and 86 percent of Central Americans had entered without documents, while 73 percent from other countries had overstayed past their nonimmigrant status. (See Table 2.2.)

When LPS2 was conducted (1992), the median age of the legalized aliens was 36. Nearly 3 out of 5 (58 percent) lived in California, and about 1 in 8 (13 percent) lived in Texas. Although the pre-1982 cohort came from more than 185 countries, the majority spoke a common language—Spanish. About 8 of 10 (81 percent) indicated they spoke best in Spanish, although about 7 in 10 reported being able to speak English when it was necessary to communicate with sales clerks, doctors, teachers, and over the telephone. Many also reported improvements in oral English skills by the time of the second survey. About 81 percent spoke Spanish or Spanish/English during the LPS2 interview. (See Table 2.3.) In 1992, after more than 10 years of continuous residence in the United States, 22 percent admitted to not speaking any English.

More than one-fifth (22 percent) of LPRs age 25 and older had attended some school (up to 4 years). Nearly 3 in 10 (29 percent) finished high school or beyond. (See Table 2.3.) In addition, 16 percent attended vocational, trade, or business school in the years following application for legalization.

The educational attainment of the LPRs was significantly lower than that of U.S. natives. LPRs 25 years and older who were at least high school graduates made up 28 percent of all legalized aliens, compared to 81 percent of all non-Hispanic white natives, 78 percent of Hispanic natives, 65 percent of black natives, and 59 percent of Hispanic immigrants (also called foreign-born Hispanics). Only 17 percent of Mexican and 31 percent of Central American LPRs completed high school, compared to nearly 75 percent of LPRs from other countries.

IRCA barred newly legalized aliens from receiving most federally funded public assistance for five years. Exceptions included access to Medicaid for pregnant women, children, the elderly, the handicapped, and for emergency care. The State Legalization Impact Assistance Grant (SLIAG) program reimbursed state and local governments for their costs of providing public assistance, education, and public health services to the legalized aliens. During its seven years of operation (fiscal years 1987 to 1994), the federal SLIAG program reimbursed states $3.5 billion, averaging $1,167 per eligible legalized alien. (The federal fiscal year begins on October 1 and ends on September 30 of the following calendar year. It is identified by the calendar year in which it ends.)

Employer Sanctions

The employer sanctions provision of IRCA prohibits employers from hiring, recruiting, or referring for a fee aliens known to be unauthorized to work in the United States. Violators of the law are subject to a series of civil fines or criminal penalties when there is a pattern or practice of violations. For the first offense, an employer is subject to a fine of $250 to $2,000 for each illegal alien hired. A second offense results in a fine ranging from $2,000 to $5,000. For later offenses, the employer could be fined from $3,000 to $10,000 for each illegal alien. If the employer is found guilty of a pattern of hiring illegal aliens, the employer could be fined up to $3,000 and sent to jail for up to six months. All employers are forbidden to hire illegal aliens. The burden of proof is on employers, so they must ask each hired person for documentation showing proofs of identity and employment eligibility. Table 2.4 lists the acceptable documents.

TABLE 2.3

Age, educational attainment, English-speaking ability, and place of residence of legalized adults, 1992

Characteristic	Legalized Adults[a] (percent)		U.S. Adults[a] (percent)
	At Application[b]	1992	1990
Age			
Total, ages 18 and above	**100**	**100**	**100**
18–19	4	0	4
20–29	37	22	21
20–24	14	6	10
25–29	23	16	11
30–39	36	45	23
30–34	22	24	12
35–39	14	21	11
40 and above	**23**	**33**	**52**
40–44	9	13	10
45–49	6	8	7
50–54	4	5	6
55–59	2	3	6
60 and above	2	4	23
Median age	32	36	40
Years of School Completed[c]			
Total	**100**	**100**	**100**
0 to 4	25	22	3
5 to 8	35	33	8
9 to 11	14	16	14
12 (high school graduate)	15	14	30
13 or more (beyond high school)	12	15	45
English Language Skills			
Total	**100**	**100**	**NA**
Interview conducted in:			
Spanish or Spanish/English	85	81	NA
Other	15	19	NA
Percent able to speak English			
with sales clerk	65	71	NA
with doctor, nurse, teacher	63	68	NA
on telephone	60	71	NA
Place of U.S. Residence			
Total	**100**	**100**	**100**
California	58	58	12
Texas	13	13	7
New York	7	7	7
Other	21	22	74

NA: Not available.
[a]Legalized alien ages 16 and above by January 1987; U.S. adults ages 18 to 64.
[b]In most cases, 1987 or 1988.
[c]Educational attainment of population ages 25 and above.
Note: Some percentages may not add to 100 due to rounding.

SOURCE: *Effects of the Immigration Reform and Control Act: Characteristics and Labor Market Behavior of the Legalized Population Five Years Following Legislation*, U.S. Department of Labor, Division of Immigration Policy and Research, Washington, D.C., 1996

TABLE 2.4

Documents that can be used to demonstrate employment eligibility

LIST A Documents that Establish Both Identity and Employment Eligibility	OR	LIST B Documents that Establish Identity	AND	LIST C Documents that Establish Employment Eligibility
1. U.S. Passport (unexpired or expired)		1. Driver's license or ID card issued by a state or outlying possession of the United States provided it contains a photograph or information such as name, date of birth, sex, height, eye color and address		1. U.S. social security card issued by the Social Security Administration *(other than a card stating it is not valid for employment)*
2. Certificate of U.S. Citizenship *(INS Form N-560 or N-561)*		2. ID card issued by federal, state or local government agencies or entities, provided it contains a photograph or information such as name, date of birth, sex, height, eye color and address		2. Certification of Birth Abroad issued by the Department of State *(Form FS-545 or Form DS-1350)*
3. Certificate of Naturalization *(INS Form N-550 or N-570)*		3. School ID card with a photograph		3. Original or certified copy of a birth certificate issued by a state, county, municipal authority or outlying possession of the United States bearing an official seal
4. Unexpired foreign passport, with *I-551 stamp* or attached *INS Form I-94* indicating unexpired employment authorization		4. Voter's registration card		
5. Alien Registration Receipt Card with photograph *(INS Form I-151 or I-551)*		5. U.S. Military card or draft record		4. Native American tribal document
6. Unexpired Temporary Card *(INS Form I-688)*		6. Military dependent's ID card		5. U.S. Citizen ID Card *(INS Form I-197)*
7. Unexpired Employment Authorization Card *(INS Form I-688A)*		7. U.S. Coast Guard Merchant Mariner Card		
8. Unexpired Reentry Permit *(INS Form I-327)*		8. Native American tribal document		6. ID Card for use of Resident Citizen in the United States *(INS Form I-179)*
9. Unexpired Refugee Travel Document *(INS Form I-571)*		9. Driver's license issued by a Canadian government authority		
		For persons under age 18 who are unable to present a document listed above:		7. Unexpired employment authorization document issued by the INS *(other then those listed under List A)*
10. Unexpired Employment Authorization Document issued by the INS which contains a photograph *(INS Form I-688B)*		10. School record or report card		
		11. Clinic, doctor or hospital record		
		12. Day-care or nursery school record		

SOURCE: "Lists of Acceptable Documents," U.S. Department of Justice, Immigration and Naturalization Service: Washington, D.C. Last modified 09/22/00. [Online] http://www.ins.usdoj.gov/graphics/formsfee/forms/files/i-9.pdf [accessed 04/06/01]

Employers are required to complete the Employment Eligibility Verification form, otherwise known as Form I-9 (Figure 2.1), certifying that they have examined the proofs of identity and that these documents appear genuine. Employers must keep I-9 forms for a minimum of three years and not dispose of them until one year after the worker's employment ends. An officer of the INS or the Department of Labor may ask to see the I-9 forms at any time as verification of the employee's legitimacy. Failure to complete or keep the I-9 forms can result in fines from $100 to $1,000.

Special Agricultural Workers (SAWs)

Section 210 of IRCA created a new classification of seasonal, temporary agricultural workers and provided for the legalization of certain such workers, referred to as Special Agricultural Workers (SAWs). A new nonimmigrant category (H-2A) was created to clarify the process by which employers can hire these seasonal, temporary agricultural workers and make their entry easier. This category was created because many fruit and vegetable farmers feared they would lose their workers, many of whom

were illegal aliens, if the IRCA provisions regarding the continuous residence and the length of residence were applied to seasonal laborers. Most of these workers were migrant laborers who often returned home to live in Mexico when there was no work available in the fields.

The SAW program permitted aliens who had performed labor in perishable agricultural commodities for a minimum of 90 days between May 1985 and May 1986 to apply for legalization. Unlike Section 245A, the SAW program involved just one admission process. The 18-month application period began June 1, 1987, and ended November 30, 1988. Approximately 1.3 million Special Agricultural Workers filed an application. By August 1992, 84 percent of these applicants had attained lawful permanent resident status. (See Table 2.1.)

IMMIGRATION MARRIAGE FRAUD AMENDMENTS OF 1986

A number of marriages between American citizens or LPRs and foreigners occur to attain permanent residence for the foreigner in the United States. Some American

FIGURE 2.1

U.S. Department of Justice
Immigration and Naturalization Service

OMB No. 1115-0136

Employment Eligibility Verification

Please read instructions carefully before completing this form. The instructions must be available during completion of this form. ANTI-DISCRIMINATION NOTICE: It is illegal to discriminate against work eligible individuals. Employers CANNOT specify which document(s) they will accept from an employee. The refusal to hire an individual because of a future expiration date may also constitute illegal discrimination.

Section 1. Employee Information and Verification. To be completed and signed by employee at the time employment begins.

Print Name: Last	First	Middle Initial	Maiden Name

Address (Street Name and Number)	Apt. #	Date of Birth (month/day/year)

City	State	Zip Code	Social Security #

I am aware that federal law provides for imprisonment and/or fines for false statements or use of false documents in connection with the completion of this form.

I attest, under penalty of perjury, that I am (check one of the following):
- ☐ A citizen or national of the United States
- ☐ A Lawful Permanent Resident (Alien # A _____)
- ☐ An alien authorized to work until ___/___/___
(Alien # or Admission #) _____

Employee's Signature	Date (month/day/year)

Preparer and/or Translator Certification. (To be completed and signed if Section 1 is prepared by a person other than the employee.) I attest, under penalty of perjury, that I have assisted in the completion of this form and that to the best of my knowledge the information is true and correct.

Preparer's/Translator's Signature	Print Name

Address (Street Name and Number, City, State, Zip Code)	Date (month/day/year)

Section 2. Employer Review and Verification. To be completed and signed by employer. Examine one document from List A OR examine one document from List B and one from List C, as listed on the reverse of this form, and record the title, number and expiration date, if any, of the document(s)

List A	OR	List B	AND	List C
Document title: _____		_____		_____
Issuing authority: _____		_____		_____
Document #: _____		_____		_____
Expiration Date (if any): ___/___/___		___/___/___		___/___/___
Document #: _____				
Expiration Date (if any): ___/___/___				

CERTIFICATION - I attest, under penalty of perjury, that I have examined the document(s) presented by the above-named employee, that the above-listed document(s) appear to be genuine and to relate to the employee named, that the employee began employment on (month/day/year) ___/___/___ and that to the best of my knowledge the employee is eligible to work in the United States. (State employment agencies may omit the date the employee began employment.)

Signature of Employer or Authorized Representative	Print Name	Title

Business or Organization Name	Address (Street Name and Number, City, State, Zip Code)	Date (month/day/year)

Section 3. Updating and Reverification To be completed and signed by employer.

A. New Name (if applicable)	B. Date of rehire (month/day/year) (if applicable)

C. If employee's previous grant of work authorization has expired, provide the information below for the document that establishes current employment eligibility.

Document Title: _____ Document #: _____ Expiration Date (if any): ___/___/___

I attest, under penalty of perjury, that to the best of my knowledge, this employee is eligible to work in the United States, and if the employee presented document(s), the document(s) I have examined appear to be genuine and to relate to the individual.

Signature of Employer or Authorized Representative	Date (month/day/year)

Form I-9 (Rev. 11-21-91)N Page 2

SOURCE: U.S. Department of Justice, Immigration and Naturalization Service: Washington, D.C. Last modified 09/22/00. [Online] http://www.ins.usdoj.gov/graphics/formsfee/forms/files/i-9.pdf [accessed 04/06/01]

citizens or LPRs have agreed to marry aliens for money. After the alien gains permanent residence, the marriage is dissolved. Other cases involve aliens entering marriages by deceiving U.S. citizens or LPRs with promises of love, only to seek divorce after gaining permanent residence.

Prior to 1986 the INS granted permanent residence fairly quickly to the foreign spouses of U.S. citizens or LPRs. Concerns regarding alleged marriage frauds led to the passage of the Immigration Marriage Fraud Amendments of 1986 (Public Law 99-639). The law specified that aliens deriving their immigrant status based on a marriage of less than two years are considered conditional immigrants. To remove the conditional immigrant status, the alien must apply for permanent residence within 90 days after the second-year anniversary of receiving conditional status. The alien and his or her spouse must show that the marriage was and is a valid one; otherwise, conditional immigrant status will be terminated, and the alien can be deported.

Battered Brides

Unfortunately, an unintentional result of the two-year conditional immigrant status is that some husbands become abusive while their brides are dependent on them to obtain permanent residence. Reports have surfaced about husbands abusing wives who are virtual prisoners of the marriage while they wait to be granted permanent residence. Since the law requires that the U.S. citizen-spouse sponsor the conditional immigrant for permanent residence, the husband is given power over the wife that she cannot defy for fear of deportation. In addition the beliefs and customs of some cultures make it very difficult for a woman to complain or file for divorce. For example, she might be rejected by her own family because of the shame she would bring to them.

The Violence Against Women (VAWA) Act of 1994, part of the Violent Crime Control and Law Enforcement Act of 1994 (Public Law 103-322), addressed the plight of these abused women and their children. The law allowed the women and/or children to self-petition for immigrant status without the abusers' participation or consent. Abused males can also file a self-petition under this law.

On October 28, 2000, the Victims of Trafficking and Violence Prevention Act (Public Law 106-386) was enacted. The Violence Against Women Act portion of this law re-authorized the provision that allowed victims of domestic violence to self-petition for permanent residence. In addition, the law created a new nonimmigrant U visa (with a 10,000 annual cap) for victims of serious crimes. Recipients of the U visa, including victims of crimes against women, can adjust to lawful permanent resident status based on humanitarian grounds as determined by the U.S. attorney general.

THE IMMIGRATION ACT OF 1990 (IMMACT)

It took six years of commitment and negotiation to pass the Immigration Reform and Control Act. Almost as soon as that law was passed, Senators Edward Kennedy (D-MA) and Alan Simpson (R-WY) began to work to change the Immigration and Nationality Act Amendments of 1965 (Public Law 89-236) that determined legal immigration into the United States. Senators Kennedy and Simpson claimed that the "family-oriented" system allowed one legal immigrant to bring too many relatives into the country, which distorted the character of immigration. Instead, they wanted immigration policy to cut back the number of dependents admitted and replace those with individuals who have skills or money to immediately benefit the American economy.

The result was the Immigration Act of 1990 (IMMACT; Public Law 101-649). Enacted on November 29, 1990, IMMACT represented a major overhaul of immigration law. The law's focus was to increase the numerical limits of immigrants and change the preference system, giving a greater priority to employment-based immigration than there had been in the past. The law also created a category of Diversity Program admissions to enable immigrants from countries that had been ignored in the recent past (mainly western Europeans) to be admitted more easily to the United States.

The total number of immigrants was set at 700,000 annually from FY (fiscal year) 1992 through FY 1994 and then revised to an annual level of 675,000 beginning in FY 1995. The 675,000 level would consist of 480,000 family-sponsored immigrants, 140,000 employment-based immigrants, and 55,000 Diversity Program immigrants.

IMMACT almost tripled the level of employment-based immigration—from 54,000 to 140,000. The goal was to attract professional people with skills that would promote economic development in the United States. This was in contrast to the unskilled workers who were legalized through IRCA. IMMACT allocations are listed below:

• Preference 1—40,000 visas for priority workers with extraordinary ability, outstanding professors and researchers, and certain multinational executives and managers.

• Preference 2—40,000 visas for members of the professions holding advanced degrees or aliens of exceptional ability, both requiring labor certification (the Secretary of Labor must certify that U.S. workers are not available and will not be hurt by the aliens' admission).

• Preference 3—40,000 visas for skilled workers with at least two years of vocational training or experience, professionals with the equivalent of a college degree, or needed unskilled workers (limited to 10,000), all requiring labor certification.

- Preference 4—10,000 visas for special immigrants, including ministers of religion, persons working for religious organizations, foreign medical graduates, alien employees of the U.S. government abroad, and alien retired employees of international organizations, of which not more than 5,000 may be religious workers.

- Preference 5—10,000 visas for employment-creation investors who invest at least $1 million (or $500,000 in rural areas or areas of high unemployment), which will create at least 10 new jobs.

The allotment of 140,000, however, includes both workers and their families so that the actual number of workers is considerably lower. In 1998 only about 43 percent of the visas set aside for workers actually went to them; the rest went to their families.

Diversity Program Immigrants

IMMACT made new provisions for the admission of "diversity immigrants" from countries with low rates of immigration to the United States. (Ironically, this refers, in part, to European immigrants, originally the vast majority of immigrants to the United States.) The temporary program (1992 to 1994) created 40,000 visas annually for aliens from 34 countries, at least 40 percent of which were designated for Ireland. The transition period also provided 1,000 visas for displaced Tibetans living in India or Nepal.

In the first year of the Diversity Program (1992) the INS ran a lottery, and the "winners" were chosen based on the chronological order of the receipt of the visa applications. Applicants were permitted to file multiple applications to improve their chances. About 20,000 visas were granted to Irish applicants; visas also went to natives of Poland (12,060), Japan (6,413), the United Kingdom (3,054), and Indonesia (2,947).

In 1993 and 1994 selections were made randomly rather than by chronological receipt of applications. In addition, only one application per immigrant was permitted. Ireland and Poland received nearly 87 percent of the visas. The permanent Diversity Program began in 1995. Fifty-five thousand visas were available annually to natives of foreign states from which immigration was less than 50,000 over the preceding five years.

Under the permanent program, no country is permitted more than 7 percent (3,500) of the total, and Northern Ireland is treated as a separate state. Aliens must have a high school education or its equivalent or two years experience in an occupation that requires at least two years of training or experience. Starting with fiscal year 1999, the number of visas was reduced to 50,000 so that 5,000 visas may be allotted to NACARA participants. In 2000, 8 million persons qualified for the diversity lottery, with the INS disqualifying an additional 2.5 million for failing to follow instructions. Table 2.5 shows the breakdown of the regions and countries that won the lottery.

A person who is selected under the lottery program may apply for permanent residence. If permanent residence is granted, the person will be authorized to work in the United States. The individual's spouse and unmarried children under the age of 21 are also allowed to enter the United States.

Political and Ideological Grounds

IMMACT changed the political and ideological grounds for exclusion and deportation. The law repealed the ban against the admission of communists and representatives of other totalitarian regimes as nonimmigrants. In addition immigration applicants previously excluded because of associations with communism were provided exceptions if the applicants had been involuntary members of the communist party, had terminated membership, or merely had close family relationships with people affiliated with communism.

Temporary Protected Status

IMMACT authorizes the U.S. attorney general to grant temporary protected status (TPS) to undocumented alien nationals present in the United States when a natural disaster or ongoing armed conflict poses a danger to their personal safety. TPS lasts for 6 to 18 months unless conditions in the alien national's country warrant an extension of stay.

TPS does not lead to permanent resident status, although these aliens may obtain work authorization. Foreign nationals who have been convicted in the United States of either a felony or two or more misdemeanors are not eligible for TPS. Once the TPS designation ends, the foreign nationals will resume the same immigrant status they had before TPS (unless that status has expired) or return to any other status obtained while in TPS.

As of March 29, 2001, nationals of El Salvador and Angola were the most recent groups of aliens granted temporary protected status. (See Table 2.6.) In January and February 2001 two major earthquakes hit El Salvador, resulting in at least 1,100 deaths and over 7,800 injuries. About 2,500 persons were reported missing. The TPS designation, made by Attorney General John Ashcroft, was estimated to cover as many as 150,000 potential Salvadoran applicants.

On March 29, 2001, the TPS designation for Angolans expired. However, Attorney General Ashcroft extended their TPS status for another year. He determined that the ongoing armed conflict in Angola continued to pose a serious threat to the safety of its nationals who were required to return under U.S. immigration law. About 3,372 Angolans were eligible to renew their status. Another 3,300 Angolans were eligible to apply for initial TPS.

THE WELFARE REFORM LAW OF 1996

Under Title IV of the Personal Responsibility and Work Opportunity Reconciliation Act of 1996 (also called the

TABLE 2.5

Number of Diversity Immigrant Visas issued by country, 2000

Africa

Algeria	1,499	Eritrea	220	Namibia	10
Angola	12	Ethiopia	2,284	Niger	22
Benin	89	Gabon	24	Nigeria	8,550
Botswana	8	Gambia, The	122	Rwanda	35
Burkina Faso	31	Ghana	8,662	Sao Tome and Principe	0
Burundi	13	Guinea	332	Senegal	207
Cameroon	860	Guinea-Bissau	1	Seychelles	3
Cape Verde	3	Kenya	1,514	Sierra Leone	2,617
Central African Rep.	18	Lesotho	3	Somalia	1,678
Chad	29	Liberia	1,762	South Africa	663
Comoros	2	Libya	79	Sudan	2,294
Congo	51	Madagascar	20	Swaziland	2
Congo, Democratic	386	Malawi	47	Tanzania	267
Republic of the		Mali	86	Togo	664
Cote D'Ivoire	333	Mauritania	47	Tunisia	175
Djibouti	12	Mauritius	28	Uganda	169
Egypt	3,301	Morocco	3,007	Zambia	72
Equatorial Guinea	5	Mozambique	7	Zimbabwe	97

Asia

Afghanistan	59	Iraq	49	Nepal	128
Bahrain	7	Israel	67	Oman	4
Bangladesh	9,175	Japan	367	Pakistan	3,187
Bhutan	0	Jordan	86	Qatar	6
Brunei	0	North Korea	3	Saudi Arabia	83
Burma	553	Kuwait	29	Singapore	33
Cambodia	103	Laos	7	Sri Lanka	220
Hong Kong	136	Lebanon	47	Syria	66
Special Admin Region		Malaysia	102	Thailand	117
Indonesia	758	Maldives	0	United Arab Emirates	42
Iran	489	Mongolia	4	Yemen	63

Oceania

Australia	656	Nauru	0	Solomon Islands	0
Fiji	1,069	New Zealand	357	Tonga	178
Kiribati	0	Palau	2	Tuvalu	0
Marshall Islands	7	Papua New Guinea	9	Vanuatu	0
Micronesia,	0	Samoa	24		
Federated State of					

Europe

Albania	6,401	Greece	107	Northern Ireland	73
Andorra	0	Hungary	219	Norway	39
Armenia	1,214	Iceland	35	Portugal	67
Austria	170	Ireland	564	Macau	16
Azerbaijan	423	Italy	294	Romania	3,494
Belarus	896	Kazakhstan	689	Russia	6,481
Belgium	83	Kyrgyzstan	181	San Marino	0
Bosnia and Herzegovina	83	Latvia	288	Serbia-Montenegro	597
Bulgaria	4,381	Liechtenstein	1	Slovakia	375
Croatia	123	Lithuania	1,316	Slovenia	26
Cyprus	37	Luxembourg	4	Spain	123
Czech Republic	215	Macedonia, Former	397	Sweden	272
Denmark	88	Yugoslav Rep. of		Switzerland	420
Estonia	152	Malta	27	Tajikistan	190
Finland	72	Moldova	418	Turkey	1,368
France	602	Monaco	1	Turkmenistan	66
Martinique	3	Netherlands	112	Ukraine	8,035
Guadeloupe	0	Aruba	2	Uzbekistan	964
Georgia	423	Netherlands Antilles	7	Vatican City	0
Germany	3,417				

North America

Bahamas, The	36

South America, Central America, and The Caribbean

Antigua and Barbuda	11	Dominica	58	Peru	1,040
Argentina	404	Ecuador	496	Saint Kitts and Nevis	7
Barbados	23	Grenada	36	Saint Lucia	22
Belize	18	Guatemala	302	Saint Vincent and	26
Bolivia	78	Guyana	166	The Grenadines	
Brazil	940	Honduras	143	Suriname	23
Chile	75	Nicaragua	38	Trinidad and Tobago	607
Costa Rica	150	Panama	100	Uruguay	39
Cuba	1,286	Paraguay	7	Venezuela	526

Natives of the following countries were not eligible to participate in DV-2000: Canada, China (mainland and Taiwan, except Hong Kong S.A.R.), Colombia, Dominican Republic, El Salvador, Haiti, India, Jamaica, Mexico, the Philippines, Poland, South Korea, United Kingdom (except Northern Ireland) and its dependent territories, and Vietnam.

SOURCE: Roger G. Kramer, *Developments in International Migration to the United States: 1999*. U.S. Department of Labor, Bureau of International Labor Affairs, Washington, DC, 1999

welfare reform law; Public Law 104-193), benefits for legal immigrants would be cut by about 44 percent. (Illegal immigrants were already ineligible for most major welfare programs.) The law is designed to ensure that available welfare benefits do not serve as an incentive for immigration and that immigrants admitted to the United States be self-reliant.

In the past, legal immigrants had generally been eligible for the same welfare benefits as citizens. Immigrants who entered the United States prior to passage of the welfare reform law on August 22, 1996 (pre-reform immigrants) retained eligibility for Supplemental Security Income (SSI) for the aged, blind, or disabled. The law, however, gave states the option of barring or limiting the pre-reform immigrants from Medicaid and the Temporary Assistance for Needy Families (TANF) benefits that they had previously been eligible to receive. Pre-reform immigrants also lost their food stamp benefits. (See Table 2.7.)

Medicaid is a joint federal-state health insurance program for certain low-income and needy people, while Temporary Assistance for Needy Families (TANF) is a federal block grant program for needy families with dependent children.

The welfare reform law also barred legal immigrants arriving after August 22, 1996 (new immigrants) from receiving SSI benefits and food stamps until they became naturalized citizens. They were not eligible for Medicaid and TANF benefits for five years after arrival. After that time the states would have the option of whether or not to grant these benefits. (See Table 2.7.) The welfare reform law also requires some sponsors of new immigrants to sign affidavits of support, which are legally binding contracts by which these sponsors agree to financially aid the immigrants.

Several groups of immigrants were exempted from the provisions of the welfare reform law barring receipt of benefits. Refugees, asylees, and persons granted withholding of deportation could apply for food stamps and TANF benefits during the first five years and for Medicaid benefits and SSI during the first seven years of living in the United States. Also exempted were immigrants who had worked at least 10 years, as well as veterans and active-duty military personnel and their spouses and dependent children.

Restoration of Government Benefits

On August 15, 1997, the Balanced Budget Act (Public Law 105-34) restored SSI and Medicaid benefits to legal immigrants who were receiving these benefits when the welfare reform law was passed. In June 1998 the Agricultural Research, Extension, and Education Reform Act (Public Law 105-185) restored food stamp benefits to certain pre-reform immigrants. Effective November 1, 1998, pre-reform immigrants (including those who had been receiving food stamp benefits or SSI), the disabled, and people younger than 18, or age 65 and older as of August 22, 1996, recovered their food stamp eligibility. This group comprised an estimated 250,000 immigrants.

On October 28, 1998, the Noncitizen Benefit Clarification and Other Technical Amendments Act of 1998 (Public Law 105-306) amended the welfare reform law. The amendment required that nonqualified aliens who were receiving SSI and Medicaid benefits on August 22, 1996, could retain these benefits.

Some States Provide Food Stamps to Ineligible Legal Immigrants

In 1997, when the food stamp restrictions went into effect, an estimated 940,000 of the 1.4 million legal immigrants receiving food stamps lost their eligibility. Nearly one-fifth were immigrant children. In *Welfare Reform: Many States Continue Some Federal or State Benefits for Immigrants* (Washington, D.C., 1998), the U.S. General Accounting Office reported to the U.S. Senate Subcommittee on Children and Families that, in 1997 and 1998, 14 states had created food stamp programs that served about one-quarter of this immigrant group nationwide. Most recipients were children, the elderly, and the disabled.

Some states have continued to provide food assistance to ineligible legal immigrants. As of February 2001, 13 states provided food stamps to these immigrants. An estimated 85,863 recipients cost the states over $4 million monthly. (See Table 2.8.)

ANTITERRORISM AND EFFECTIVE DEATH PENALTY ACT (AEDP) OF 1996

On April 24, 1996, the Antiterrorism and Effective Death Penalty Act was passed in response to the Oklahoma City bombing in 1995. Among its provisions that pertained to immigrants was the expedited removal of

TABLE 2.6

Temporary protected status

Country	Currently Designated?	Designation Date*	Expiration Date
Angola	No	3/29/2000	3/29/2001
Angola II[a]	Yes	3/29/2001	3/29/2002
Bosnia-Herzegovina	No	8/10/1992	2/10/2001
Burundi	No	11/3/1997	11/2/2001
Burundi II[a]	Yes	11/9/1999	11/2/2001
El Salvador	No	1/1/1991	6/30/1992 (DED to 12/31/1994)
El Salvador II[b]	Yes	3/9/2001	9/9/2002
Guinea-Bissau	No	3/11/1999	9/10/2000
Honduras	Yes	1/5/1999 (CR from 12/30/1998)	7/5/2001
Kosovo (province ofYugoslavia)	No	6/9/1998	12/8/2000
Kosovo II[a] (province of Yugoslavia) (redesignation)	No	6/8/1999	12/8/2000
Kuwait	No	3/27/1991	3/27/1992
Lebanon	No	3/27/1991	3/28/1993
Liberia I	No	3/27/1991	9/28/1998 (DED)
Liberia II	No	4/7/1997 (CR from 6/1/1996)	9/28/1998 (DED)
Liberia III	No (DED through 9/29/2001)	9/29/1998	9/28/1999** (DED through 9/29/2001)
Montserrat	Yes	8/28/1997 (CR from 8/22/1997)	8/27/2001
Nicaragua	Yes	1/5/1999 (CR from 12/30/1998)	7/5/2001
Rwanda	No	6/7/1994	12/6/1997
Sierra Leone	No	11/4/1997	11/2/2001
Sierra Leone II[a]	Yes	11/09/1999	11/2/2001
Somalia	Yes	9/16/1991	9/17/2001
Sudan	No	11/4/1997	11/2/2001
Sudan II[a]	Yes	11/9/1999	11/2/2001

[a] Subsequent listings of these countries indicate a re-designation under the TPS program.

[b] The most recent designation of El Salvador under the TPS program is not a "re-designation" of the original, statutory designation under Section 303 of the IMMACT of 1990. The original designation was based upon Congress' determination that there was an ongoing world conflict in El Salvador, whereas the new designation is based on the Attorney General's determination that recent earthquakes have resulted in a substantial, but temporary, disruption of living conditions, such that El Salvador is temporarily unable to handle adequately the return of its nationals.

* Unless otherwise indicated, continuous residence (CR) and continuous physical presence (CPP) are required from designation date.

** The President has directed the Attorney General to extend deferred enforced departure (DED) and related employment authorization benefits to eligible Liberians in the United States until 9/29/2001.

SOURCE: U.S. Department of Justice, Immigration and Naturalization Service: Washington, D.C. [Online] http://www.ins.usdoj.gov/graphics/services/tps_inter.htm [accessed April 6, 2001]

criminal aliens. It also authorized state and local law enforcement officials to arrest and detain illegal aliens.

ILLEGAL IMMIGRATION REFORM AND IMMIGRANT RESPONSIBILITY ACT (IIRIRA) OF 1996

On September 30, 1996, the Illegal Immigration Reform and Immigrant Responsibility Act (IIRIRA; Public Law 104-208) became law. In an effort to reduce illegal immigration, IIRIRA, among its many provisions,

TABLE 2.7

Overview of Federal Welfare Program eligibility for immigrants, 1998

Federal program	Immigrants[a]	
	Pre-reform (entered United States before Aug. 22, 1996)	New (entered United States on or after Aug. 22, 1996)
TANF: Assistance for needy families with dependent children who meet state eligibility criteria	State's option to continue benefits.[b]	No benefits available for first 5 years, then at state's option.
Medicaid:[c] Medical assistance to needy individuals who meet federal and state eligibility criteria	Benefits continued for those receiving SSI and state's option to continue benefits for others.[b]	No benefits available for first 5 years, then at state's option.
SSI: Cash assistance to needy blind, disabled, or aged individuals who meet federal eligibility criteria	Benefits continued for those receiving SSI[b] and those who are or become blind or disabled can apply in the future.	No benefits available until citizenship.
Food stamps: Food assistance to needy individuals who meet federal eligibility criteria	No benefits available until citizenship.	No benefits available until citizenship.

Note: This reflects the welfare reform provisions as of May 1998. In June 1998, P.L. 105-185 was enacted to restore food stamp eligibility to certain pre-reform immigrants.

[a]Exceptions allow for benefits to be provided to aliens entering the United States as refugees or asylees, Amerasian immigrants, Cuban or Haitian entrants, and those whose deportation is withheld. These individuals are eligible to apply for TANF and Food Stamp benefits during the first 5 years and for Medicaid and SSI during their first 7 years of U.S. residency. In addition, benefits may be provided to immigrants who are honorably discharged veterans, active-duty personnel, or their spouses and dependent children, and pre-reform or new immigrants (after 5 years of U.S. residency) who can be credited with 40 work quarters through their own or their parents' or spouse's work.

[b]Certain noncitizens who remain in the country legally but do not meet the definition of "qualified alien," such as those Permanently Residing Under the Color of Law (PRUCOL) may no longer meet the eligibility criteria for TANF, Medicaid, and SSI. PRUCOL status denotes those aliens who have legally resided in the country for an indefinite period of time but are not lawfully admitted for permanent residence. Such status was used in determining an alien's eligibility for certain welfare benefits.

[c]Immigrants who are no longer eligible for Medicaid retain eligibility for Medicaid's emergency services.

SOURCE: *Welfare Reform: Many States Continued Some Federal or State Benefits for Immigrants,* U.S. General Accounting Office, Washington, D.C., 1998

- Required doubling the number of U.S. Border Patrol agents to 10,000 by the year 2001 and increasing equipment and technology at air and land ports of entry.

- Authorized improvements of southwest border barriers.

- Toughened penalties for immigrant smuggling (up to 10 years in prison, 15 years for third and subsequent offenses) and document fraud (up to 15 years in prison).

- Increased INS investigators for work site enforcement, visa overstayers, and alien smuggling.

- Increased detention space for criminals and other deportable aliens.

- Instituted a new "expedited removal" proceeding (denial of an alien's entry into the United States without a hearing) to speed deportation of aliens with no documents or with fraudulent documents.

- Authorized three voluntary pilot programs to enable employers to verify the immigrant status of job applicants and to reduce the number and types of documents needed for identification and employment eligibility.

- Required a legally binding affidavit of support from immigrant sponsors, who must have an income of at least 125 percent of the poverty level. (In 2000 the poverty level was $17,761 for a family of four and $24,636 for a family of six.)

- Instituted a bar on admissibility for aliens seeking to reenter the United States after having been unlawfully present in the country—a bar of three years for aliens unlawfully present from six months to a year and a bar of 10 years for those unlawfully present for more than a year.

Employment Verification Process

As mandated by IIRIRA, the U.S. General Accounting Office (GAO) reported to Congress about the state of the current employment verification process as it pertained to the hiring of unauthorized aliens. In *Illegal Aliens: Significant Obstacles to Reducing Unauthorized Alien Employment Exist* (Washington, D.C., April 1999), the GAO concluded that, although IRCA established a process by which employers can verify an applicant's eligibility to work in the United States, the continued prevalence of fraudulent documentation and employers who seek "cheap labor" present obstacles to the implementation of IIRIRA.

During 9,600 work site investigations between October 1996 and May 1998, the INS arrested about 27,500 unauthorized aliens. In over half (55 percent) of the 4,755 completed investigations involving employers seemingly compliant with Form I-9 paperwork requirements, the INS found nearly 13,000 unauthorized aliens working. Unauthorized aliens were also found in 82 percent of the 1,655 completed investigations involving noncompliant

TABLE 2.8

State-funded food programs for legal immigrants

The table below shows programs states have initiated to provide food assistance to legal immigrants who are ineligible for federal Food Stamp (FS) benefits as a result of welfare reform.

States	Starting Date	February 2001 Targeted Population	Persons Served (Monthly Estimate)*	Issuance (Monthly Estimate)
California	9-1-97	Legal immigrants otherwise eligible.	72,457 EBT - 9,887	$3,480,005 EBT - $490,162
Illinois	1-1-98	Parents of FS eligible children; 60-60-64-year-olds. Must have been in the U.S. on 8/22/96.	EBT - 266	EBT - $16,067
Maine	9-1-98	Legal immigrants otherwise eligible.	411	$22,851
Maryland	10-1-97	Children under 18 arriving in U.S. after 8/22/96.	EBT - 233	EBT - $19,407
Mebraska	8-1-97	Legal immigrants otherwise eligible.	696	$56,797
New York	9-1-97	Elderly (60-67-year-olds) living in in the same county since 8/22/96.	83 EBT - 868	$8,567 EBT - $98,435
Ohio (Phasing out program)	4-1-98	SSI recipients who resided in Ohio as of 8/22/96.	EBT - 7	EBT - $521
Wisconsin	8-1-98	Legal immigrants otherwise eligible.	EBT - 955	EBT - $45,756
Total			**Coupons - 73,647** **EBT - 12,216** **85,863**	**$3,568,220** **EBT - $670,348** **$4,238,568**
		Other Activity		
Connecticut	4-1-98 State EBT	Legal immigrants otherwise eligible.	Unknown	Unknown
Massachusetts	10-1-97 State EBT	Legal immigrants otherwise eligible.	Unknown	Unknown
New Jersey	3-10-99 State EBT	Parents of FS-eligible children complying with work requirements; elderly (65 or Older) arriving after 8/22/96.	Unknown	Unknown
Rhode Island	10-1-98 State EBT	Legal immigrants otherwise eligible.	Unknown	Unknown
Washington	11-1-99 State EBT	Legal immigrants otherwise eligible.	Unknown	Unknown

* Estimates are based on information reported by states to USDA and are an average of the prior 3 months.
SSI - Supplemental Security Income
EBT - Electronic Benefits Transfer; operates like a bank card that a store uses to debit a Food Stamp account. It will eventually replace the paper food stamp coupons.

SOURCE: "State-Funded Food Programs For Legal Immigrants" U.S. Department of Agriculture, Food and Nutrition Service, Washington, D.C., (last modified 2/26/01), http://www.fns.usda.gov/fsp/MENU/APPS/ELGIBILITY/WorkandAliens/Statesprogram.htm [Accessed on 4/1/01]

employers who were subject to fines. The INS arrested 7,055 unauthorized aliens working for noncompliant employers. (See Figure 2.2.)

The INS arrested unauthorized aliens in 48 percent of the investigations involving targeted industries and 43 percent of non-targeted industries. In the targeted-industry investigations, the INS made arrests in two-thirds (66 percent) of completed investigations in the landscape and horticultural services and 61 percent in the miscellaneous food preparation industry. (See Table 2.9.)

It took 10 years after IRCA for Congress, through the IIRIRA, to require the Immigration and Naturalization Service to test three pilot programs to enable employers to electronically verify employees' work eligibility. However, employer participation in the programs is generally voluntary and, as of June 2000, the INS achieved just 10 percent of its target participation rate of 16,000 employers, down from 16 percent in 1998. The INS found that employers have been reluctant to participate in electronic verification, fearing that employees rejected by the system may find employment with competitors not enrolled in the program. Some employers are also worried about further INS inspections, such as those involving compliance with Form I-9 paperwork requirements.

IIRIRA also authorized the reduction of the number and types of documents needed for identification and employment eligibility. However, the INS has not resolved this matter. As of May 2001 the documents in Table 2.4 remained acceptable for verification purposes. In the meantime, the INS began issuing new documents with increased security features. According to the General Accounting Office, the new security features do not seem to deter unauthorized aliens from using counterfeit versions of the new documents.

FIGURE 2.2

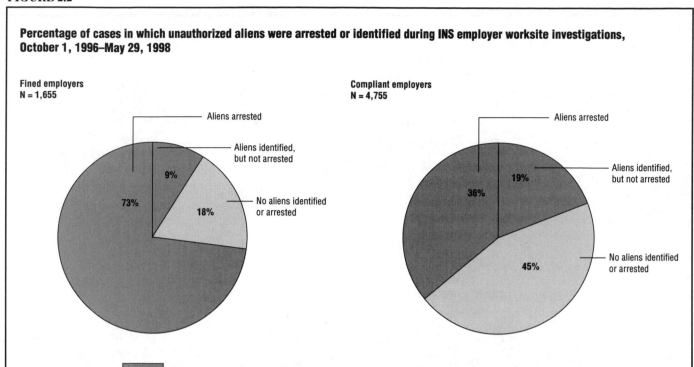

Percentage of cases in which unauthorized aliens were arrested or identified during INS employer worksite investigations, October 1, 1996–May 29, 1998

Fined employers
N = 1,655

Aliens arrested

Aliens identified, but not arrested

No aliens identified or arrested

9%

73%

18%

Compliant employers
N = 4,755

Aliens arrested

Aliens identified, but not arrested

No aliens identified or arrested

19%

36%

45%

Percentage of cases in which INS found unauthorized aliens during employer worksite investigations

Note 1: Figure does not include investigations that are completed with the issuance of a warning notice; categorized as NIFs but with no information on the size and type of the fine; or completed without the determination of fine, warning, or compliance. The figure also does not include cases with missing data regarding the number of aliens arrested or identified.

Note 2: "Identified" refers to unauthorized aliens identified during worksite operations, but not arrested. This category includes unauthorized aliens identified through the I-9 audit that left employment, but were not arrested.

GAO analysis of INS Employer Sanctions database.

SOURCE: *Illegal Aliens: Significant Obstacles to Reducing Unauthorized Alien Employment Exist,* U.S. General Accounting Office, Washington, D.C., 1999

INS Fails to Develop Effective Work Site Investigation Program

In February 1996 President Bill Clinton signed an executive order prohibiting companies that knowingly hire undocumented immigrants from receiving federal contracts or even competing for federal contracts for a year. However, the INS has yet to develop an effective work site enforcement program. In 1998 the INS completed about 6,500 investigations of employers, or just 3 percent of the estimated number of employers of undocumented workers. In 1999 this proportion was down to about 2 percent (3,900 investigations).

In 2000 the U.S. General Accounting Office reported to Congress that the INS had changed its work site enforcement strategy. Instead of focusing on work site raids, it will educate employers about denying employment to undocumented workers and will pursue criminal investigation of offending employers. This strategy will be implemented over the next five years.

BACKLASH FROM THE 1996 LAWS

Detention and Deportation of Criminal Aliens

IIRIRA mandated that the INS detain and remove any noncitizen convicted of crimes that Congress called "aggravated felonies." IIRIRA's definition of aggravated felony includes drug offenses, as well as minor crimes for which a sentence of one year or more has been imposed, even if a judge suspends the sentence.

In addition, the 1996 law can be applied retroactively, which means that the alien can be deported even if the crime was committed before IIRIRA was enacted. Persons who had already served time for a crime can be arrested and held without bail pending a final order of deportation. The law forbids these individuals from appealing for a deportation waiver from a judge or to file a habeas corpus petition to determine the legality of their detention. (A habeas corpus refers to a prisoner's petition to be heard in federal court.) In some cases, legal permanent immigrants are detained even if the crime was committed many years

TABLE 2.9

Results of INS worksite investigations completed in targeted and nontargeted industries, October 1996–May 1998

		Fines[a]		Arrests	
Type of industry[b]	Number of investigations completed	Percentage assessed substantive fine	Percentage assessed paperwork fine	Percentage of investigations with aliens arrested	Number of aliens arrested
Targeted industries	**5,265**	**11**	**8**	**48**	**14,434**
Eating and drinking places	2,672	14	10	49	4,559
Hotels and motels	678	2	3	28	544
General building contractors	354	6	5	58	1,398
Apparel and textile products	343	32	12	55	2,643
Landscape and horticultural services	293	7	8	66	1,154
Masonry, stonework, tile, plaster insulation	192	9	6	55	538
Roofing, siding, sheet metal	159	6	8	54	575
Services to dwellings, buildings (includes janitorial)	139	4	6	57	462
General farm and field crops	99	4	6	57	468
Nursing homes, nursing care facilities	82	2	4	29	42
Miscellaneous food preparation (includes seafood)	81	16	12	61	672
Meat products, preparation	76	3	4	57	1,135
Heavy construction (not buildings)	70	6	4	33	152
Forestry	20	10	0	40	61
Farm labor contractors and labor management services	7	0	0	43	31
Nontargeted industries	4,203	7	8	43	12,649
Total	**9,468**	**9**	**10**	**46**	**27,083**

[a] Category does not include investigations reported as ending with dispositions of Notice of Intent to Fine and where the Employer Sanctions database had no information regarding the type of fine assessed.
[b] Does not include investigations where no standard industry code was recorded (n=166).

SOURCE: *Illegal Aliens: Significant Obstacles to Reducing Unauthorized Alien Employment Exist,* U.S. General Accounting Office, Washington, D.C., 1999

ago. Some have never committed another crime and have become productive members of society.

U.S. Supreme Court Hears Deportation Cases

In 1998 three appellate courts ruled that aliens subject to removal have the right to federal court review of final deportation orders. The Clinton administration appealed these cases to the Supreme Court. The Supreme Court refused to review two of the cases (*Reno v. Navas,* No. 98-996, and *Reno v. Goncalves,* No. 98-835) and sent the third case (*INS v. Magana-Pisano,* No. 98-836) back to the appellate court for further proceedings.

On April 24, 2001, the U.S. Supreme Court began hearing oral arguments on two other appellate court decisions relating to the 1996 laws (IIRIRA and AEDP) to determine whether Congress went too far in divesting the district court of jurisdiction to hear a defendant's habeas corpus petition and whether the AEDP and IIRIRA can be applied retroactively.

One of the cases involves Deboris Calcano-Martinez, who was admitted to the United States at age three as a legal permanent resident in 1971. In 1997 Calcano-Martinez was ordered deported to the Dominican Republic after pleading guilty to selling heroin. The mother of four appealed to the Second Circuit Court of Appeals for a habeas review. In *Calcano-Martinez v. INS* (232 F.3d 328; September 1, 2000), a unanimous Second Circuit Court of

Appeals held that, since the 1996 laws do not explicitly mention their intent to strip federal courts of habeas jurisdiction over criminal aliens' constitutional challenges, a federal court can review the alien's legal claim against final deportation order.

The second case involves Enrico St. Cyr, a Haitian national, who was admitted to the United States as a lawful permanent resident in 1986. In March 1996 St. Cyr pleaded guilty to a charge of drug trafficking and was ordered deported. At the time the Board of Immigration Appeals allowed for aliens to appeal their deportation order. An immigration judge could waive St. Cyr's deportation if he could show that his deportation would cause extraordinary hardship to his family in the United States.

However, the Antiterrorism and Effective Death Penalty Act and the Illegal Immigration Reform and Immigrant Responsibility Act were passed before St. Cyr's deportation proceedings started in 1997, and he was considered subject to the provisions of the 1996 laws. In 1998 the Board of Immigration Appeals dismissed his appeal for a waiver of deportation. In 1999 St. Cyr filed a habeas corpus petition in the U.S. District Court for the District of Connecticut, arguing that the 1996 laws should not be applied retroactively, making him ineligible for a waiver of deportation. The district court held that it had the jurisdiction to hear the habeas corpus petition. Moreover, it ruled that the 1996 laws may not be applied to an alien if the crime, criminal proceedings, and conviction occurred before the passage of the laws. On September 1, 2000, in *St. Cyr v. INS* (229 F.3d 406), the Second Circuit Court of appeals (with one justice dissenting) affirmed the district court's decision.

On June 25, 2001, in a 5-4 decision, the Supreme Court ruled that legal immigrants convicted of a crime have the right to challenge their deportation in court (*Calcano-Martinez v. INS*, No. 00-1011, and *INS v. St. Cyr*, No. 00-767). On June 28, 2001, the Court ruled on related cases (*Zadvydas v. Davis*, No. 99-7791, and *Ashcroft v. Ma*, No. 00-38). The Court held, again by a 5-4 decision, that the government may not detain deportable aliens indefinitely just because their home countries would not accept them.

Many Aliens are Detained in U.S. Jails

To allow for the construction of more detention facilities, Congress delayed the mandatory detention provisions of the 1996 laws from going into effect until October 9, 1998. However, the INS continues to rely on county jails, federal prisons, and private lockups to accommodate the increasing number of detained noncitizens. Some aliens with no criminal convictions, such as asylum seekers, are held with some of the nation's toughest criminals.

On April 1, 2001, the *Dallas Morning News* (Dallas, Texas) released its findings on aliens detained in U.S. jails. The *News* obtained this information under the federal Freedom of Information Act and after settlement of a lawsuit with the INS who initially refused to provide the information. The *News* found that 851 persons from 69 countries have been detained by the INS for at least three years. About 60 percent had been convicted of aggravated felony. However, over 360 inmates have no criminal convictions. These include asylum seekers.

Cubans comprised about 70 percent of the longest-held prisoners. Of the 588 Cuban detainees, 160 have been in jail for 10 years or more. The *Dallas Morning News* believes the Cuban detainees had come in 1980 as part of the Mariel boatlift. Nationals of Vietnam, Laos, and Cambodia accounted for about 10 percent of those in jail. They will most probably remain in jail indefinitely because their countries refuse to accept deportees from the U.S. According to the *News*, on any given day, about 20,000 aliens are in INS detention.

NEWLY ENACTED LAWS

Legal Immigration and Family Equity Act (LIFE)

On December 21, 2000, the Legal Immigration and Family Equity Act (LIFE) became law. Among its provisions was the temporary reinstatement of Section 245(i) of the Immigration and Nationality Act of 1952 (Public Law 82-414), allowing undocumented immigrants to apply for visas without first leaving the United States. A visa allows an illegal alien to stay in the country and wait for adjustment to lawful permanent resident status. Prior to this time, most illegal aliens were required to leave the country and apply for a visa at a U.S. consulate abroad. Illegal aliens who were in the United States for at least six months could be barred from re-entry for up to 10 years. In 1994 Congress had initially added Section 245(i) to the 1952 law but let it expire in 1998.

About 640,000 illegal aliens were affected by Section 245(i). An alien had to be sponsored by either a relative who is a U.S. citizen or a lawful permanent resident or by an employer. U.S. citizens could apply on behalf of their spouses, children, parents, or siblings. Lawful permanent residents could apply on behalf of their spouses and unmarried children. The application had to be filed on or before April 30, 2001. When a visa becomes available, the applicant must pay a $1,000 penalty fee and other filing fees.

CHILD CITIZENSHIP ACT OF 2000

Congress passed the Child Citizenship Act of 2000 (Public Law 106-395) on October 30, 2000, granting automatic U.S. citizenship to foreign-born children of Americans, including adopted children. About 150,000 persons became U.S. citizens on February 27, 2001, the day the law took effect.

To be eligible for automatic U.S. citizenship, a child must satisfy the definition of "child" for naturalization purposes under the Immigration and Nationality Act (INA) of 1952 and meet the following requirements:

- The child has at least one U.S. citizen parent (by birth or naturalization).

- The child is under 18 years of age.

- The child is currently residing permanently in the United States in the legal and physical custody of the U.S. citizen parent.

- The child is a lawful permanent resident.

- If the child is adopted, he or she must meet the requirements of the INA as it applies to an adopted child.

The new law, however, is not retroactive. Persons age 18 or older on February 27, 2001, do not qualify for citizenship. If they seek naturalization, they have to fulfill the same eligibility requirements that currently exist for adult lawful permanent residents.

CHAPTER 3
CURRENT IMMIGRATION STATISTICS

To understand the scope of the immigration issue in the United States, it is important to know how many immigrants are in the country, where they come from, why they come here, and why some do not get to stay here. Because legislation is written and projects are funded based on immigrant statistics, it is also vital to know immigrants' ages, the skills they bring, their ability to work, and where they settle in the United States.

Immigrants, as defined by U.S. immigration law, are persons legally admitted for permanent residence in the United States. Some arrive in the United States with immigrant visas issued abroad at a consular office of the U.S. Department of State. (Visas are government authorizations permitting entry into a country.) Others who already reside in the United States adjust their status from temporary to permanent residence. They include illegal immigrants, foreign students, temporary workers, and refugees and asylees.

A HUGE INCREASE

Figure 3.1 shows the number of immigrants admitted between 1901 and 1998. The Immigration Reform and Control Act of 1986 (IRCA) (Public Law 99-603) helped boost the number of immigrants admitted to the United States to over 1.5 million in 1990. The IRCA status adjustments of about 1.1 million (part of the nearly 2.7 million ultimately legalized) pushed the number of admitted immigrants to over 1.8 million in 1991. Since then, the number of legal immigrants has decreased, dropping to 660,477 in 1998.

FIGURE 3.1

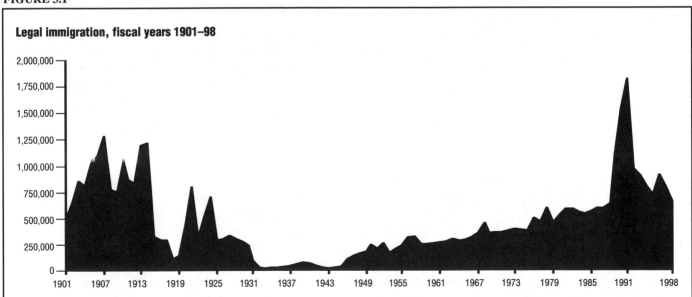

Legal immigration, fiscal years 1901–98

SOURCE: "Chart 1. Legal Immigration: Fiscal Years 1901–98," in *Legal Immigration, Fiscal Year 1998.* U.S. Department of Justice, Immigration and Naturalization Service: Washington, D.C., July 1999

FIGURE 3.2

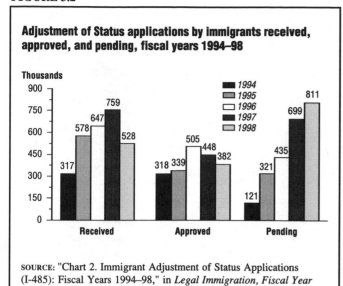

Adjustment of Status applications by immigrants received, approved, and pending, fiscal years 1994–98

SOURCE: "Chart 2. Immigrant Adjustment of Status Applications (I-485): Fiscal Years 1994–98," in *Legal Immigration, Fiscal Year 1998*. U.S. Department of Justice, Immigration and Naturalization Service: Washington, D.C., July 1999

ADJUSTMENT OF STATUS

Adjustment of status refers to the procedure that permits certain aliens already in the United States who are eligible to receive an immigrant visa to apply for immigrant status with the Immigration and Naturalization Service (INS). According to the INS, the increase in status adjustments starting in 1995 has resulted in fewer admissions of legal immigrants. In FY (fiscal year) 1997 (October 1, 1996, to September 30, 1997), the number of aliens granted legal permanent residence (798,378) declined 13 percent from FY 1996 (915,900). The 1997 total included 380,718 aliens previously living abroad who were granted immigrant visas through the U.S. Department of State. The remaining 417,660 legal immigrants included former illegal aliens, refugees, and asylees who had lived an average of three years in the United States and adjusted their status through the INS. The decrease in the number of aliens granted legal permanent residence between 1996 and 1997 was not due to a decline in immigrant applications but to the increase in adjustment-of-status applications pending (awaiting decision) at the INS.

Before FY 1995 applications pending averaged about 120,000 per year. Previously, most illegal residents were required to leave the country and apply for an immigrant visa at a U.S. consulate abroad. At the end of 1994 Congress added Section 245(i) to the Immigration and Nationality Act of 1952 (Public Law 82-414), allowing illegal residents eligible to adjust to permanent resident status to do so without leaving the United States. Consequently, during the three years (FYs 1995–1997) that 245(i) was in effect, a great portion of the visa processing became the responsibility of the INS instead of the State Department.

The 245(i) applications pending more than doubled to 321,000 in 1995 from 121,000 in 1994. In 1998 applications pending reached 811,000. (See Figure 3.2.) Section 245(i) officially expired in January 1998, but adjustments of status under this provision continued for some time. By 1999 applications pending totalled 951,000. In December 2000 Section 245(i) under the Legal Immigration and Family Equity Act (LIFE) was revived, with an application expiration date of April 30, 2001. The INS expected about 640,000 eligible illegal aliens to file visa petitions. In a letter to Congress in May 2001, President George W. Bush asked for an extension of the program, noting that about 200,000 applicants did not meet the deadline. On May 21, 2001, the House of Representatives voted for a limited four-month extension, but as of June 1, 2001, the Senate had not voted for any extension and no legislation had been enacted.

Immigrant-rights advocates applauded the president's efforts, but those favoring reduced immigration claimed that extending the program would show the world that the United States is not really serious about curtailing illegal immigration. Critics cited statistics showing that, in cities with large numbers of immigrants, there was a rise in marriages immediately before Section 245(i) expired. In Dallas, Texas, the Dallas County Clerk's office reported that it had issued over 1,250 marriage licenses during March of 2001, up from 860 licenses in March 2000. Los Angeles County issued nearly 13,000 marriage licenses in January and February of 2001, a 59 percent increase over the same period in 2000. The borough of Manhattan in New York City saw the applications for marriage licenses rise from 100 a day to over 300 a day before the expiration of 245(i). Opponents of Section 245(i) pointed out that such law encourages fraudulent marriages.

A CHANGING BLEND OF IMMIGRANTS

Over the past several decades, the main regional source of immigrants to the United States has been shifting away from Europe toward Asia and South and Central America. The changes were caused both by the effect of American involvement in Southeast Asia, which led to a growing proportion of Southeast Asians seeking a new home in the United States, and by recent changes in the immigration laws.

Between 1901 and 1910 about 9 of 10 (91.6 percent) legal immigrants came from Europe. By 1951–60, just slightly half (52.7 percent) of those who entered the United States came from Europe, with more than one-third (36 percent) arriving from North America (mainly Mexico, the Caribbean, and Central America). By 1961–1970, the proportion from Europe had dropped sharply to 33.8 percent, while the percentage from Asia increased dramatically to 43.9 percent. Between 1971 and 1980 North America (37.5 percent) and Asia (35.3 percent) accounted for nearly three-quarters of immigrant admissions. From 1991 through 1998 the proportion of immigrants from

FIGURE 3.3

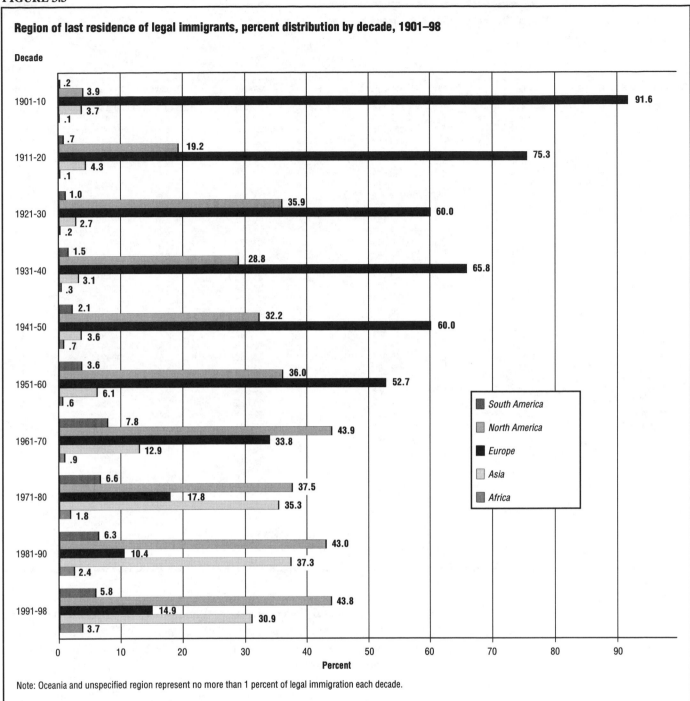

Region of last residence of legal immigrants, percent distribution by decade, 1901–98

Note: Oceania and unspecified region represent no more than 1 percent of legal immigration each decade.

SOURCE: "Chart B. Region of Last Residence of Legal Immigrants, Percent Distribution by Decade," in *1998 Statistical Yearbook of the Immigration and Naturalization Service*. U.S. Department of Justice, Immigration and Naturalization Service: Washington, D.C., November 2000

Europe was barely 15 percent. North America remained the main sending region (43.8 percent), followed by Asia (30.9 percent). (See Figure 3.3.)

In 1998 North Americans (38.3 percent) made up the largest proportion of immigrants, followed by Asians (33.3 percent), and Europeans (13.7 percent). Although African immigrants made up only 6.2 percent of the total immigrants in 1998, their numbers nearly doubled from

26,712 (3.3 percent) in 1994 (not shown) to 52,889 (5.8 percent) in 1996. (See Table 3.1.) This is due primarily to the Diversity Program begun in 1995 as provided by the Immigration Act of 1990 (IMMACT).

Country of Birth

In 1998 by individual country, Mexico was the country of birth of the greatest number of immigrants (131,575

TABLE 3.1

Immigrants admitted to the United States by region of birth and by selected country of birth, fiscal years 1995–98

Region and country of birth	1998 Number	1998 Percent	1997 Number	1997 Percent	1996 Number	1996 Percent	1995 Number	1995 Percent
All countries	**660,477**	**100.0**	**798,378**	**100.0**	**915,900**	**100.0**	**720,461**	**100.0**
Africa	40,660	6.2	47,790	6.0	52,889	5.8	42,456	5.9
Asia	219,696	33.3	265,786	33.3	307,807	33.6	267,931	37.2
Europe	90,793	13.7	119,898	15.0	147,581	16.1	128,185	17.8
North America	**252,996**	**38.3**	**307,488**	**38.5**	**340,540**	**37.2**	**231,526**	**32.1**
Caribbean	75,521	11.4	105,299	13.2	116,801	12.8	96,788	13.4
Central America	35,679	5.4	43,676	5.5	44,289	4.8	31,814	4.4
Other North America	141,796	21.5	158,513	19.9	179,450	19.6	102,924	14.3
Oceania	3,935	.6	4,342	.5	5,309	.6	4,695	.7
South America	45,394	6.9	52,877	6.6	61,769	6.7	45,666	6.3
Unknown	7,003	1.1	197	Z	5	Z	2	Z
1. Mexico	131,575	19.9	146,865	18.4	163,572	17.9	89,932	12.5
2. China, People's Republic	36,884	5.6	41,147	5.2	41,728	4.6	35,463	4.9
3. India	36,482	5.5	38,071	4.8	44,859	4.9	34,748	4.8
4. Philippines	34,466	5.2	49,117	6.2	55,876	6.1	50,984	7.1
5. Dominican Republic	20,387	3.1	27,053	3.4	39,604	4.3	38,512	5.3
6. Vietnam	17,649	2.7	38,519	4.8	42,067	4.6	41,752	5.8
7. Cuba	17,375	2.6	33,587	4.2	26,466	2.9	17,937	2.5
8. Jamaica	15,146	2.3	17,840	2.2	19,089	2.1	16,398	2.3
9. El Salvador	14,590	2.2	17,969	2.3	17,903	2.0	11,744	1.6
10. Korea	14,268	2.2	14,239	1.8	18,185	2.0	16,047	2.2
11. Haiti	13,449	2.0	15,057	1.9	18,386	2.0	14,021	1.9
12. Pakistan	13,094	2.0	12,967	1.6	12,519	1.4	9,774	1.4
13. Colombia	11,836	1.8	13,004	1.6	14,283	1.6	10,838	1.5
14. Russia	11,529	1.7	16,632	2.1	19,668	2.1	14,560	2.0
15. Canada	10,190	1.5	11,609	1.5	15,825	1.7	12,932	1.8
16. Peru	10,154	1.5	10,853	1.4	12,871	1.4	8,066	1.1
17. United Kingdom	9,011	1.4	10,651	1.3	13,624	1.5	12,427	1.7
18. Bangladesh	8,621	1.3	8,681	1.1	8,221	.9	6,072	.8
19. Poland	8,469	1.3	12,038	1.5	15,772	1.7	13,824	1.9
20. Iran	7,883	1.2	9,642	1.2	11,084	1.2	9,201	1.3
Subtotal	443,058	67.1	545,541	68.3	611,602	66.8	465,232	64.6
Other	217,419	32.9	252,837	31.7	304,298	33.2	255,229	35.4

Z Rounds to less than .05 percent.

SOURCE: "Table 2. Immigrants Admitted by Region and Selected Country of Birth: Fiscal Years 1995–98," in *Legal Immigration, Fiscal Year 1998*. U.S. Department of Justice, Immigration and Naturalization Service: Washington, D.C., July 1999

persons), followed by the People's Republic of China (36,884), India (36,482), the Philippines (34,466), and the Dominican Republic (20,387). These five countries combined accounted for nearly 40 percent of all legal immigrants in 1998. (See Table 3.1.)

CATEGORIES OF ADMISSION

There are various ways to qualify for immigration to the United States, but admissions are generally classified by the INS into four major groups:

• Family-reunification immigrants.

• Employment-based immigrants.

• Refugees and asylees.

• Diversity Program immigrants.

IMMACT (Public Law 101-649) established a flexible annual limit of 675,000 immigrants (not counting refugee and asylee adjustments and other categories) to be granted permanent resident status per year. The annual limit is flexible in that it may exceed 675,000 if the maximum number of visas were not issued in the preceding year.

The INS grants visas based on a system consisting of two general categories—family-sponsored and employment-based immigration. (See Table 3.2.) Limits on the number of visas issued are determined annually. Those not qualifying under any of the preferences may apply under the nonpreference category, but very few visas are granted under this category.

The immigration cap can also be overcome based on the number of family-sponsored immigrants. IMMACT put no limit on the number of immediate relatives (spouses, children, and parents) of adult U.S. citizens and children born abroad to alien permanent residents. However, their number is used to calculate the limit of family-sponsored preference visas.

TABLE 3.2

Categories of immigrants included in world-wide annual limit specified in section 201 of the Immigration and Nationality Act, unadjusted and fiscal year 1998 limits

Preference	Description	Unadjusted Limit	Limit
Family-sponsored immigrants		**480,000** [1]	**480,000** [1]
Family-sponsored preferences		**226,000**	**226,000**
First	Unmarried sons and daughters of U.S. citizens and their children	23,400 [2]	23,400 [2]
Second	Spouses, children, and unmarried sons and daughters of permanent resident aliens	114,200 [3]	114,200 [3]
Third	Married sons and daughters of U.S. citizens	23,400 [3]	23,400 [3]
Fourth	Brothers and sisters of U.S. citizens (at least 21 years of age)	65,000 [3]	65,000 [3]
Immediate relatives of adult U.S. citizens (spouses, children, and parents) and children		Not limited; assumed to be	
born abroad to alien residents		254,000 [1]	254,000 [1]
Employment-based preferences		**140,000**	**140,000**
First	Priority workers	40,040 [4]	40,040 [4]
Second	Professionals with advanced degrees or aliens of exceptional ability	40,040 [3]	40,040 [3]
Third	Skilled workers, professionals, needed unskilled workers, and Chinese Student Protection Act immigrants	40,040 [3]	40,040 [3]
Fourth	Special immigrants	9,940	9,940
Fifth	Employment creation ("Investors")	9,940	9,940
Diversity		**55,000**	**55,000**
TOTAL		**675,000**	**675,000**

Note: The annual limits are adjusted based on visa usage in the previous year.

[1] The number of immediate relatives of U.S. citizens included in these figures is assumed to be 254,000. Immediate relatives may enter without any limitation, however, the limit for family-sponsored preference immigrants in a fiscal year is equal to 480,000 minus the number of immediate relatives admitted in the preceding year. The limit of family-sponsored preference visas cannot go below a minimum of 226,000—the worldwide limit of 480,000 minus 254,000.

[2] Plus unused family 4th preference visas.

[3] Visas not used in higher preferences may be used in these categories.

[4] Plus unused employment 4th and 5th preference visas.

SOURCE: "Categories of immigrants included in world-wide annual limit specified in section 201 of the Immigration and Nationality Act: unadjusted and fiscal year 1998 limits," in *Legal Immigration, Fiscal Year 1998*. U.S. Department of Justice, Immigration and Naturalization Service: Washington, D.C., July 1999

In 1998 the worldwide annual limit of family-sponsored preference visas was calculated as 480,000 minus the number of immediate relative visas issued in 1997 (this becomes the assumed number of immediate relatives of U.S. citizens for 1998, which was 254,000). This number, however, is not permitted to go below 226,000—the difference between the worldwide limit of 480,000 and 254,000. (See Table 3.2.)

In 1998 a total of 475,750 family-sponsored persons (accounting for 72 percent of legal immigrants) were admitted to the country. In addition, 77,517 employment-based immigrants (11.7 percent of total immigration) and 45,499 Diversity Program immigrants (6.9 percent) were granted entry to the United States. Refugees and asylees (54,709) made up another 8.3 percent of immigrants. (See Table 3.3.)

The number of family-sponsored preference immigrants in 1998 (191,480) decreased by about 6 percent from 1997 (213,331), below the limit of 226,000. Between 1997 and 1998 immediate relatives of U.S. citizens decreased in number (from 322,440 to 284,270) but increased as a percentage of all immigrants (from 40.4 to 43 percent). (See Table 3.3.)

Also included in the category of immediate relatives are orphans adopted by American citizens. In 1998 14,867 children were in this group. The leading source of orphans was Russia (4,320), followed by the People's Republic of China (3,988) and Korea (1,705). Romania, which has many orphans and abandoned children in institutions, at one point permitted many children to be adopted but has since changed its policy. Only 388 Romanian children were adopted by U.S. families in 1998. A total of 938 Guatemalan children and 576 Vietnamese children were also adopted in 1998. (See Table 3.4.)

In the decade before 1991, employment-based preference immigrants accounted for less than 4 percent of all immigration because their spouses and children used more than half of the visas available in this category. One of the major goals of IMMACT was to increase the number of highly skilled workers entering the United States, from 54,000 in 1991 to 140,000 starting in 1992 (the year IMMACT was implemented). However, the actual number of employment-based immigrants has been lower than 140,000 since 1992. During fiscal years 1994–1998, these workers (not including their families) accounted for about 5 percent of the yearly immigration. (See Table 3.5.)

First-preference employment-based immigrants (priority workers, or workers with needed skills) and second-

TABLE 3.3

Immigrants admitted by major category of admission, fiscal years 1995–98

Category of admission	1998 Number	1998 Percent	1997 Number	1997 Percent	1996 Number	1996 Percent	1995 Number	1995 Percent
Total	660,477	100.0	798,378	100.0	915,900	100.0	720,461	100.0
New arrivals	357,037	54.1	380,718	47.7	421,405	46.0	380,291	52.8
Adjustments of status	303,440	45.9	417,660	52.3	494,495	54.0	340,170	47.2
Categories related to world-wide limits	598,787	90.7	675,816	84.6	772,737	84.4	593,234	82.3
Family-sponsored immigrants	475,750	72.0	535,771	67.1	596,264	65.1	460,376	63.9
Family-sponsored preferences	191,480	29.0	213,331	26.7	294,174	32.1	238,122	33.1
Unmarried sons/daughters of U.S. citizens	17,717	2.7	22,536	2.8	20,909	2.3	15,182	2.1
Spouses and children of alien residents	88,488	13.4	113,681	14.2	182,834	20.0	144,535	20.1
Married sons/daughters of U.S. citizens	22,257	3.4	21,943	2.7	25,452	2.8	20,876	2.9
Siblings of U.S. citizens	63,018	9.5	55,171	6.9	64,979	7.1	57,529	8.0
Immediate relatives of U.S. citizens [1]	284,270	43.0	322,440	40.4	302,090	33.0	222,254	30.8
Spouses	151,172	22.9	170,263	21.3	169,760	18.5	123,238	17.1
Parents	61,724	9.3	74,114	9.3	66,699	7.3	48,382	6.7
Children	70,472	10.7	76,631	9.6	63,971	7.0	48,740	6.8
Children born abroad to alien residents	902	.1	1,432	.2	1,660	.2	1,894	.3
Legalization dependents	21	Z	64	Z	184	Z	277	Z
Employment-based preferences	77,517	11.7	90,607	11.3	117,499	12.8	85,336	11.8
Priority workers	21,408	3.2	21,810	2.7	27,501	3.0	17,339	2.4
Professionals with advanced degree or of exceptional ability	14,384	2.2	17,059	2.1	18,462	2.0	10,475	1.5
Skilled, professionals, unskilled	34,317	5.2	42,596	5.3	62,756	6.9	50,245	7.0
Chinese Student Protection Act	41	Z	142	Z	401	Z	4,213	.6
Needed unskilled workers	6,255	.9	8,702	1.1	11,849	1.3	7,884	1.1
Other skilled, professionals	28,021	4.2	33,752	4.2	50,506	5.5	38,148	5.3
Special immigrants	6,584	1.0	7,781	1.0	7,844	.9	6,737	.9
Investors	824	.1	1,361	.2	936	.1	540	.1
Diversity programs	45,499	6.9	49,374	6.2	58,790	6.4	47,245	6.6
Permanent	45,499	6.9	49,360	6.2	58,245	6.4	40,301	5.6
Transition	X	X	14	Z	545	.1	6,944	1.0
Other categories	61,690	9.3	122,562	15.4	143,163	15.6	127,227	17.7
Amerasians	346	.1	738	.1	956	.1	939	.1
Parolees, Soviet and Indochinese	1,225	.2	1,844	.2	2,269	.2	3,086	.4
Refugees and asylees	54,709	8.3	112,158	14.0	128,565	14.0	114,664	15.9
Refugee adjustments	44,709	6.8	102,052	12.8	118,528	12.9	106,827	14.8
Asylee adjustments [2]	10,000	1.5	10,106	1.3	10,037	1.1	7,837	1.1
Cancellation of removal [2]	4,000	.6	4,628	.6	5,811	.6	3,168	.4
Total, IRCA legalization	955	.1	2,548	.3	4,635	.5	4,267	.6
Residents since 1982	954	.1	1,439	.2	3,286	.4	3,124	.4
Special Agricultural Workers	1	Z	1,109	.1	1,349	.1	1,143	.2
Other	455	.1	646	.1	927	.1	1,103	.2

[1] May enter without limitation; the number admitted may affect the limit on family-sponsored preference immigrants in the following year.
[2] Estimated.
X Not applicable.
Z Rounds to less than .05 percent.

SOURCE: "Immigrants Admitted by Major Category of Admission: Fiscal Years 1995–98," in *Legal Immigration, Fiscal Year 1998*. U.S. Department of Justice, Immigration and Naturalization Service: Washington, D.C., July 1999

preference employment-based immigrants (professionals with advanced degrees or of exceptional ability) accounted for about 46 percent of employment-based immigrants. About 44 percent (34,317) of the employment-based immigrants admitted in 1998 entered under the third preference. They included skilled workers, professionals, needed unskilled workers, their families, and aliens subject to the Chinese Student Protection Act. (See Table 3.5.) The Chinese Student Protection Act of 1992 (Public Law 102-404) allowed nearly 27,000 students from the People's Republic of China who were in the United States after June 4, 1989, but before April 11, 1990, to adjust to permanent resident status. Following the Tiananmen Square incident of June 4, 1989, the United States had offered safe haven to these students.

Immigrant Visa Waiting List

The demand for immigrant visas always far exceeds the limit. In January 1997 more than 3.6 million active registrants were on the waiting list at consular offices abroad. Nearly 1.1 million persons were waiting for visas in the family-sponsored second-preference category (spouses and unmarried children of permanent residents). The wait to enter in this category can be as long as 10 to 15 years. About 3 in 10 (29 percent) persons on the waiting list were Mexicans, primarily relatives of newly legal-

TABLE 3.4

Immigrant orphans adopted by U.S. citizens by gender, age, and region and country of birth, fiscal year 1998

Region and country of birth	Total	Sex			Age				
		Male	Female	Unknown	Under 1 year	1–4 years	5–9 years	Over 9 years	Unknown
All countries	14,867	5,355	9,511	1	6,776	6,420	1,175	487	9
Europe	5,457	2,742	2,715	—	1,739	2,781	727	208	2
Albania	9	2	7	—	—	8	—	1	—
Bulgaria	147	66	81	—	1	111	32	3	—
Czechoslovakia	3	1	2	—	—	3	—	—	—
Czech Republic	1	—	1	—	—	1	—	—	—
Slovak Republic	2	1	1	—	—	2	—	—	—
Estonia	9	6	3	—	—	4	3	2	—
Germany	2	1	1	—	—	1	—	—	1
Greece	4	2	2	—	—	4	—	—	—
Hungary	29	15	14	—	4	20	5	—	—
Latvia	73	33	40	—	31	23	13	6	—
Lithuania	71	38	33	—	16	38	14	3	—
Poland	70	40	30	—	4	36	28	2	—
Portugal	8	3	5	—	—	1	4	3	—
Romania	388	173	215	—	37	293	36	22	—
Soviet Union, former	4,621	2,351	2,270	—	1,639	2,229	590	162	1
Armenia	7	3	4	—	7	—	—	—	—
Belarus	2	—	2	—	—	—	2	—	—
Georgia	7	3	4	—	1	5	—	1	—
Kazakhstan	54	18	36	—	32	14	7	1	—
Kyrgyzstan	4	1	3	—	—	—	—	4	—
Moldova	57	27	30	—	8	49	—	—	—
Russia	4,320	2,227	2,093	—	1,560	2,049	563	147	1
Ukraine	168	70	98	—	31	111	18	8	—
Uzbekistan	1	1	—	—	—	—	—	1	—
Unknown republic	1	1	—	—	—	1	—	—	—
Spain	1	1	—	—	—	—	—	1	—
United Kingdom	6	2	4	—	—	3	—	3	—
Yugoslavia, former	16	8	8	—	7	7	2	—	—
Croatia	4	1	3	—	2	2	—	—	—
Macedonia	8	6	2	—	4	2	2	—	—
Unknown	4	1	3	—	1	3	—	—	—
Asia	7,393	1,702	5,691	—	3,965	3,098	216	110	4
Afghanistan	3	1	2	—	—	—	—	3	—
Bangladesh	6	2	4	—	3	2	—	1	—
Cambodia	241	118	123	—	164	65	6	6	—
China, People's Rep.	3,988	77	3,911	—	1,523	2,387	65	10	3
Hong Kong	24	12	12	—	4	17	2	1	—
India	462	130	332	—	156	237	47	22	—
Indonesia	4	2	2	—	1	2	1	—	—
Iran	4	1	3	—	2	—	—	2	—
Japan	35	21	14	—	25	9	—	1	—
Jordan	1	1	—	—	1	—	—	—	—
Korea	1,705	940	765	—	1,601	97	5	2	—
Lebanon	13	8	5	—	11	2	—	—	—
Nepal	16	4	12	—	6	8	2	—	—
Pakistan	25	13	12	—	13	10	1	1	—
Philippines	189	99	90	—	19	94	36	40	—
Singapore	1	1	—	—	—	1	—	—	—
Sri Lanka	2	2	—	—	1	—	—	1	—
Taiwan	18	5	13	—	13	4	—	1	—
Thailand	78	41	37	—	2	60	11	5	—
Turkey	2	1	1	—	2	—	—	—	—
Vietnam	576	223	353	—	418	103	40	14	1

ized immigrants, followed by Filipinos (15.8 percent), Indians (6.7 percent), and nationals of the People's Republic of China (6.5 percent). (See Figure 3.4.)

CHARACTERISTICS OF IMMIGRANTS

Where Do They Want to Live?

Incoming immigrants are most likely to consider locations that will provide jobs and a community in which they will feel comfortable, usually the area where their relatives or friends who speak their language and have similar customs have already settled and can help them out. As a result, immigrants mostly settle in certain states and metropolitan areas that are already populated with people of similar national backgrounds.

In 1998, of 660,477 incoming immigrants, over 40 percent wanted to live in just two states—California (25.8 percent) and New York (14.6 percent). Other popular destinations for immigrants were Florida (9.1 per-

TABLE 3.4

Immigrant orphans adopted by U.S. citizens by gender, age, and region and country of birth, fiscal year 1998 [CONTINUED]

Region and country of birth	Total	Sex			Age				
		Male	Female	Unknown	Under 1 year	1–4 years	5–9 years	Over 9 years	Unknown
Africa	**171**	**69**	**102**	**—**	**25**	**50**	**45**	**50**	**1**
Algeria	1	—	1	—	1	—	—	—	—
Benin	1	—	1	—	1	—	—	—	—
Cameroon	2	—	2	—	—	—	—	2	—
Egypt	5	1	4	—	3	2	—	—	—
Equatorial Guinea	1	1	—	—	—	—	1	—	—
Eritrea	2	1	1	—	—	—	—	2	—
Ethiopia	88	35	53	—	14	30	27	17	—
Ghana	10	2	8	—	1	—	1	8	—
Kenya	7	2	5	—	1	3	2	1	—
Lesotho	2	2	—	—	—	—	1	1	—
Liberia	9	4	5	—	1	—	2	6	—
Morocco	2	1	1	—	2	—	—	—	—
Nigeria	13	7	6	—	1	7	1	3	1
Rwanda	1	—	1	—	—	—	—	1	—
Sierra Leone	1	—	1	—	—	—	—	1	—
South Africa	17	7	10	—	—	6	8	3	—
Tanzania	1	1	—	—	—	—	—	1	—
Uganda	4	3	1	—	—	—	2	2	—
Zambia	3	1	2	—	—	1	—	2	—
Zimbabwe	1	1	—	—	—	1	—	—	—
Oceania	**3**	**—**	**3**	**—**	**1**	**1**	**—**	**1**	**—**
Fiji	2	—	2	—	—	1	—	1	—
Tonga	1	—	1	—	1	—	—	—	—
North America	**1,344**	**610**	**733**	**1**	**797**	**343**	**130**	**72**	**2**
Mexico	170	79	90	1	86	35	36	12	1
Caribbean	**170**	**61**	**109**	**—**	**23**	**68**	**43**	**36**	**—**
Dominican Republic	9	1	8	—	2	1	3	3	—
Grenada	3	—	3	—	—	—	3	—	—
Haiti	113	44	69	—	20	52	22	19	—
Jamaica	34	14	20	—	1	13	12	8	—
San Lucia	2	1	1	—	—	—	2	—	—
St. Vincent & Grenadines	4	1	3	—	—	2	1	1	—
Trinidad & Tobago	5	—	5	—	—	—	—	5	—
Central America	**1,004**	**470**	**534**	**—**	**688**	**240**	**51**	**24**	**1**
Belize	4	1	3	—	3	—	—	1	—
Costa Rica	5	2	3	—	5	—	—	—	—
El Salvador	14	6	8	—	—	12	2	—	—
Guatemala	938	441	497	—	671	210	37	19	1
Honduras	9	4	5	—	1	3	5	—	—
Nicaragua	16	8	8	—	7	2	5	2	—
Panama	18	8	10	—	1	13	2	2	—
South America	**497**	**231**	**266**	**—**	**248**	**146**	**57**	**46**	**—**
Bolivia	69	31	38	—	31	36	2	—	—
Brazil	86	42	44	—	19	17	24	26	—
Chile	23	12	11	—	1	21	—	1	—
Colombia	221	97	124	—	163	33	17	8	—
Ecuador	53	31	22	—	24	23	5	1	—
Guyana	8	3	5	—	—	1	2	5	—
Paraguay	7	4	3	—	—	5	2	—	—
Peru	22	7	15	—	5	9	5	3	—
Surinam	2	1	1	—	—	—	—	2	—
Venezuela	6	3	3	—	5	1	—	—	—
Unknown	**2**	**1**	**1**	**—**	**1**	**1**	**—**	**—**	**—**

— Represents zero.

SOURCE: "Table 15. Immigrant-orphans adopted by U.S. citizens by sex, age, and region and selected country of birth, fiscal year 1998," in *1998 Statistical Yearbook of the Immigration and Naturalization Service*. U.S. Department of Justice, Immigration and Naturalization Service: Washington, D.C., November 2000

cent), Texas (6.7 percent), New Jersey (5.3 percent), and Illinois (5 percent). (See Table 3.6.) Since 1971, these six states have been the principal states of intended residence for new immigrants, with California the leading state since 1976.

Not surprisingly, almost all the metropolitan areas where the immigrants wanted to live were located in the six states indicated above. The leading metropolitan area was New York City with 82,175 immigrants, followed by Los Angeles-Long Beach, California (59,598); Chicago,

TABLE 3.5

Employment-based immigration by preference, fiscal years 1994–98

	Fiscal Years				
	1994	**1995**	**1996**	**1997**	**1998**
Employment-Based Preference					
Total, Employment 1st preference	**21,053**	**17,339**	**27,501**	**21,810**	**21,408**
Aliens with extraordinary ability	1,313	1,194	2,060	1,717	1,691
Outstanding professors or researchers	1,809	1,617	2,633	2,097	1,835
Multinational executives or managers	4,975	3,922	6,354	5,325	5,183
Spouses and children of 1st preference	12,956	10,606	16,454	12,671	12,699
Total, Employment 2nd preference	**14,432**	**10,475**	**18,462**	**17,059**	**14,384**
Members of professions holding advanced degrees or persons of exceptional ability	6,807	4,952	8,870	8,393	6,933
Spouses and children of 2nd preference	7,625	5,523	9,592	8,666	7,451
Total, Employment 3rd preference	**76,956**	**50,245**	**62,756**	**42,596**	**34,317**
Skilled workers	10,139	9,094	16,001	10,564	8,515
Baccalaureate holders	7,732	5,792	5,507	3,972	3,927
Spouse and child of the above	28,398	23,262	28,998	19,216	15,579
Chinese Student Protection Act	21,297	4,213	401	142	41
Principals	21,008	4,134	373	132	32
Spouses and children	289	79	28	10	9
Other workers (unskilled workers)	4,136	3,636	6,010	4,036	2,701
Spouse & child of unskilled worker	5,254	4,248	5,839	4,666	3,554
Total, Employment 4th preference	**10,406**	**6,737**	**7,844**	**7,781**	**6,584**
Special immigrants	4,647	2,929	3,494	3,652	2,695
Spouse and child of 4th preference	5,759	3,808	4,350	4,129	3,889
Total, Employment of 5th preference	**444**	**540**	**936**	**1,361**	**824**
Employment creation, not targeted area	106	95	143	129	83
Spouses and children	190	190	301	211	156
Employment creation, targeted area	51	79	152	315	176
Spouses and children	97	176	340	706	409
Excluding Chinese Protection Act:					
Total, employment preference, principals	41,715	33,310	51,224	40,200	33,739
Percent of all immigration	5.2	4.6	5.6	5.0	5.1
Total, employment preference, dependents	60,279	47,813	65,874	50,265	43,737
Percent of all immigration	7.5	6.6	7.2	6.3	6.6
TOTAL, employment preferences	101,994	81,123	117,098	90,465	77,476
Percent of all immigration	12.7	11.3	12.8	11.3	11.7
Including Chinese Student Protection Act:					
GRAND TOTAL, employment preferences	123,291	85,336	117,499	90,607	77,517

Notes: Percentages may not add to totals due to rounding. Also, the number of admissions in a given year may exceed the numerical ceiling on visa issuances as immigrant visas may be used up to 6 months after issuance.

SOURCE: Roger G. Kramer, "Table 3. Employment-based Immigration, by Preference: Fiscal Years 1994–98," in *Developments in International Migration to the United States: 1999*. U.S. Department of Labor, Bureau of International Labor Affairs, Washington, DC, 1999

Illinois (30,355), Miami, Florida (28,853); and Washington, D.C., and its surrounding areas in Maryland and Virginia (24,032). (See Table 3.6.)

Occupations

In 1998 about 34 percent of all legal immigrants ages 16 to 64 reported having an occupation at the time of entry or status adjustment. The occupations most frequently mentioned by immigrants were professional specialty and technical occupations (9.2 percent); machine operators, fabricators, and laborers (6.7 percent); and service occupations (5.1 percent). (See Table 3.7.)

Gender and Age

In 1993, for the first time since 1987, female immigrants outnumbered male immigrants. Historically, more females have immigrated to the United States than males; however, from 1988 to 1992, this trend was reversed because the immigrants legalized under IRCA were primarily male. In 1998, 53.5 percent of the aliens admitted were female. The median age of immigrants was 29 years. Nearly one-third were ages 15 to 29. Just 4.7 percent were 65 years old and over. (See Table 3.8.)

NATURALIZATION—BECOMING A CITIZEN

Naturalization is the conferring of U.S. citizenship, by any means, upon a person after birth. A naturalization court grants citizenship if the naturalization occurs within the United States, while a representative of the INS confers naturalization if it is performed outside the United States. Beginning in 1992 the Immigration Act of 1990

FIGURE 3.4

Immigrant waiting list by country, January 1997

Mexico (29.0%)
Other (18.7%)
Guyana (1.4%)
Pakistan (1.5%)
Poland (1.7%)
Jamaica (1.7%)
Hong Kong (1.8%)
Haiti (1.9%)
El Salvador (1.9%)
Vietnam (2.1%)
South Korea (2.1%)
China-Taiwan born (3.0%)
Dominican Republic (4.2%)
Philippines (15.8%)
India (6.7%)
China-mainland born (6.5%)

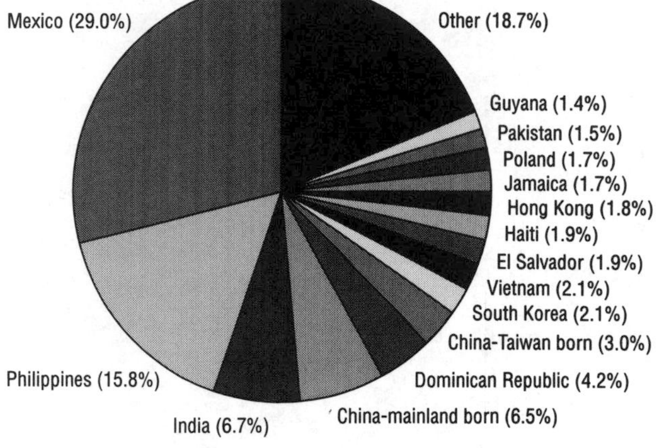

A breakdown of the worldwide waiting list by region is:

	Family Preferences (% of Family Total)		Employment Preferences (% of Employment Total)		Total (% of Total Waiting List)	
Africa	68,745	(1.9%)	3,608	(4.3%)	72,353	(2.0%)
Asia	1,602,761	(45.3%)	43,204	(51.1%)	1,645,965	(45.4%)
Europe	133,219	(3.8%)	11,005	(13.0%)	144,224	(4.0%)
North America*	1,566,452	(44.3%)	18,966	(22.5%)	1,585,418	(43.8%)
Oceania	14,338	(0.4%)	476	(0.6%)	14,814	(0.4%)
South America	152,915	(4.3%)	7,208	(8.5%)	160,123	(4.4%)
Total	**3,538,430**	**(100.0%)**	**84,467**	**(100.0%)**	**3,622,897**	**(100.0%)**

*North America includes Canada, Mexico, Central America and the Caribbean.

SOURCE: "Immigrant Waiting List by Country, January 1997," in *Report of the Visa Office 1998*. U.S. Department of State, Bureau of Consular Affairs: Washington, D.C., 2000

also permitted persons to naturalize through administrative hearings with the INS. When individuals become United States citizens, they pledge allegiance to the United States and renounce allegiance to their former country of nationality.

In order to naturalize most immigrants must meet certain general requirements. They must be at least 18 years old, have been legally admitted to the United States for permanent residence, and have lived in this country continuously for at least five years. They must also be able to speak, read, and write English; know how the U.S. government works; have a basic knowledge of U.S. history; and be of good character. In 1998, 96 percent of the immigrants who became naturalized did so by meeting these general provisions.

Special Provisions

A small proportion of those seeking naturalization do so under special provisions of the naturalization laws that exempt them from one or more of the general requirements. Spouses and children of U.S. citizens and military personnel make up most of those attaining citizenship through special provisions. Spouses of U.S. citizens can become naturalized in only three years instead of the normal five. Children who immigrate with their parents generally do not naturalize but receive their U.S. citizenship through the naturalization of their parents. Aliens who served honorably during U.S. military campaigns may, under certain conditions, become naturalized without first having to become permanent residents. They also do not have to live in the country for any length of time. In 1998, 4 percent of all new citizens naturalized under these special provisions.

Naturalization Rates

Not all immigrants choose to become U.S. citizens. Naturalization rates (the proportions of immigrants gaining citizenship through naturalization) differ considerably among different groups of immigrants. Immigrants who arrive in the United States as young adults, those who come from distant parts of the world such as Africa or Asia, and refugees are the most likely to seek citizenship. Persons who were single when they entered as immigrants are more likely to apply for naturalization than those who were married.

Asian immigrants are often more likely to become citizens because they have come a great distance, often through difficult conditions. The great distance often makes it more difficult to maintain contacts with their mother country. In addition, especially in the case of China and Vietnam, many people arriving from Asia left because they rejected the political system in their native country, and they may no longer be able to return. Canadians and Mexicans, on the other hand, live very close to their countries of origin and find it easier to maintain contact with family and travel back and forth. Most have come for economic reasons and have not necessarily rejected the political systems of their home countries.

In general, people in high-status positions, particularly medical professionals and engineers, have the highest naturalization rates. Those without a substantial attachment to the labor force, such as homemakers and retired or unemployed persons, have low naturalization rates.

National Origins

In 1998, 463,060 persons became U.S. citizens through naturalization, the fourth-highest naturalization rate in U.S. history. The all-time record number of naturalizations occurred in 1996 (1,044,689), followed by 1997 (598,225) and 1944 (441,979). (See Figure 3.5 and Table 3.9.) Prior to the 1970s the majority of naturalized

TABLE 3.6

Immigrants admitted by selected states and metropolitan areas of intended residence, fiscal years 1995–98

State and metropolitan area	1998		1997		1996		1995	
	Number	Percent	Number	Percent	Number	Percent	Number	Percent
All states	**660,477**	**100.0**	**798,378**	**100.0**	**915,900**	**100.0**	**720,461**	**100.0**
1. California	170,126	25.8	203,305	25.5	201,529	22.0	166,482	23.1
2. New York	96,559	14.6	123,716	15.5	154,095	16.8	128,406	17.8
3. Florida	59,965	9.1	82,318	10.3	79,461	8.7	62,023	8.6
4. Texas	44,428	6.7	57,897	7.3	83,385	9.1	49,963	6.9
5. New Jersey	35,091	5.3	41,184	5.2	63,303	6.9	39,729	5.5
6. Illinois	33,163	5.0	38,128	4.8	42,517	4.6	33,898	4.7
7. Washington	16,920	2.6	18,656	2.3	18,833	2.1	15,862	2.2
8 Massachusetts	15,869	2.4	17,317	2.2	23,085	2.5	20,523	2.8
9 Virginia	15,686	2.4	19,277	2.4	21,375	2.3	16,319	2.3
10 Maryland	15,561	2.4	19,090	2.4	20,732	2.3	15,055	2.1
11 Michigan	13,943	2.1	14,727	1.8	17,253	1.9	14,135	2.0
12 Pennsylvania	11,942	1.8	14,553	1.8	16,938	1.8	15,065	2.1
13 Georgia	10,445	1.6	12,623	1.6	12,608	1.4	12,381	1.7
14 Connecticut	7,780	1.2	9,528	1.2	10,874	1.2	9,240	1.3
15 Ohio	7,697	1.2	8,189	1.0	10,237	1.1	8,585	1.2
16 Minnesota	6,981	1.1	8,233	1.0	8,977	1.0	8,111	1.1
17 Colorado	6,513	1.0	7,506	.9	8,895	1.0	7,713	1.1
18 North Carolina	6,415	1.0	5,935	.7	7,011	.8	5,617	.8
19 Arizona	6,211	.9	8,632	1.1	8,900	1.0	7,700	1.1
20 Nevada	6,106	.9	6,541	.8	5,874	.6	4,306	.6
Other	73,076	11.1	81,023	10.1	100,018	10.9	79,348	11.0
All metropolitan areas	**660,477**	**100.0**	**798,378**	**100.0**	**915,900**	**100.0**	**720,461**	**100.0**
1 New York, NY	82,175	12.4	107,434	13.5	133,168	14.5	111,687	15.5
2 Los Angeles-Long Beach, CA	59,598	9.0	62,314	7.8	64,285	7.0	54,669	7.6
3 Chicago, IL	30,355	4.6	35,386	4.4	39,989	4.4	31,730	4.4
4 Miami, FL	28,853	4.4	45,707	5.7	41,527	4.5	30,935	4.3
5 Washington, DC-MD-VA	24,032	3.6	31,444	3.9	34,327	3.7	25,717	3.6
6 San Francisco, CA	14,540	2.2	16,892	2.1	18,171	2.0	15,773	2.2
7 Oakland, CA	13,437	2.0	15,723	2.0	15,759	1.7	12,011	1.7
8 Houston, TX	13,183	2.0	17,439	2.2	21,387	2.3	14,379	2.0
9 Boston-Lawrence, MA [1]	12,725	1.9	13,937	1.7	18,726	2.0	16,750	2.3
10 San Jose, CA	12,656	1.9	17,374	2.2	13,854	1.5	12,855	1.8
11 Orange County, CA	10,954	1.7	18,190	2.3	17,580	1.9	18,187	2.5
12 Fort Lauderdale, FL	9,951	1.5	10,646	1.3	10,290	1.1	8,373	1.2
13 Riverside-San Bernardino, CA	9,967	1.5	9,518	1.2	10,314	1.1	7,568	1.1
14 San Diego, CA	9,840	1.5	14,758	1.8	18,226	2.0	12,077	1.7
15 Detroit, MI	9,811	1.5	10,019	1.3	11,929	1.3	9,899	1.4
16 Dallas, TX	9,602	1.5	11,061	1.4	15,915	1.7	9,843	1.4
17 Newark, NJ	9,553	1.4	10,801	1.4	17,939	2.0	11,162	1.5
18 Seattle-Bellevue-Everett, WA	9,385	1.4	10,692	1.3	10,429	1.1	9,652	1.3
19 Philadelphia, PA-NJ	9,129	1.4	10,858	1.4	13,034	1.4	11,440	1.6
20 Bergen-Passaic, NJ	8,597	1.3	9,788	1.2	15,682	1.7	9,385	1.3
Other	272,134	41.2	318,397	39.9	373,369	40.8	286,369	39.7

[1] Includes Lowell and Brockton.

SOURCE: "Immigrants Admitted by Selected State and Metropolitan Area of Intended Residence: Fiscal Years 1995–98," in *Legal Immigration, Fiscal Year 1998*. U.S. Department of Justice, Immigration and Naturalization Service: Washington, D.C., July 1999

citizens were born in Europe. Between 1961 and 1970 nearly two-thirds (62.4 percent) of persons naturalized were Europeans. (See Figure 3.6.) After the Immigration and Nationality Act Amendments of 1965 (Public Law 89-236) dropped the national origins quota system in favor of family reunification and the admission of persons with needed occupational skills, the proportion of Europeans naturalized as U.S. citizens declined. Asia's share started to increase, partly because of these provisions and partly due to the admission of Indo-Chinese refugees in the 1970s and 1980s.

Between 1971 and 1980 Europe, North American, and Asia each accounted for about one-third of naturalized citizens (30.8 percent, 28.1 percent, and 33.5 percent, respectively). By the 1980s Asia had become the leading region of birth, representing nearly half (48.8 percent) of all naturalized citizens. During 1991–1998, the proportion of naturalized aliens who were of Asian background fell to 38.1 percent, while that of North Americans rose to 38.9 percent. (See Figure 3.6.) In 1996, for the first time, North America became the leading region of birth of persons naturalized in the United States.

TABLE 3.7

Immigrants admitted ages 16 to 64, by occupation, fiscal years 1995–98

Occupation	1998		1997		1996		1995	
	Number	Percent	Number	Percent	Number	Percent	Number	Percent
Immigrants aged 16-64	479,849	100.0	586,830	100.0	669,814	100.0	514,993	100.0
Professional specialty and technical	44,297	9.2	61,733	10.5	74,220	11.1	58,214	11.3
Architects	1,229	.3	539	.1	565	.1	472	.1
Engineers, surveyors and mapping scientists	7,863	1.6	10,281	1.8	11,605	1.7	8,990	1.7
Mathematical and computer scientists	2,541	.5	2,606	.4	3,276	.5	2,127	.4
Natural scientists	2,490	.5	3,516	.6	3,729	.6	2,371	.5
Health diagnosing occupations	4,650	1.0	6,012	1.0	6,853	1.0	4,866	.9
Physicians	3,824	.8	5,237	.9	5,922	.9	4,072	.8
Other	826	.2	775	.1	931	.1	794	.2
Health assessment and treating	3,612	.8	9,023	1.5	12,482	1.9	11,654	2.3
Nurses	2,485	.5	6,161	1.0	8,243	1.2	8,118	1.6
Other	1,127	.2	2,862	.5	4,239	.6	3,536	.7
Teachers, postsecondary	2,553	.5	3,338	.6	4,664	.7	3,650	.7
Teachers, except postsecondary	5,614	1.2	7,757	1.3	8,701	1.3	7,221	1.4
Counselors, educational and vocational	195	Z	259	Z	255	Z	186	Z
Librarians, archivists, and curators	96	Z	124	Z	223	Z	153	Z
Social scientists and urban planners	618	.1	710	.1	832	.1	577	.1
Social, recreation, and religious workers	2,983	.6	3,463	.6	3,665	.5	2,725	.5
Lawyers and judges	662	.1	827	.1	984	.1	810	.2
Writers, artists, entertainers and athletes	3,583	.7	5,161	.9	6,453	1.0	5,036	1.0
Health technologists and technicians	3,532	.7	1,471	.3	1,062	.2	737	.1
Technologists and technicians, except health	2,076	.4	6,646	1.1	8,871	1.3	6,639	1.3
Executive, administrative, managerial	18,002	3.8	25,651	4.4	31,115	4.6	24,306	4.7
Sales occupations	10,123	2.1	13,906	2.4	14,955	2.2	11,329	2.2
Administrative support occupations	12,514	2.6	18,172	3.1	21,526	3.2	18,177	3.5
Precision production, craft, and repair	11,905	2.5	20,131	3.4	23,421	3.5	18,068	3.5
Operators, fabricators, and laborers	32,354	6.7	70,433	12.0	75,551	11.3	50,755	9.9
Farming, forestry, and fishing	10,185	2.1	11,809	2.0	13,195	2.0	11,282	2.2
Service occupations	24,241	5.1	52,051	8.9	60,722	9.1	45,609	8.9
No occupation	171,620	35.8	277,749	47.3	317,349	47.4	239,704	46.5
Homemakers	79,412	16.5	113,868	19.4	125,714	18.8	88,890	17.3
Unemployed or retired	34,682	7.2	84,198	14.3	98,761	14.7	78,093	15.2
Students and/or children under age 16	57,526	12.0	79,683	13.6	92,874	13.9	72,721	14.1
Unknown or not reported	144,608	30.1	35,195	6.0	37,760	5.6	37,549	7.3

Z Rounds to less than .05 percent.

SOURCE: "Immigrants Aged 16 to 64 Admitted by Occupation: Fiscal Years 1995–98," in *Legal Immigration, Fiscal Year 1998*. U.S. Department of Justice, Immigration and Naturalization Service: Washington, D.C., July 1999

In 1998 Mexico was the leading country of origin of naturalized citizens (109,065), accounting for nearly 24 percent of the total. Two-thirds (67 percent) of the Mexicans who naturalized were composed of those who legalized under the Immigration Reform and Control Act of 1986. In FY 1994 the first of the nearly 2.7 million amnestied illegal aliens became eligible to naturalize. For the next several years, the IRCA-legalized population is expected to add to the annual naturalization numbers. In 1998, 19 percent had naturalized. Vietnam (29,125) was the second leading origin country for naturalized citizens, followed by the Philippines (23,809), India (16,003), Cuba (15,114), and the People's Republic of China (14,737). (See Table 3.9.)

In 1998 the overall median number of years of residence in the United States between acquiring legal permanent residence to becoming naturalized was nine years.

The median years for each region of birth varied. Persons from Europe and Africa spent a median of eight years in permanent resident status before naturalizing, compared to nine years for Asians, 10 years each for North and South Americans, and 12 years for those from Oceania (countries of the South Pacific area). (See Table 3.10.)

Rise in Naturalization in the 1990s

Between 1990 and 1992, the INS received an average of 260,000 applications for naturalization. In 1996 and 1997 the number of applications rose to about 1.2 million and 1.5 million, respectively. In 1999 the number of naturalization applicants was nearly three times that of the early 1990s. The INS attributes this increase to four factors:

• In FY 1992 the INS's Green Card Replacement Program, requiring legal permanent immigrants to apply

TABLE 3.8

Immigrants admitted by gender and age, fiscal years 1995–98

Gender and age	1998		1997		1996		1995	
	Number	Percent	Number	Percent	Number	Percent	Number	Percent
Total	660,477	100.0	798,378	100.0	915,900	100.0	720,461	100.0
Gender								
Male	299,946	45.4	365,484	45.8	422,740	46.2	333,859	46.3
Female	353,426	53.5	432,699	54.2	493,142	53.8	386,582	53.7
Unknown	7,105	1.1	195	Z	18	Z	20	Z
Age								
Under 15 years	129,291	19.6	157,089	19.7	186,362	20.3	157,325	21.8
15-29 years	213,360	32.3	264,183	33.1	304,855	33.3	237,385	32.9
30-44 years	177,942	26.9	212,937	26.7	246,823	26.9	185,838	25.8
45-64 years	101,884	15.4	124,923	15.6	135,980	14.8	105,863	14.7
65 years and over	30,717	4.7	39,070	4.9	41,780	4.6	33,993	4.7
Unknown age	7,283	1.1	176	Z	100	Z	57	Z
Gender and age								
Male								
Under 15 years	64,515	9.8	79,006	9.9	94,105	10.3	79,494	11.0
15-29 years	99,146	15.0	120,842	15.1	141,874	15.5	109,270	15.2
30-44 years	79,566	12.0	95,565	12.0	110,421	12.1	84,524	11.7
45-64 years	42,782	6.5	52,685	6.6	58,373	6.4	46,028	6.4
65 years and over	13,353	2.0	17,301	2.2	17,912	2.0	14,513	2.0
Unknown age	584	.1	85	Z	55	Z	30	Z
Female								
Under 15 years	64,640	9.8	78,050	9.8	92,249	10.1	77,824	10.8
15-29 years	113,820	17.2	143,278	17.9	162,975	17.8	128,110	17.8
30-44 years	97,973	14.8	117,311	14.7	136,398	14.9	101,310	14.1
45-64 years	58,985	8.9	72,208	9.0	77,607	8.5	59,832	8.3
65 years and over	17,340	2.6	21,765	2.7	23,868	2.6	19,479	2.7
Unknown age	668	.1	87	Z	45	Z	27	Z
Median Age	**29**	**X**	**28**	**X**	**28**	**X**	**28**	**X**
Male	28	X	28	X	27	X	27	X
Female	29	X	29	X	29	X	29	X

Note: Male and female totals by age may not sum to total by age because of records with unknown gender.
X Not applicable.
Z Rounds to less than .05 percent.

SOURCE: "Table 4. Immigrants Admitted by Gender and Age: Fiscal Years 1995–98," in *Legal Immigration, Fiscal Year 1998*. U.S. Department of Justice, Immigration and Naturalization Service: Washington, D.C., July 1999

---

for a new, more fraud-resistant card, caused some immigrants to apply for U.S. citizenship instead.

• In 1994 the first of the nearly 2.7 million IRCA-legalized aliens became eligible for naturalization.

• In 1994 Proposition 187 prohibited noncitizens from receiving public benefits in California, and in 1996 the welfare reform law barred legal permanent immigrants access to federally funded benefits.

• In 1995 the Citizenship USA (CUSA) initiative, implemented by the INS to remedy the backlog of pending naturalization applications, resulted in increased processing of applications.

An Investigation of Citizenship USA

Between 1992 and mid-1995 the number of naturalization applications awaiting processing increased fourfold, from 135,652 to 481,580. On August 31, 1995, INS commissioner Doris M. Meissner announced Citizenship

USA (CUSA) to help ease the backlog of naturalization applications. The goal of the initiative was to streamline the naturalization process so that an eligible applicant would be naturalized within six months of application.

In 1996 media reports questioned the expedited naturalization process. At the same time, INS employees started voicing criticisms and concerns about their superiors' strategy. Allegations surfaced, claiming that CUSA had been implemented to help President Bill Clinton get re-elected with the help of new citizens who would lean toward the Democratic Party.

In April 1997 the Office of the Inspector General (OIG) of the U.S. Department of Justice started an investigation of the CUSA initiative. On July 31, 2000, the OIG reported that its three-year investigation of CUSA found that the INS rushed to naturalize 1 million people in 1996 but that the allegations involving the Clinton administration were false. This investigation was the largest of its kind ever undertaken by the OIG.

FIGURE 3.5

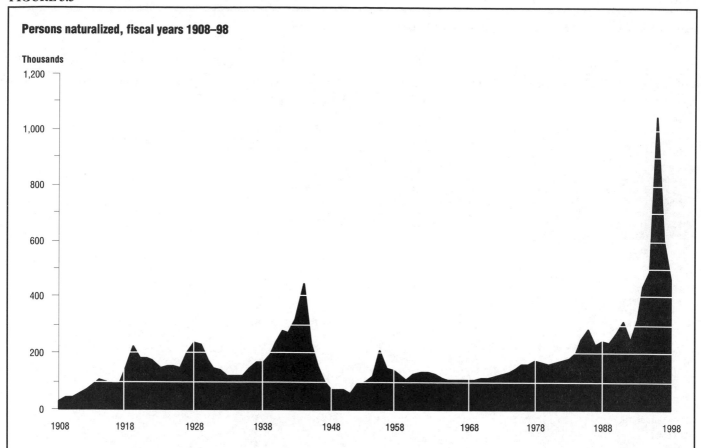

Persons naturalized, fiscal years 1908–98

SOURCE: "Chart N: Persons Naturalized: Fiscal Years 1908–98," in *1998 Statistical Yearbook of the Immigration and Naturalization Service*. U.S. Department of Justice, Immigration and Naturalization Service: Washington, D.C., November 2000

According to the OIG report, prior to CUSA, "naturalization processing already suffered from systemic weaknesses. INS lacked standards for the consistent evaluation of an applicant's 'good moral character' and other qualifications for citizenship. INS had become reliant on the use of temporary files, thus preventing adjudicators from learning as much as possible about an applicant's background, including information concerning possible grounds for disqualification. Applicant criminal history checks were poorly administered."

As a result, the INS failed to acquire complete criminal background investigations for 18 percent of the more than one million persons naturalized in 1996. About 600 cases of citizenship were improperly conferred. Further audit by an independent firm found that as many as 8,400 immigrants should not have been naturalized.

NONIMMIGRANTS

Tourists, Business People, Foreign Government Officials, and Foreign Students

Under U.S. immigration law a nonimmigrant is "an alien admitted to the United States for a specified purpose and temporary period but not for permanent residence." In FY 1998 more than 30.1 million nonimmigrants arrived in the United States, the largest number ever to visit and a 10.2 percent (5.3 million) annual average increase from 1996. About 6.3 million nonimmigrants entered the United States during 1975. The number nearly doubled to 11.8 million in both 1981 and 1982. Between 1983 and 1985 the number declined to about 9.5 million, gradually increasing over the next 13 years. (See Figure 3.7.)

Half (50.1 percent) of all nonimmigrants entering the United States in 1998 were citizens of four countries—Japan (17.5 percent), the United Kingdom (14 percent), Mexico (11.6 percent), and Germany (7 percent). (See Figure 3.8.) Most of the nonimmigrants came as tourists (77.1 percent) or for business (14.6 percent). Nearly 565,000 students entered the United States to attend academic institutions. They were accompanied by almost 34,000 spouses and children. An additional 251,000 academics, with over 42,000 spouses and children, came to teach, study, or do research. More than 225,000 (less than 1 percent of the total entries) were foreign government officials and representatives of international organiza-

TABLE 3.9

Persons naturalized by region and country of former allegiance, fiscal years 1989–98

Region and country of former allegiance	1989	1990	1991	1992	1993	1994	1995	1996	1997	1998
All countries	233,777	270,101	308,058	240,252	314,681	434,107	488,088	1,044,689	598,225	463,060
Europe	35,079	37,264	37,808	30,781	42,162	63,915	69,005	108,966	66,850	61,055
Albania	143	91	80	109	98	125	122	340	399	342
Andorra	11	6	3	5	3	6	5	5	2	—
Austria	71	83	113	100	199	281	284	347	171	160
Belgium	131	147	170	151	193	264	223	291	149	164
Bulgaria	137	160	225	171	165	250	240	493	288	226
Czechoslovakia, former	949	916	843	676	629	691	613	613	372	277
Czech Republic	X	X	X	X	—	6	5	11	16	6
Slovak Republic	X	X	X	X	—	2	21	44	33	43
Unknown republic	949	916	843	676	629	683	587	558	323	228
Denmark	109	153	177	126	162	255	225	279	159	165
Estonia	19	17	33	14	20	62	63	78	56	51
Finland	61	83	85	91	103	135	137	152	82	106
France	940	1,091	1,413	1,124	1,239	1,758	1,518	2,257	1,281	1,250
Germany	2,196	2,395	2,197	1,901	2,554	3,706	3,546	4,245	2,588	2,345
Germany, East	190	187	X	X	X	X	X	X	X	X
Germany, West	2,006	2,208	X	X	X	X	X	X	X	X
Greece	2,768	2,270	1,820	1,769	2,135	2,596	2,114	2,769	1,645	1,268
Hungary	580	743	814	608	624	824	844	936	488	502
Iceland	26	25	23	37	34	38	38	37	29	31
Ireland	787	742	746	738	1,079	1,659	1,928	3,010	1,682	1,392
Italy	2,492	2,453	1,976	1,618	3,495	5,703	4,032	4,617	2,282	2,383
Latvia	45	55	52	53	64	131	193	371	200	201
Liechtenstein	2	1	3	2	1	5	4	2	3	2
Lithuania	68	71	71	50	85	119	230	273	156	143
Luxembourg	8	6	16	9	12	11	8	19	7	3
Malta	59	72	77	56	74	98	44	113	44	35
Monaco	3	2	4	5	3	9	4	3	1	—
Netherlands	410	410	508	378	471	714	727	1,015	577	480
Norway	79	115	141	107	129	176	160	217	107	86
Poland	5,002	5,972	5,493	4,681	5,551	7,036	8,030	13,200	7,553	5,643
Portugal	2,698	2,491	1,848	1,884	3,978	6,106	3,925	6,173	3,769	4,658
Romania	2,190	2,914	3,471	2,457	2,699	3,454	3,316	4,451	2,573	2,063
San Marino	3	4	6	3	8	4	8	—	2	2
Soviet Union, former	3,020	2,847	2,822	1,648	2,763	7,249	17,406	36,265	25,965	25,101
Armenia	X	X	X	6	136	645	1,240	3,524	4,151	4,701
Azerbaijan	X	X	X	—	—	4	32	233	321	346
Belarus	X	X	X	—	1	7	198	657	856	983
Georgia	X	X	X	—	1	8	24	94	81	72
Kazakhstan	X	X	X	—	2	35	27	32	42	61
Kyrgyzstan	X	X	X	—	—	—	2	3	3	19
Moldova	X	X	X	—	7	61	190	520	711	636
Russia	X	X	X	31	315	1,240	3,846	8,909	7,172	6,535
Tajikistan	X	X	X	—	2	1	1	43	24	39
Turkmenistan	X	X	X	—	—	1	2	8	5	6
Ukraine	X	X	X	11	173	793	3,375	8,392	6,415	7,173
Uzbekistan	X	X	X	—	—	10	62	436	329	291
Unknown republic	3,020	2,847	2,822	1,600	2,126	4,444	8,407	13,414	5,855	4,239
Spain	490	535	436	462	615	812	778	1,714	671	827
Sweden	129	166	208	186	228	317	261	335	201	197
Switzerland	246	302	357	310	393	574	451	505	290	296
United Kingdom [1]	7,865	8,286	9,935	7,800	10,158	15,753	14,823	20,052	11,418	9,351
Yugoslavia, former	1,342	1,640	1,642	1,452	2,198	2,994	2,705	3,789	1,640	1,305
Bosnia-Herzegovina	X	X	X	—	4	25	31	47	48	28
Croatia	X	X	X	—	33	144	242	496	222	192
Macedonia	X	X	X	X	X	52	107	329	214	140
Slovenia	X	X	X	—	3	8	23	22	8	18
Unknown	1,342	1,640	1,642	1,452	2,158	2,765	2,212	2,895	1,148	927

tions, such as the North Atlantic Treaty Organization (NATO), including their families and staff.

There are no restrictions on the number of nonimmigrants allowed to enter the United States. In fact, the United States, like most other countries, encourages tourism and tries to attract as many visitors as possible. However, while it is easy to get in, strict rules do apply

to the conditions of the visit. For example, students may stay only long enough to complete their studies, and business people may stay only six months (although a six-month extension is available). Most nonimmigrants may not hold jobs while they are here, although exceptions are made for students and the families of diplomats. However, a certain undetermined number, amounting to many tens of thousands, choose to over-

TABLE 3.9

Persons naturalized by region and country of former allegiance, fiscal years 1989–98 [CONTINUED]

Region and country of former allegiance	1989	1990	1991	1992	1993	1994	1995	1996	1997	1998
Asia	**111,488**	**124,675**	**160,367**	**121,965**	**145,318**	**186,963**	**182,570**	**267,334**	**169,658**	**143,927**
Afghanistan	1,051	1,141	1,392	1,047	1,539	1,994	2,014	3,936	1,724	1,693
Bahrain	5	12	11	12	9	18	17	21	6	7
Bangladesh	496	696	874	967	942	1,175	1,291	5,120	3,122	1,161
Bhutan	6	3	8	6	9	10	7	—	3	1
Brunei	4	7	12	12	8	11	7	6	3	8
Burma	479	597	827	454	469	757	780	1,085	484	373
Cambodia	3,234	3,525	4,786	2,749	3,149	4,125	3,605	5,077	4,936	5,321
China, People's Republic	11,664	13,563	16,783	13,488	16,851	22,018	20,917	30,656	17,552	14,737
Cyprus	229	185	167	170	188	194	170	212	106	112
Hong Kong [1]	[1]	[1]	[1]	[1]	[1]	[1]	[1]	[1]	[1]	542
India	9,833	11,499	12,961	13,413	16,506	20,886	18,331	28,932	18,812	16,003
Indonesia	352	350	603	309	408	532	569	883	462	530
Iran	4,485	5,973	10,411	6,778	7,029	10,054	11,659	17,326	10,553	9,936
Iraq	1,387	1,855	1,641	1,196	1,522	1,772	1,609	2,157	1,519	1,951
Israel	1,703	2,102	2,789	2,376	2,609	3,241	2,821	3,577	1,918	1,543
Japan	727	736	938	621	989	1,427	1,415	1,803	1,108	1,800
Jordan	1,872	2,408	2,493	2,297	2,678	2,901	2,556	3,019	1,795	1,586
Korea	11,301	10,500	12,266	8,297	9,611	12,313	15,445	24,693	13,996	9,866
Kuwait	198	247	301	299	344	426	350	380	234	177
Laos	3,463	3,329	3,594	3,052	3,945	5,638	4,064	7,845	8,092	7,218
Lebanon	2,213	2,797	3,570	2,881	3,402	4,611	4,159	4,978	2,796	2,308
Malaysia	362	426	477	388	418	513	424	580	377	339
Maldives	—	—	1	1	1	—	3	—	2	—
Mongolia	—	—	—	—	—	—	—	—	—	1
Nepal	35	37	56	43	48	62	55	88	52	73
Oman	3	2	2	7	5	5	5	1	1	2
Pakistan	2,443	3,330	3,670	3,350	3,777	4,539	4,883	10,278	6,430	3,450
Philippines	24,802	25,936	33,714	28,579	33,864	40,711	37,645	45,210	28,075	23,809
Qatar	7	7	6	15	17	14	11	17	7	6
Saudi Arabia	48	63	91	94	139	132	112	119	79	60
Singapore	141	162	180	145	157	209	170	237	123	116
Sri Lanka	298	335	464	333	445	531	514	756	486	436
Syria	908	1,146	1,480	1,200	1,312	1,809	1,776	2,148	1,370	1,125
Taiwan	5,779	6,895	10,876	6,408	7,384	10,757	10,007	12,431	6,489	5,317
Thailand	1,167	1,145	1,379	962	1,169	1,645	1,675	3,399	1,808	1,825
Turkey	1,085	1,214	1,349	1,124	1,229	1,655	1,559	1,885	1,341	1,120
United Arab Emirates	2	6	2	7	13	20	11	10	5	7
Vietnam	19,357	22,027	29,603	18,357	22,427	29,486	31,432	47,625	33,349	29,125
Yemen	349	419	590	528	706	772	502	844	443	243
Africa	**7,209**	**8,770**	**10,230**	**9,628**	**11,293**	**15,719**	**17,702**	**21,842**	**13,862**	**11,070**
Algeria	86	95	111	102	120	173	177	208	138	123
Angola	48	58	30	35	50	77	38	57	55	45
Benin	3	8	10	13	10	6	13	9	4	11
Botswana	—	—	1	4	1	3	2	5	5	—
Burkina Faso	—	2	2	1	5	7	7	9	6	7
Burundi	4	3	1	10	4	10	6	4	5	2
Cameroon	33	38	48	75	105	171	164	195	129	104
Cape Verde	223	272	178	226	216	518	524	457	347	491
Central African Republic	11	2	6	2	4	1	6	4	1	1
Chad	3	2	5	2	1	2	1	2	2	3
Comoros	—	1	2	—	2	2	—	1	—	—
Congo, Democratic Republic [2]	36	55	50	48	68	86	81	131	60	61
Congo, Republic [2]	4	9	4	2	4	5	1	4	2	8
Cote d'Ivoire	10	14	27	36	47	76	77	139	89	75
Djibouti	3	1	6	7	7	5	8	5	3	2
Egypt	1,638	1,945	2,644	2,098	2,045	2,616	2,625	3,486	2,021	1,354
Equatorial Guinea	1	2	4	2	1	2	2	5	2	1
Eritrea	X	X	X	X	—	69	371	541	399	488

stay their nonimmigrant visas and continue to live in the United States illegally.

Temporary Foreign Workers

The INS defines a temporary worker as "an alien worker coming to the United States to work for a temporary period of time." The major nonimmigrant category for legal temporary workers is the H visa, which includes the H-2/H-2A and H-1B visas.

THE H-2/H-2A PROGRAM. The H-2 Temporary Agricultural Worker Program, authorized by the Immigration and Nationality Act (Public Law 82-414) of 1952, was a flexible response to seasonal agricultural labor demands. Since 1964 it has been the only legal temporary foreign agricultural worker program in the United States. (The year 1964 marked the end of the Mexican Bracero program, a temporary foreign agricultural worker program negotiated between the United States and Mexico.) In

TABLE 3.9

Persons naturalized by region and country of former allegiance, fiscal years 1989–98 [CONTINUED]

Region and country of former allegiance	1989	1990	1991	1992	1993	1994	1995	1996	1997	1998
Ethiopia	1,246	1,370	1,453	1,505	1,858	2,359	2,558	2,563	1,813	1,727
Gabon	6	1	4	2	-	-	1	2	1	1
Gambia, The	4	13	19	11	18	26	51	82	39	40
Ghana	567	714	669	692	722	1,110	1,557	2,519	1,418	1,024
Guinea	5	15	7	7	3	10	8	23	22	26
Guinea-Bissau	—	1	2	3	1	6	3	6	1	2
Kenya	202	257	273	237	307	360	335	458	350	271
Lesotho	2	2	3	3	3	5	6	4	4	6
Liberia	229	283	356	359	455	613	728	794	657	536
Libya	103	137	135	147	142	158	196	137	112	81
Madagascar	7	6	10	15	3	13	12	21	8	11
Malawi	9	13	11	16	13	32	29	23	14	20
Mali	4	5	2	5	9	8	17	23	25	17
Mauritania	5	3	2	2	3	1	6	3	4	1
Mauritius	14	15	11	13	14	22	18	42	23	22
Morocco	243	320	365	396	482	687	653	937	483	343
Mozambique	20	30	24	22	24	43	22	18	27	15
Namibia	11	6	6	7	11	12	8	6	10	6
Niger	21	22	—	—	—	6	211	263	116	207
Nigeria	932	1,415	1,775	1,862	2,378	3,772	4,541	5,368	3,292	1,911
Rwanda	1	—	5	5	3	3	9	8	6	3
Sao Tome & Principe	—	—	—	1	—	2	2	—	1	1
Senegal	32	58	30	41	61	74	75	226	211	103
Seychelles	15	20	20	18	17	10	15	12	13	5
Sierra Leone	137	163	194	187	292	396	561	566	396	376
Somalia	64	90	107	122	130	154	211	248	157	288
South Africa	687	697	883	650	830	1,145	798	956	559	589
Sudan	55	68	79	99	129	138	177	258	216	174
Swaziland	5	3	8	4	4	2	5	3	1	8
Tanzania	170	187	221	180	187	227	192	347	171	145
Togo	7	13	16	13	17	23	19	29	17	14
Tunisia	67	55	78	68	123	85	112	129	80	67
Uganda	122	124	131	118	133	172	239	267	195	134
Zambia	56	65	111	65	113	110	108	113	74	68
Zimbabwe	58	92	91	90	118	106	116	126	78	52
Oceania	**868**	**881**	**1,045**	**891**	**1,208**	**1,726**	**1,731**	**2,676**	**1,620**	**1,464**
Australia	81	110	116	140	230	321	271	454	275	256
Fiji	436	374	477	398	544	705	698	1,336	628	484
Kiribati	2	1	1	—	1	1	1	3	3	2
Marshall Islands	—	—	—	—	—	2	4	5	3	1
Micronesia, Federated States	1	2	—	2	3	3	5	5	1	7
Nauru	—	2	1	1	4	3	3	-	1	—
New Zealand	124	116	191	110	178	262	254	336	214	193
Palau	21	23	23	22	15	11	2	2	6	14
Papua New Guinea	3	2	3	1	3	2	7	9	3	—
Samoa [3]	130	150	142	102	131	189	207	267	149	206
Solomon Islands	1	1	2	27	11	46	54	2	6	7
Tonga	68	100	89	86	86	170	213	257	330	291
Tuvalu	—	—	—	—	2	1	1	—	1	3
Vanuatu	1	—	—	2	—	10	11	—	—	—
North America	**61,954**	**64,730**	**71,838**	**56,710**	**87,751**	**130,108**	**172,513**	**454,954**	**257,027**	**201,717**
Canada	2,922	3,644	4,441	4,067	6,662	9,128	7,949	10,324	6,094	6,012
Mexico	18,520	17,564	22,066	12,880	23,630	46,186	79,614	217,418	134,494	109,065
Caribbean	**31,952**	**34,320**	**34,025**	**32,272**	**47,061**	**57,915**	**55,515**	**155,178**	**78,263**	**59,607**
Antigua-Barbuda	490	339	478	376	439	617	658	899	714	808
Bahamas, The	98	161	151	156	140	234	208	628	303	248
Barbados	931	970	852	669	855	1,423	1,270	2,394	1,873	1,137
Cuba	9,514	10,291	9,554	7,703	13,105	10,421	17,401	62,100	12,000	15,114

1986 the H-2 program was amended as the H-2A program. No numerical limit has been set for this program.

Under the program, employers file petitions for the temporary admission of foreign agricultural workers for temporary work for which U.S. workers cannot be found. The employer pays the prevailing wage (at least the minimum wage) and provides workers' compensation insurance. The employer also provides funds for round-trip transportation, meals and/or facilities for food preparation, and housing for workers who do not commute.

The numbers of certified H-2A jobs have varied over the years. Between 1989 and 1991 the average number of jobs certified was about 26,000, dropping to about 17,500 between 1992 and 1994 and to about 15,000 in 1995. Since 1995 the number of certifications has been rising, reaching over 23,350 in 1997. Compared to the total num-

TABLE 3.9

Persons naturalized by region and country of former allegiance, fiscal years 1989–98 [CONTINUED]

Region and country of former allegiance	1989	1990	1991	1992	1993	1994	1995	1996	1997	1998
Dominica	436	399	550	308	285	381	399	694	535	642
Dominican Republic	6,454	5,984	6,368	8,464	12,274	11,415	9,934	27,293	19,450	11,324
Grenada	413	459	456	421	552	815	722	1,564	1,136	601
Haiti	3,692	5,009	4,436	3,993	5,202	7,997	7,876	24,556	15,667	10,168
Jamaica	6,455	6,762	6,838	6,765	7,976	12,216	11,049	24,270	18,746	14,468
St. Kitts-Nevis	405	265	699	307	372	581	557	539	540	661
St. Lucia	249	204	286	194	236	377	400	549	429	402
St. Vincent & Grenadines	263	279	324	254	328	533	477	1,005	737	415
Trinidad & Tobago	2,552	3,198	3,033	2,602	3,293	4,905	4,484	8,619	5,273	3,619
Central America	**8,560**	**9,202**	**11,306**	**7,491**	**10,398**	**16,879**	**29,435**	**72,034**	**38,176**	**27,033**
Belize	373	389	499	304	381	636	856	1,765	1,280	951
Costa Rica	676	589	792	547	672	1,063	1,145	2,603	1,488	1,077
El Salvador	2,001	2,410	3,653	2,056	3,057	5,675	13,667	33,240	17,818	12,160
Guatemala	1,281	1,280	1,832	1,086	1,682	3,001	5,159	13,383	7,522	5,444
Honduras	1,167	1,259	1,306	1,248	1,713	2,208	2,943	7,494	4,022	2,651
Nicaragua	1,271	1,520	1,732	1,100	1,500	2,442	3,930	10,614	4,178	3,306
Panama	1,791	1,755	1,492	1,150	1,393	1,854	1,735	2,935	1,868	1,444
South America	**16,503**	**19,548**	**20,928**	**19,982**	**26,464**	**34,988**	**38,058**	**79,918**	**39,475**	**26,733**
Argentina	1,246	1,466	1,850	1,237	1,611	2,488	2,700	5,040	2,112	1,608
Bolivia	424	471	519	423	571	810	1,168	2,066	980	812
Brazil	564	674	683	679	922	1,342	1,278	2,685	2,192	1,927
Chile	887	866	920	713	862	1,203	1,295	2,775	1,291	959
Colombia	4,736	5,540	5,513	6,439	9,976	12,299	12,724	26,115	10,911	6,730
Ecuador	1,671	2,052	2,215	1,857	2,703	3,951	5,366	14,206	7,129	4,539
Guyana	3,654	4,306	4,826	4,717	4,938	6,043	5,584	10,618	7,008	4,479
Paraguay	127	127	133	138	175	257	236	420	140	104
Peru	2,267	2,829	3,088	2,633	3,274	4,740	5,889	12,073	5,898	4,191
Suriname	25	33	34	45	26	90	58	129	59	42
Uruguay	381	433	400	371	577	670	678	1,289	599	385
Venezuela	521	751	747	730	829	1,095	1,082	2,502	1,156	957
U.S. possessions	52	52	53	51	76	105	134	136	35	61
Stateless or not reported	624	14,181	5,789	244	409	583	6,375	108,863	49,698	17,033

— Represents zero.
X Not applicable.

[1] On July 1, 1997, sovereignty over Hong Kong passed from the United Kingdom to the People's Republic of China. Naturalizations of former Hong Kong residents may have been counted under United Kingdom prior to this date.
[2] In May 1997 Zaire was formally recognized as the Democratic Republic of the Congo; the Congo is referred to by its conventional name, the Republic of the Congo.
[3] In August 1997 Western Samoa was formally recognized as Samoa (Independent State).

SOURCE: "Table 48. Persons Naturalized by Region and Country of Former Allegiance, Fiscal Years 1989–98," in *1998 Statistical Yearbook of the Immigration and Naturalization Service*. U.S. Department of Justice, Immigration and Naturalization Service: Washington, D.C., November 2000

---

ber of U.S. farm workers, the number of H-2A workers has been small. In 1999 there were about 1.2 million agricultural workers and workers in related occupations in the United States, excluding farm operators and managers. The 41,827 H-2A job certifications approved by the U.S. Department of Labor constituted just 3.5 percent of the total number of agricultural jobs.

Until the early 1990s the Florida sugarcane industry, the predominant employer of H-2A workers, had brought in workers mostly from Jamaica. Over the last decade, as the sugarcane industry mechanized, the number of Jamaicans who entered the United States as H-2A workers declined from 13,881 in 1990 to 4,231 in 1996. On the other hand, the number of Mexican workers under the program increased from 4,993 to 10,353 over the same time period. In 1999, 96 percent of all H-2A visas went to workers from Mexico.

In 1999 workers in the tobacco industry accounted for 42 percent of H-2A certifications, followed by workers in vegetable harvesting (21 percent) and apple harvesting (10 percent). Other crop and livestock activities included nursery/horticulture, farm machinery (custom combine), sheep herding, and harvesting of fruits other than apples. North Carolina, with 10,279 job certifications approved, accounted for 25 percent of these jobs, followed by Georgia (14 percent), Virginia (9 percent), Kentucky (7 percent), New York (5.5 percent), and Tennessee (5 percent). (See Table 3.11.)

THE H-1B PROGRAM. The largest classification of H visas is granted to foreign workers in specialty occupations and fashion models "of distinguished merit and ability." Foreign nationals in specialty occupations include architects, engineers, computer programmers, accountants, medical personnel, professors, researchers, and computer

FIGURE 3.6

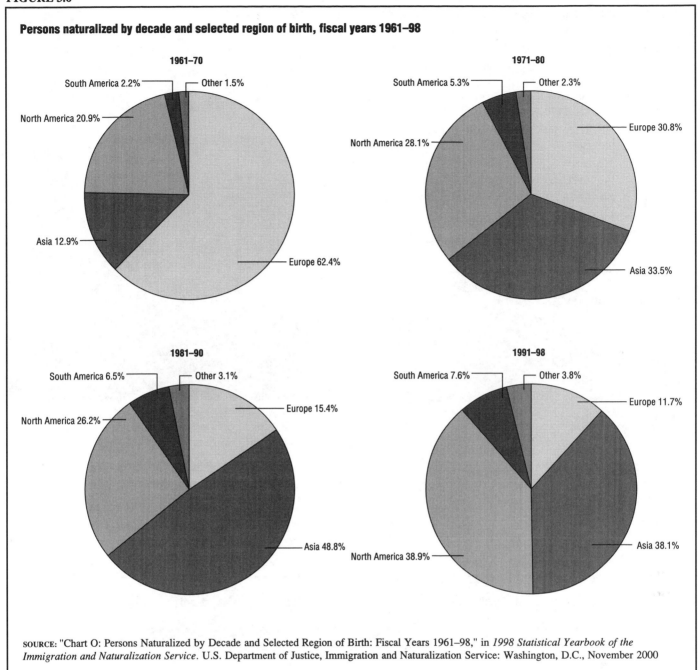

Persons naturalized by decade and selected region of birth, fiscal years 1961–98

SOURCE: "Chart O: Persons Naturalized by Decade and Selected Region of Birth: Fiscal Years 1961–98," in *1998 Statistical Yearbook of the Immigration and Naturalization Service*. U.S. Department of Justice, Immigration and Naturalization Service: Washington, D.C., November 2000

professionals. Visa petitions are approved for up to three years and may be extended to six years. The H-1B category is different from permanent immigration that is employer-based. In the latter category, the employer sponsors an alien, who, when approved for any of the three employer-based preferences, becomes a legal permanent resident.

In 2000 the U.S. General Accounting Office (GAO) provided information to the Committee on Government Reform of the House of Representatives regarding the implementation of the H-1B program and its implications for American workers (*H-1B Foreign Workers: Better Controls Needed to Help Employers and Protect Workers*,

Washington, D.C., September 2000). The Immigration Act of 1990 set the ceiling for H-1B admissions at 65,000. In recent years the demand for H-1B workers has grown. In FY 1992, the first year the annual limit took effect, 48,645 visas were issued. In FY 1997, for the first time, the maximum limit was reached before the end of the year; in FY 1998 the ceiling was reached in May.

On October 21, 1998, the American Competitiveness and Workforce Improvement Act (Public Law 105-277) temporarily raised the maximum limit to 115,000 for FY 1999. Among its provisions, the law required employers to offer H-1B workers benefits and wages comparable to those offered to U.S. workers. It also imposed on employers a $500 fee per alien to fund the education and training of U.S. workers. Both the INS and the Department of Labor (DOL) would administer the H-1B program. In FY 1999 the visas issued exceeded the maximum limit by 20,000. (See Figure 3.9.)

According to the GAO, in FY 1999 computer-related occupations accounted for 59 percent of H-1B visas approved, with systems analysis and programming accounting for 54 percent of the visas. Another 5 percent of visas went to electrical or electronics engineering jobs, which may also involve computer development. The remaining 36 percent of visas were allocated to college and university education, accounting and auditing, biolog-

TABLE 3.10

Median years of residence by year of naturalization and region of birth, fiscal years 1965–98

Region of birth	1998	1995	1990	1985	1980	1975	1970	1965
Persons naturalized	9	9	8	8	8	7	8	7
Europe	8	9	10	9	10	8	9	7
Asia	9	7	7	7	7	6	6	6
Africa	8	6	7	7	7	6	6	6
Oceania	12	11	10	8	8	7	9	8
North America	10	14	11	13	11	9	7	9
South America	10	10	9	8	9	10	7	7

SOURCE: "Table I: Median Years of Residence by Year of Naturalization and Region of Birth: Selected Fiscal Years 1965–98," in *1998 Statistical Yearbook of the Immigration and Naturalization Service*. U.S. Department of Justice, Immigration and Naturalization Service: Washington, D.C., November 2000

FIGURE 3.7

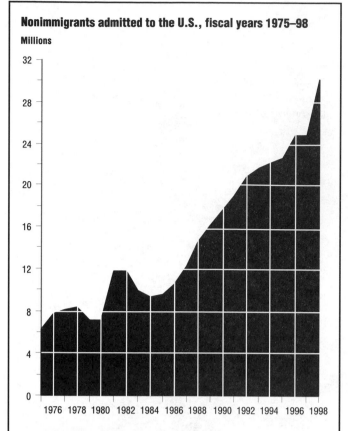

Nonimmigrants admitted to the U.S., fiscal years 1975–98

NOTE: Data estimated for last quarter of 1979 and no data available for 1980 and 1997.

SOURCE: "Chart F: Nonimmigrants Admitted: Fiscal Years 1975–98," in *1998 Statistical Yearbook of the Immigration and Naturalization Service*. U.S. Department of Justice, Immigration and Naturalization Service: Washington, D.C., November 2000

FIGURE 3.8

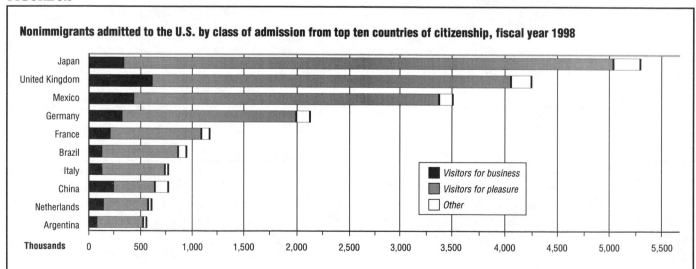

Nonimmigrants admitted to the U.S. by class of admission from top ten countries of citizenship, fiscal year 1998

NOTE: China includes People's Republic of China and Taiwan.

SOURCE: "Chart I: Nonimmigrants Admitted by Selected Class of Admission from Top Ten Countries of Citizenship: Fiscal Year 1998," in *1998 Statistical Yearbook of the Immigration and Naturalization Service*. U.S. Department of Justice, Immigration and Naturalization Service: Washington, D.C., November 2000

TABLE 3.11

Workers approved under H2-A visas, by state and crop, 1999

State	Crop/Agricultural Work	No. workers approved	State	Crop/Agricultural work	No. workers approved
Alabama	Horticulture, fruit, sweet potatoes, sheep	364	Nevada	Onions/garlic, irrigation, sheepherder, livestock	1,063
Alaska	Sheep shearer	6	New Hampshire	Apples, diversified crops, vegetables	318
Arizona	Sheepherder, citrus, farm machinery	92	New Jersey	Fruits, nursery	54
Arkansas	Vegetables, livestock, farm machinery	1,313	New Mexico	Farm work, sheep shearing	9
California	Sheepherder onions, grapes	514	New York	Apples, nursery, greenhouse, cabbage, cranberry	2,304
Colorado	Sheep, livestock, farm machinery, orchard work	186	North Carolina	Tobacco, hay/straw, vegetables, Christmas trees, fruits, horticulture	10,279
Connecticut	Tobacco, diversified crops, apples, nursery, Christmas trees, sod, dairy/poultry, vegetables	1,613	North Dakota	Farm work, beekeeping, goatherder	22
Delaware	None		Ohio	Horticulture, vegetable, tobacco, fruits	551
D.C.	None		Oklahoma	Farm machinery, strawberries, farm work	447
Florida	Strawberry, tomato, horticulture, trees, sugar	237	Oregon	Nursery, sheepherder, farm work	137
Georgia	Vegetables, fruits, tobacco, pecans, sod, hay	5,845	Pennsylvania	Nursery, Christmas trees	39
Hawaii	None		Rhode Island	Apples	12
Idaho	Sheepherder/shearing, irrigation, farm worker	807	South Carolina	Fruits, vegetables, horticulture, grain	1,040
Illinois	Horticulture	26	South Dakota	Sheepherder, farm machinery, livestock	8
Indiana	None		Tennessee	Tobacco, horticulture, hay/straw, vegetables, sod, grain, fruits	1,908
Iowa	Poultry, dairy, farm work, farm machinery	72			
Kansas	Farm machinery nursery	200	Texas	Farm machinery/work, diversified crops, cabbage, livestock, vegetables, horticulture, citrus, berries	1,502
Kentucky	Tobacco, vegetables, horticulture, sod, hay/straw	3,029			
Louisiana	Farm work, horticulture, nursery, sugar cane	784	Utah	Sheepherder, sheep shearing	162
Maine	Apples, blueberries, horticulture	416	Vermont	Apples, diversified crops, poultry, dairy	418
Maryland	Nursery, vegetables, tobacco, dairy, vineyard	320	Virginia	Tobacco, produce, hay, apples, vegetables, nursery, fruits, Christmas trees, vineyard, sod	3,856
Massachusetts	Apples, diversified crops, tobacco, vegetables Horticulture, farm work, sod	737			
Michigan	Horticulture, Christmas trees, vegetables	180	Washington	Sheepherder	13
Minnesota	Grain, horticulture, vegetables	36	West Virginia	Apples, tobacco	93
Mississippi	Fruits, horticulture, fish, vegetable, soybean	438	Wisconsin	Grain, dairy, vegetables	10
Missouri	Goat herding, dairy	8	Wyoming	Sheepherder, sheep shearing, wool grading, livestock	201
Montana	Irrigation, sheepherder, farm work/machinery	261			
Nebraska	Potatoes, farm work, livestock, dairy	60			

U.S. DOL – U.S. Department of Labor
ETA – Employment and Training Administration of the DOL

SOURCE: Ruth Ellen Wasem and Geoffrey K. Collver. "FY1999 H2-A Workers Approved, by State and Crop." in *Immigration of Agricultural Guest Workers: Policy, Trends, and Legislative Issues.* Congressional Research Service, The Library of Congress: Washington, D.C., February 15, 2001

---

ical sciences, economics, mechanical engineering, medicine, and commercial art. (See Figure 3.10.) The GAO report included only workers in the IT (information technology)-related industry.

H-1B workers had a median age of 28.3 years. More than 4 of 5 were under age 35. Over half (57 percent) had a bachelor's degree, while 41 percent had an advanced degree. More than one-third (35 percent) of workers approved for IT-related jobs had obtained advanced degrees, compared to 50 percent for workers in the other occupations. H-1B workers for IT-related jobs, as compared to those with non-IT-related jobs, tended to be recruited from outside the United States. Indian nationals represented nearly half (48 percent) of H-1B workers and three-fourths of workers in IT-related jobs. Nationals from the People's Republic of China, the United Kingdom, Canada, and the Philippines comprised 18 percent of H-1B visa holders. (See Figure 3.11.) Taiwan, Korea, Japan, Pakistan, and Russia were the other leading sources of H-1B workers.

The GAO found that employers were dissatisfied with the administration of the H-1B program by the INS and DOL,

especially the long processing time of applications. The restrictions imposed by the law limited DOL's legal authority to enforce it. Moreover, the INS lacked an effective system to ensure proper review of each application. These implementation weaknesses were likely to lead to worker abuse.

In May 2000 John R. Fraser, deputy administrator of the Wage and Hour Division of DOL's Employment Standards Administration, testified before the House Subcommittee on Immigration and Claims about H-1B workers' complaints regarding their employers. The complaints included employers failing to pay the workers when no work was available, requiring the workers to reimburse the employer for the $500 fee, and withholding wages when the workers left for other employment. Some workers also complained that they received less pay than what the employer indicated on the application. Fraser reported that the 135 complaints his office received in FY 1999 was nearly triple the average of about 50 complaints received each year through FY 1998.

In July 2000, before the end of the fiscal year, the INS announced that it had issued the maximum limit of

FIGURE 3.9

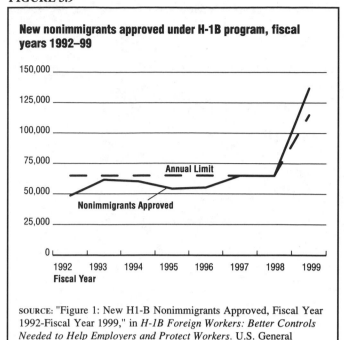

New nonimmigrants approved under H-1B program, fiscal years 1992–99

SOURCE: "Figure 1: New H1-B Nonimmigrants Approved, Fiscal Year 1992-Fiscal Year 1999," in *H-1B Foreign Workers: Better Controls Needed to Help Employers and Protect Workers.* U.S. General Accounting Office: Washington, D.C., September 2000

FIGURE 3.10

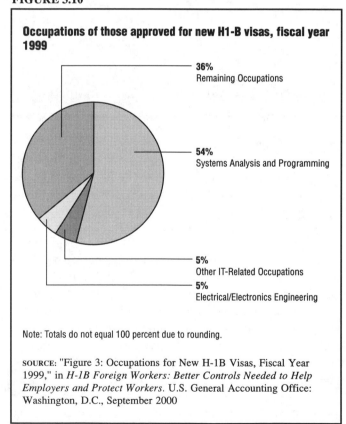

Occupations of those approved for new H1-B visas, fiscal year 1999

- 36% Remaining Occupations
- 54% Systems Analysis and Programming
- 5% Other IT-Related Occupations
- 5% Electrical/Electronics Engineering

Note: Totals do not equal 100 percent due to rounding.

SOURCE: "Figure 3: Occupations for New H-1B Visas, Fiscal Year 1999," in *H-1B Foreign Workers: Better Controls Needed to Help Employers and Protect Workers.* U.S. General Accounting Office: Washington, D.C., September 2000

FIGURE 3.11

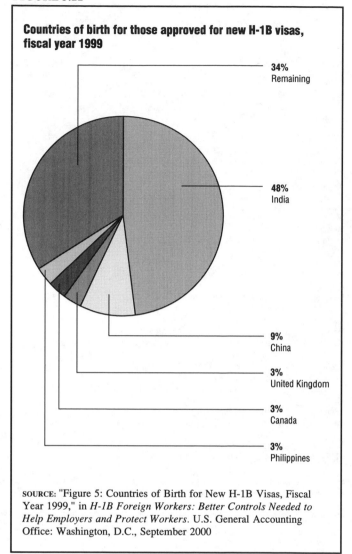

Countries of birth for those approved for new H-1B visas, fiscal year 1999

- 34% Remaining
- 48% India
- 9% China
- 3% United Kingdom
- 3% Canada
- 3% Philippines

SOURCE: "Figure 5: Countries of Birth for New H-1B Visas, Fiscal Year 1999," in *H-1B Foreign Workers: Better Controls Needed to Help Employers and Protect Workers.* U.S. General Accounting Office: Washington, D.C., September 2000

be accompanied by a $1,000 fee in addition to the $110 filing fee. The $1,000 fee will be used to assist U.S. citizens, legal permanent residents and other U.S. workers through job training, scholarships, and grants for mathematics and engineering- or science-enrichment courses. In addition, the law exempted aliens employed by an institution of higher education or certain research organizations from being counted against the FY 2001 limit.

ALIENS TURNED AWAY FROM THE UNITED STATES

Expedited Removal

Immigration inspectors at designated ports of entry to the United States determine which aliens may not enter the country. In 1998, of approximately 300 million aliens who applied for admission at ports of entry, about 600,000 were found inadmissible. Under the Illegal Immigration Reform and Immigrant Responsibility Act (IIRIRA) of 1996, inspectors are authorized to put some inadmissible aliens through expedited removal proceed-

115,000 H-1B visas. On October 17, 2000, Congress passed the American Competitiveness in the Twenty-First Century Act (Public Law 106-311), increasing the annual limit to 195,000 for 2001, 2002, and 2003. After that date the cap reverts back to 65,000. All H- 1B petitions have to

FIGURE 3.12

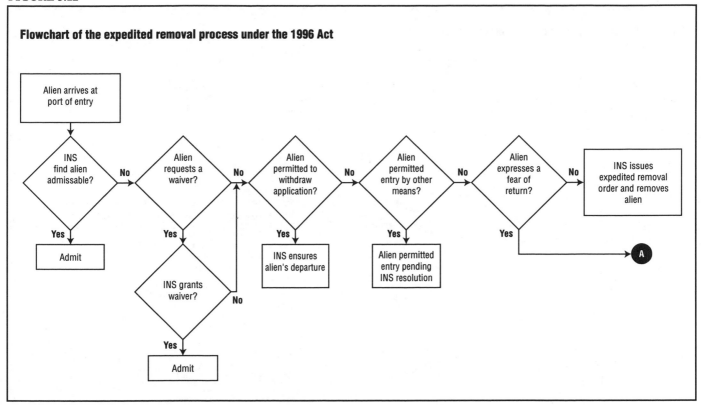

Flowchart of the expedited removal process under the 1996 Act

ings. These aliens are the ones who arrive with improper, fraudulent, or no documents. Inspectors can remove inadmissible aliens within days or weeks. In the past, the old exclusion process of removing aliens took months or even years.

Aliens who express a credible fear of persecution or torture if they are returned to their home country or country of last residence are interviewed by an asylum officer. If the officer finds their fear to be credible, the officer refers the alien to a hearing before an immigration judge to request asylum. Figure 3.12 shows the expedited removal process, including the credible-fear process.

In 1998 immigration inspectors placed 76,671 inadmissible aliens at ports of entry under expedited removal. These removals represented 44 percent of the total removals. Over 2,500 aliens who were found to have a credible fear of persecution were referred to an asylum officer and eventually for a hearing before an immigration judge. Over 9 of 10 aliens (93 percent) placed in expedited removals were from Mexico. The rest of the aliens came from such countries as Jamaica, the Dominican Republic, Canada, and Ecuador.

Aliens with AIDS

Aliens with AIDS (acquired immune deficiency syndrome) are barred from the United States under the ruling that persons with "communicable diseases of public health significance" are not permitted to enter. In 1990

the U.S. Department of Health and Human Services, as part of the Immigration Act of 1990, declared that tuberculosis and AIDS were a public health threat. In 1993 Congress added HIV (human immunodeficiency virus), the virus infection that causes AIDS, to the list of grounds for exclusion (denial of an alien's entry into the United States.) It is not, however, a legal ground for deportation (the removal of immigrants who are already in the country).

Those who opposed the ban pointed out that immigrants who have cancer or end-stage renal disease (kidney disease requiring costly dialysis treatment) are not denied immigrant status, and HIV-positive immigrants should not be treated differently. Supporters of the ban, however, argued that, unlike cancer and kidney disease, HIV is communicable and some infected immigrants would inevitably spread the disease. Furthermore, at a medical cost of about $100,000 per patient, they argued that U.S. taxpayers should not have to commit to additional, avoidable health expenses when health care is already a tremendous financial problem.

In late 1991, a large number of Haitians fled their country following the military takeover of President Jean-Bertrand Aristide's democratic government earlier in September. The U.S. Navy and Coast Guard intercepted over 8,000 Haitian refugees at sea. In 1992 and 1993 another 34,000 refugees were intercepted. Many were returned to Haiti. Some were detained at Guantánamo

FIGURE 3.12

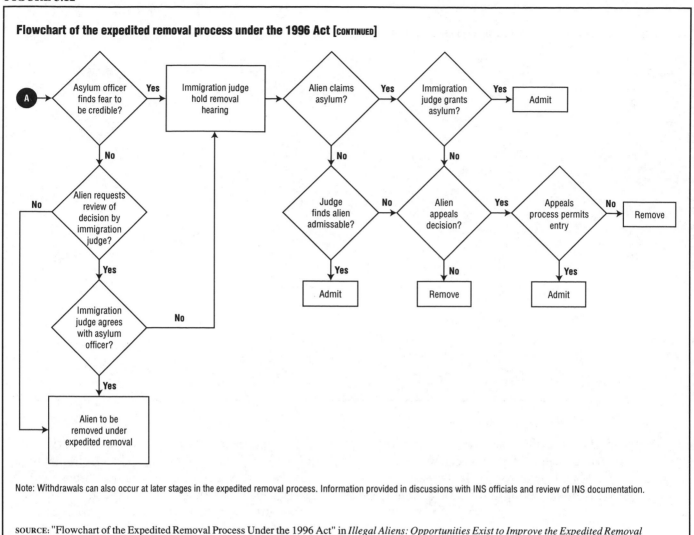

Flowchart of the expedited removal process under the 1996 Act [CONTINUED]

Note: Withdrawals can also occur at later stages in the expedited removal process. Information provided in discussions with INS officials and review of INS documentation.

SOURCE: "Flowchart of the Expedited Removal Process Under the 1996 Act" in *Illegal Aliens: Opportunities Exist to Improve the Expedited Removal Process,* U.S. General Accouting Office, Washington, D.C., 2000

Bay, site of a U.S. naval base on the island of Cuba. In 1993 HIV-infected Haitian refugees being detained at Guantánamo Bay held a hunger strike to protest being denied entry to the United States after they were approved for asylum proceedings. On June 8, 1993, a federal judge in New York ordered the U.S. government to release 158 HIV-positive Haitians who had been detained for up to 20 months.

CHAPTER 4

THE REFUGEE INFLUX

WHO IS A REFUGEE?

Before World War II, the United States government had no arrangements for admitting people seeking refuge. The only way oppressed people were able to enter the United States was through regular immigration procedures under the national quotas set by the Immigration Act of 1924, or the National Origins Act (43 Stat. 153).

After World War II refugees were admitted through special legislation passed by Congress. The Immigration and Nationality Act of 1952 (INA; Public Law 82-414) did not specifically mention refugees, but it did allow entry to large groups of people, such as Hungarians after their unsuccessful uprising in 1956, Cubans who left after Fidel Castro's takeover in 1959, and Southeast Asians after the defeat of South Vietnam in 1975.

Refugees were legally recognized for the first time in the Immigration and Nationality Act Amendments of 1965 (Public Law 89-236). This preference category was reserved for refugees from the Middle East or from countries ruled by a communist government. By 1980, 130,000 refugees had been admitted to the United States under this classification, although many more were admitted through special programs.

The Refugee Act of 1980

The Refugee Act of 1980 (Public Law 96-212) changed the definition of the term "refugee," which previously applied only to those fleeing a communist or Middle Eastern nation. The Refugee Act of 1980 adopted the definition of "refugee" contained in the 1951 United Nations Convention Relating to the Status of Refugees and its 1967 Protocol.

The definition of "refugee," found in Section 101(a)(42) of the Immigration and Nationality Act, as amended by the Refugee Act of 1980, is as follows:

The term "refugee" means (A) any person who is outside any country of such person's nationality or, in the

case of a person having no nationality, is outside any country in which such person last habitually resided, and who is unable or unwilling to return to, and is unable or unwilling to avail himself or herself of the protection of, that country because of persecution or a well-founded fear of persecution on account of race, religion, nationality, membership in a particular social group, or political opinion, or (B) in such circumstances as the President after appropriate consultation [as defined in Section 207(e) of this Act] may specify, any person who is within the country of such person's nationality or, in the case of a person having no nationality, within the country in which such a person is habitually residing, and who is persecuted or who has a well-founded fear of persecution on account of race, religion, nationality, membership in a particular social group, or political opinion.

The term "refugee" does not include any person who ordered, incited, assisted, or otherwise participated in the persecution of any person on account of race, religion, nationality, membership in a particular social group, or political opinion.

. . . a person who has been forced to abort a pregnancy or to undergo involuntary sterilization, or who has been persecuted for failure or refusal to undergo such a procedure or for other resistance to a coercive population control program, shall be deemed to have been persecuted on account of political opinion, and a person who has a well-founded fear that he or she will be forced to undergo such a procedure or be subject to persecution for such failure, refusal or resistance shall be deemed to have a well-founded fear of persecution on account of political opinion.

The Refugee Act of 1980 requires the president of the United States, at the beginning of each fiscal year, to determine the number of refugees to be admitted following meetings between executive branch officials and the Judiciary Committee of both houses of Congress. Refugee numbers are determined without consideration of any overall immigrant quota. The law also regulates U.S.

TABLE 4.1

U.S. Refugee Admissions Program eligibility for refugee processing priorities, fiscal year 2000

*P-1 Processing: All Nationalities are Eligible.

Nationalities	P – 2(1)	P – 3	P – 4
Angolans		X	
Bosnians(2)	X	X	X
Burmese	X		
Burundians		X	
Congolese (Brazzaville)		X	
Congolese (DROC)		X	
Cubans	X		
Eritreans		X	
Ethiopians		X	
Former Soviet Union(3)	X		
Guinea Bissauans		X	
Iranians	X	X	
Iraqis		X	
Rwandans		X	
Sierra Leoneans		X	
Somalis(6)		X	
Sudanese		X	
Togolese		X	
Vietnamese(5)	X		

Notes:
* The UNHCR or U.S. Embassies may refer members of any nationality group —not only those listed in the table above – for consideration of admission to the United States under Priority 1 (P-1). (For certain nationalities – Libyans, Palestinians, and North Koreans – prior consultation with DOS and INS Washington will be required.)
(1) See explanation of groups of special concern under Priority 2 (P-2).
(2) As of November 1, 1999, registration for Priority 4 Bosnian processing will be closed.
(3) While all persons who were nationals of the former Soviet Union prior to September 2, 1991 are eligible to be considered for refugee processing by establishing a well-founded fear of persecution, Jews, Evangelical Christians, and Ukrainian Catholic and Orthodox religious activists may establish refugee status for U.S. admission by asserting a fear of persecution and asserting a credible basis of concern about the possibility of such persecution. (Lautenberg Amendment).
(4) In January 1998, the USG implemented a P-2 processing program for Africa. In this program, specific and identifiable groups in designated locations will become eligible for resettlement processing. The first group was a caseload of Burundian and Rwandan families of Hutu/Tutsi mixed marriages located in a UNHCR protection camp in Tanzania. Also designated were a group of Ogoni refugees from Nigeria and a group of Togolese refugees in Benin. Other groups will also be designated for P-2 processing will follow.
(5) Certain ROVR applicants and Vietnamese who were members of certain category groups identified by the INS in 1983 may establish refugee status for U.S. admission by asserting a fear of persecution and asserting a credible basis of concern about the possibility of such persecution. (Lautenberg Amendment). Registration for consideration under the regular programs of the Orderly Departure Program ended on September 30, 1994.
(6) Given the backlog of an estimated 35,000 P-3 applications for Somalis, the filing of new affidavit of relationship will be suspended in FY 2000 while existing cases are addressed and the situation in the region is reviewed.

DESCRIPTION OF U.S. REFUGEE PROCESSING PRIORITIES FY 2000

PRIORITY ONE: UNHCR or U.S. Embassy identified cases: persons facing compelling security concerns in countries of first asylum; persons in need of legal protection because of the danger of refoulement; those in danger due to threats of armed attack in an area where they are located; persons who have experienced recent persecution because of political, religious, or human rights activities (prisoners of conscience); women-at-risk; victims of torture or violence; physically or mentally disabled persons; persons in urgent need of medical treatment not available in the first asylum country; and persons for whom other durable solutions are not feasible and whose status in the place of asylum does not present a satisfactory long-term solution. As with all other priorities, Priority One referrals must still establish a creditable fear of persecution or history of persecution in the country from which they fled.

PRIORITY TWO: Groups of Special Concern:
Africa: Specific groups (within certain nationalities) as identified by the Department of State in consultation with NGOs, UNHCR, INS, and other area experts. Only those members of the specifically identified groups are eligible for processing. Each group will be selected based on its individual circumstances.
Bosnia: Former detainees who were held on account of ethnicity or political/religious opinion; persons of any ethnic background in mixed marriages; victims of torture or systematic and significant acts of violence against members of targeted ethnic groups by governmental authorities or quasi-governmental authorities in areas under their control; surviving spouses of civilians who would have been eligible under these criteria if they had not died in detention or been killed as a result of torture or violence. (Effective Jan. 1, 1997.)
Burma: Certain members of ethnic minorities who have actively and persistently worked for political autonomy; certain political activists engaged in the pro-democracy movement.
Cuba: In-country, emphasis given to former political prisoners, members of persecuted religious minorities, human rights activists, forced-labor conscripts, persons deprived of their professional credentials or subjected to other disproportionately harsh or discriminatory treatment resulting from their perceived or actual political or religious beliefs or activities, dissidents, and other refugees of compelling concern to the United States.
Iran: Members of Iranian religious minorities.
Former Soviet Union: In-country, Jews, Evangelical Christians, and certain members of the Ukrainian Catholic or Orthodox churches. Preference among these groups is accorded to those with close family in the United States.
Vietnam: In-country, former reeducation camp detainees who spent more than three years in detention camps subsequent to April 1975 because of pre-1975 association with the U.S. government of the former South Vietnamese government; certain former U.S. Government employees and other specified individuals or groups of concern; persons who returned from first-asylum camps in Southeast Asia on or after October 1, 1995 who qualify for consideration under the Resettlement Opportunity for Vietnamese Returnees (ROVR) criteria. Completion of the processing of any residual ODP cases registered and determined eligible for consideration prior to the beginning of FY 2000.

PRIORITY THREE: Spouses, unmarried sons and daughters, and parents of persons lawfully admitted to the United States as permanent resident aliens, refugees, asylees, conditional residents, and certain parolees; the over 21 year old unmarried sons and daughters of U.S. citizens; and parents of U.S. citizens under 21 years of age. (Spouses and unmarried sons and daughters under 21 of U.S. citizens and the parents of U.S. citizens who is 21 or older are required by regulation to be admitted as immigrants rather than as refugees.)

PRIORITY FOUR: Grandparents, grandchildren, married sons and daughters, and siblings of U.S. citizens and persons lawfully admitted to the United States as permanent resident aliens, refugees, asylees, conditional residents, and certain parolees. (Currently open only to Bosnians and without regard to ethnicity. As of November 1, 1999, registration for Priority 4 Bosnian processing will be closed.)

SOURCE: "U.S. Refugee Admissions Program: Eligibility for Refugee Processing Priorities FY 2000," in *U.S. Refugee Admissions for Fiscal Year 2000: Report to Congress.* U.S. Departments of State, Justice, and Health and Human Services: Washington, D.C., October 1999

asylum policy. Whereas a refugee applies for protection while outside the United States, an asylee is already in the United States when applying for admission.

The Lautenberg Amendment

Thousands of refugees have been admitted to the United States under the Lautenberg Amendment, a provision of the Foreign Operations Appropriations Act of 1990 (Public Law 101-167). While normal refugee procedures require individuals to establish a well-founded fear of persecution on a case-by-case basis, under the Lautenberg Amendment applicants are only required to prove that they are members of a protected category with a credible but not necessarily individual fear of persecution. In the former Soviet Union, Jews, Evangelical Christians, and certain members of the Ukrainian Catholic or Ukrainian Orthodox Churches were identified as belonging to these groups. Other groups included nationals of Vietnam, Laos, and Cambodia.

Since 1990 the Lautenberg Amendment has been reauthorized each year as a provision of various laws. In fiscal year 2000 it was extended under the District of Columbia Appropriations Act 2000 (Public Law 106-113; also known as the Departments of Commerce, Justice, and State, the Judiciary, and Related Agencies Appropriations Act 2000).

PROCESSING PRIORITY SYSTEM

In 2000 the number of persons "of concern" to the United Nations High Commissioner for Refugees (UNHCR) numbered nearly 22.3 million. Almost 11.7 million were refugees and 1.2 million were asylum seekers. Over the years the United States has reorganized its categories of priorities for admitting refugees to serve the needs of those who face imminent threats to life and safety and to change the processing that routinely favored applicants from certain countries (for example, Vietnam and the former Soviet Union). Although the categories of priorities have changed, large numbers of Vietnamese and nationals of the countries of the former Soviet Union still qualify for admission to the United States. In fiscal year 2000 the United States had four priority categories under which refugees were assigned. (See Table 4.1.) Assignment to a particular priority, however, does not necessarily guarantee admission to the United States.

HOW MANY ARE ADMITTED?

Every year representatives of the Administration, Congress, state and local governments, public interest groups, private voluntary organizations, and other organizations concerned with refugees meet to discuss the refugee resettlement needs around the world. They also discuss the U.S. refugee policy and its impact on Americans and the international community.

TABLE 4.2

Refugee admissions ceilings, fiscal year 2001

Africa	20,000
East Asia	6,000
Europe	37,000
Former Yugoslavia	20,000
Kosovo Crisis Refugess	—
Former Soviet Union	17,000
Latin America/Caribbean	3,000
Near East/South Asia	10,000
Unallocated reserve	4,000
TOTAL	80,000

SOURCE: "Refugee Admissions Ceilings, FY 2001." Bureau of Population, Refugees, and Migration, U.S. Department of State: Washington, D.C. Last modified February 2001. [Online] http://www.usinfo.state.gov/ topical/global/refugees/adover.html [accessed 04/02/01]

Before the start of a new fiscal year, the president, after consultation with Congress, sets the number of refugee admissions for that fiscal year. For fiscal year (FY) 2001 the Clinton administration established a total admissions ceiling (maximum number) of 80,000 refugees, with an unfunded reserve of 4,000 refugees to allow for increases in some regions as changes in resettlement occurred. The admissions ceiling was then reallocated among five geographic regions. Under the law, unused admissions numbers in one region can be used by another region. The overall admissions ceiling can also be changed as needed. For example, in fiscal year 1999 the initial admissions ceiling for Eastern Europe and the former Soviet Union was 48,000. Due to the Kosovo crisis, this number was expanded to 61,000. That year the admissions ceiling was changed to 91,000 refugees. The unallocated reserve of 2,000 refugees was included in the 61,000 count. In 1999, about 85,000 refugees from Eastern Europe and the former Soviet Union entered the United States.

The FY 2001 East Asian worldwide ceiling of 6,000 refugees was the lowest since the Vietnam War ended in 1975. On the other hand, the African region had a worldwide ceiling of 20,000, up from 12,000 in 1999 and nearly triple the annual allocation of 7,000 for the past several years. (See Table 4.2.)

Under the provision of the Refugee Act of 1980, an annual admissions ceiling of 217,000 refugees was established for 1981. No ceiling was set for fiscal year 1980 because the law did not take effect until mid-fiscal year. In fiscal year 1980 over 207,000 refugees were admitted to the United States. In 1982 the admissions ceiling was down to 140,000 refugees. The annual ceilings continued to decline, reaching 67,000 in 1986. After that they rose steadily for six years, peaking at 142,000 in 1992. For the next five years the ceilings declined again, down to 78,000 in 1997. During the following three years, the ceil-

FIGURE 4.1

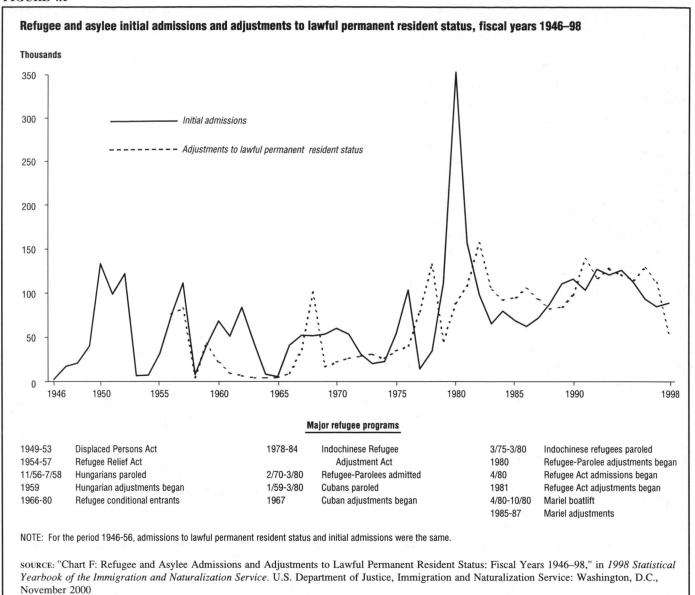

Refugee and asylee initial admissions and adjustments to lawful permanent resident status, fiscal years 1946–98

Major refugee programs

1949-53	Displaced Persons Act	1978-84	Indochinese Refugee	3/75-3/80	Indochinese refugees paroled
1954-57	Refugee Relief Act		Adjustment Act	1980	Refugee-Parolee adjustments began
11/56-7/58	Hungarians paroled	2/70-3/80	Refugee-Parolees admitted	4/80	Refugee Act admissions began
1959	Hungarian adjustments began	1/59-3/80	Cubans paroled	1981	Refugee Act adjustments began
1966-80	Refugee conditional entrants	1967	Cuban adjustments began	4/80-10/80	Mariel boatlift
				1985-87	Mariel adjustments

NOTE: For the period 1946-56, admissions to lawful permanent resident status and initial admissions were the same.

SOURCE: "Chart F: Refugee and Asylee Admissions and Adjustments to Lawful Permanent Resident Status: Fiscal Years 1946–98," in *1998 Statistical Yearbook of the Immigration and Naturalization Service*. U.S. Department of Justice, Immigration and Naturalization Service: Washington, D.C., November 2000

ings ranged from 83,000 to 91,000. The 2001 admissions ceiling of 80,000 refugees was down 10,000 from 2000.

Figure 4.1 shows the number of initial admissions and the number of refugees and asylees given permanent resident status from 1946 to 1998. Different refugee programs were implemented to serve specific purposes that existed at the time. For example, the Displaced Persons Act of 1948 (Public Law 80-774) helped resettle persons who fled or lost their homes during World War II. The largest number of refugees between 1946 and 1960 arrived from Europe mainly as a result of World War II. Throughout the 1980s most refugees came from Asia, primarily as a result of the Vietnam War.

Recent Admissions

In fiscal year 1999, 84,778 refugees were admitted to the United States. The former Yugoslavia provided the most refugees (38,620), followed by the former Soviet Union (16,917) and Vietnam (9,622). Together, these three countries accounted for about 77 percent of all refugee arrivals. A total of 4,321 Somalis were also admitted as refugees, as well as 2,493 Liberians and 2,020 Cubans. (See Table 4.3.) Between 1975 and December 31, 2000, over 2.4 million refugees had resettled in the United States. (See Table 4.4.)

Amerasians, considered a special class of immigrants under the Amerasian Homecoming Act of 1987 (Public Law 100-202), are included in the refugee admissions ceiling and are eligible for refugee benefits. Large-scale processing of Amerasian applicants ended in 1993, although a smaller number continue to be processed and admitted to the United States. In 1999, 241 Amerasians from Vietnam were admitted to the United States. Cuban (19,862) and Haitian (1,215) entrants were also admitted

TABLE 4.3

Amerasian, entrant, and refugee arrivals by country of origin, fiscal year 1999

Country of Origin	Entrant Count	Entrant Col %	Amerasian Count	Amerasian Col %	Refugee Count	Refugee Col %	Total Count	Total Col %
Afghanistan	0	0.00%	0	0.00%	361	0.40%	361	0.30%
Algeria	0	0.00%	0	0.00%	15	0.00%	15	0.00%
Albania	0	0.00%	0	0.00%	11	0.00%	11	0.00%
Bahrain	1	0.00%	0	0.00%	0	0.00%	1	0.00%
Burma	0	0.00%	0	0.00%	295	0.30%	295	0.30%
Burundi	0	0.00%	0	0.00%	223	0.30%	223	0.20%
Chad	0	0.00%	0	0.00%	22	0.00%	22	0.00%
Sri Lanka	0	0.00%	0	0.00%	5	0.00%	5	0.00%
Congo	0	0.00%	0	0.00%	27	0.00%	27	0.00%
Zaire	0	0.00%	0	0.00%	42	0.00%	42	0.00%
China	0	0.00%	0	0.00%	1	0.00%	1	0.00%
Cameroon	0	0.00%	0	0.00%	9	0.00%	9	0.00%
Central Africa	0	0.00%	0	0.00%	1	0.00%	1	0.00%
Cuba	19862	94.20%	0	0.00%	2020	2.40%	21882	20.60%
Djibouti	0	0.00%	0	0.00%	8	0.00%	8	0.00%
Eritrea	0	0.00%	0	0.00%	32	0.00%	32	0.00%
Ethiopia	0	0.00%	0	0.00%	1879	2.20%	1879	1.80%
Gambia	0	0.00%	0	0.00%	13	0.00%	13	0.00%
Ghana	0	0.00%	0	0.00%	5	0.00%	5	0.00%
Guinea	0	0.00%	0	0.00%	6	0.00%	6	0.00%
Haiti	1215	5.80%	0	0.00%	91	0.10%	1306	1.20%
Indonesia	0	0.00%	0	0.00%	26	0.00%	26	0.00%
Iran	0	0.00%	0	0.00%	1737	2.00%	1737	1.60%
Ivory Coast	0	0.00%	0	0.00%	5	0.00%	5	0.00%
Iraq	0	0.00%	0	0.00%	1962	2.30%	1962	1.80%
Kenya	0	0.00%	0	0.00%	2	0.00%	2	0.00%
Laos	0	0.00%	0	0.00%	19	0.00%	19	0.00%
Liberia	0	0.00%	0	0.00%	2493	2.90%	2493	2.30%
Macau	0	0.00%	0	0.00%	1	0.00%	1	0.00%
Mauritania	0	0.00%	0	0.00%	1	0.00%	1	0.00%
Nigeria	0	0.00%	0	0.00%	625	0.70%	625	0.60%
Peru	0	0.00%	0	0.00%	1	0.00%	1	0.00%
Poland	0	0.00%	0	0.00%	2	0.00%	2	0.00%
Romania	0	0.00%	0	0.00%	2	0.00%	2	0.00%
Rwanda	0	0.00%	0	0.00%	153	0.20%	153	0.10%
Sierra Leone	0	0.00%	0	0.00%	678	0.80%	678	0.60%
Somalia	0	0.00%	0	0.00%	4321	5.10%	4321	4.10%
Sudan	0	0.00%	0	0.00%	2389	2.80%	2389	2.30%
Syria	0	0.00%	0	0.00%	2	0.00%	2	0.00%
Togo	0	0.00%	0	0.00%	93	0.10%	93	0.10%
Tanzania	0	0.00%	0	0.00%	1	0.00%	1	0.00%
Uganda	0	0.00%	0	0.00%	12	0.00%	12	0.00%
USSR (Former)	1	0.00%	0	0.00%	16917	20.00%	16918	15.90%
Vietnam	0	0.00%	241	100.0%	9622	11.30%	9863	9.30%
Yemen	0	0.00%	0	0.00%	1	0.00%	1	0.00%
Yugoslavia (Former)	0	0.00%	0	0.00%	38620	45.60%	38620	36.40%
Unknown	0	0.00%	0	0.00%	27	0.00%	27	0.00%
Table Total	21079	100.0%	241	100.0%	84778	100.0%	106098	100.0%

NOTE: Arrival figures do not reflect secondary migration.

SOURCE: "Table IX: Amerasian, Entrant, and Refugee Arrivals by Country of Origin for FY 1999" in *Proposed Refugee Admissions for Fiscal Year 2001: Report to Congress*. U.S. Departments of State, Justice, and Health and Human Services: Washington, D.C., July 2000

in 1999. These individuals were granted parole status by the U.S. attorney general for humanitarian reasons. A parolee is an alien who is temporarily admitted to the United States for urgent humanitarian reasons and is required to leave the country when the conditions for the parole cease to exist. Nonetheless, a parolee may be allowed to adjust to permanent resident status if requirements are met.

Those Granted Lawful Permanent Residence

For a refugee or an asylee to adjust to permanent resident status, he or she must have lived in the United States for at least one year. From 1991 through 1998, over three-quarters of the nearly 915,000 refugees and asylees admitted as lawful permanent residents to the United States came from Asia (36 percent) or from Europe (41 percent). (See Table 4.5.)

TABLE 4.4

Refugee admissions fiscal years 1975–2000*

Africa	106,594
East Asia	1,273,604
Europe	263,848
Former Soviet Union	562,929
Latin America/Caribbean	82,627
Near East/South Asia	122,256
TOTAL	2,411,858

* As of December 31, 2000

SOURCE: "Refugee Admissions, FY 1975 to date." Bureau of Population, Refugees, and Migration, U.S. Department of State: Washington, D.C. Last modified February 2001. [Online] http://www.usinfo.state.gov/topical/global/refugees/adover.html [accessed April 2, 2001]

In 1998 Cuba (14,915) was the leading country of birth of refugees and asylees who became permanent residents, followed by the former Soviet Union (13,200), the former Yugoslavia (5,312), Vietnam (4,921), Thailand (1,134), and Laos (1,110). These six countries accounted for 74 percent of all refugees and asylees who adjusted to permanent resident status. (See Table 4.5.)

Where Do the Refugee Arrivals Live?

In 1999 the Office of Refugee Resettlement of the U.S. Department of Health and Human Services reported that nearly half (49.8 percent) of refugees who arrived in the United States resettled in seven states. New York (9,851) and California (9,493) were the primary destinations. The remaining popular destinations were Florida, Georgia, Illinois, Texas, and Washington.

EAST ASIAN REFUGEES

Since 1975 the overwhelming majority of refugees reaching the United States has come from Southeast Asia. This influx began when about 130,000 people left Vietnam at the time of the collapse of the American-supported South Vietnamese government in 1975. The U.S. government evacuated about 65,000 Vietnamese military and government officials, as well as Vietnamese employees of the United States and their families. Another 65,000 escaped on their own.

Orderly Departure Program (ODP)

In 1979, in response to the refugee situation created not only by the end of the Vietnam War but also by Vietnam's invasion of Cambodia and China's attack on Vietnam, the United Nations convened a conference of some 70 nations to address the problem. As a result, in 1980 the Vietnamese and the United States governments agreed to create an Orderly Departure Program (ODP) to provide a safe and legal means of leaving Vietnam.

In July 1989, as part of the ODP, Vietnam and the United States signed an agreement for the resettlement of thousands of re-education camp detainees. Tens of thousands of former South Vietnam military and civilian government officials had been placed in re-education camps by the communist government that took power in 1975. Some were kept a minimum of three years, while others spent many years in the camps before they were allowed to return home. Since then about 166,500 re-education camp prisoners and accompanying family members have been resettled in the United States. In 1994 the ODP refugee programs ceased accepting applications for resettlement. The ODP office in Bangkok, Thailand, continued to process applications until fiscal year 1999, when that office formally closed. Since then, the remaining applications have been processed at the Resettlement Section of the newly established U.S. Consulate General in Ho Chi Minh City (formerly Saigon) in Vietnam.

Amerasian Children

Amerasian children are children born of unions between an American parent and an Asian parent. The Amerasian children born of American soldiers and Vietnamese women during the Vietnam War have generally not been absorbed into Vietnamese society and have often faced lives of homelessness and poverty. Vietnamese society generally does not recognize the children of non-Vietnamese unions, and the problems these children face have been compounded because they are seen as the off-spring of enemy soldiers.

In 1988, following the passage of the Amerasian Homecoming Act of 1987, 319 Amerasian children came to the United States. In 1992, at the peak of Amerasian immigration, more than 18,000 Amerasian children and relatives entered the country. Large-scale processing of the Amerasian caseload was completed in 1993, although processing of small numbers of qualified applicants continued through 1998. Between 1980 and 1998, about 21,000 Amerasian children were admitted to the United States. They were accompanied by approximately 59,000 family members.

Winding Down

After more than 25 years, what the INS refers to as one of the longest-running migration and refugee resettlement programs in the modern era is winding down. The last phase of the Vietnamese resettlement, the Resettlement Opportunity for Vietnamese Returnees (ROVR) program, is coming to a close. The ROVR is an initiative by the United States and Vietnamese governments to offer certain designated Vietnamese returnees a final chance to enter the United States. An estimated 20,850 Vietnamese nationals were eligible for interviews with the INS for resettlement in the United States. As part of the agreement, refugees had to return to Vietnam from asylum camps in

TABLE 4.5

Refugees and asylees granted lawful permanent resident status by region and country of birth, fiscal years 1946–98

Region and country of birth	Total	1946-50	1951-60	1961-70	1971-80 [1]	1981-90 [1]	1991-96	1997	1998
All countries	**3,386,553**	**213,347**	**492,371**	**212,843**	**539,447**	**1,013,620**	**748,122**	**112,158**	**54,645**
Europe	**1,322,392**	**211,983**	**456,146**	**55,235**	**71,858**	**155,512**	**312,815**	**39,795**	**19,048**
Albania	7,283	29	1,409	1,952	395	353	3,013	76	56
Austria	17,486	4,801	11,487	233	185	424	330	20	6
Bulgaria	7,132	139	1,138	1,799	1,238	1,197	1,519	69	33
Czechoslovakia, former	37,983	8,449	10,719	5,709	3,646	8,204	1,201	40	15
Estonia	12,042	7,143	4,103	16	2	25	646	89	18
Germany	101,911	36,633	62,860	665	143	851	625	79	55
Greece	31,525	124	28,568	586	478	1,408	342	11	8
Hungary	76,439	6,086	55,740	4,044	4,358	4,942	1,231	24	14
Italy	63,636	642	60,657	1,198	346	394	378	14	7
Latvia	40,815	21,422	16,783	49	16	48	2,156	272	69
Lithuania	28,468	18,694	8,569	72	23	37	961	85	27
Netherlands	17,646	129	14,336	3,134	8	14	17	3	5
Poland	210,227	78,529	81,323	3,197	5,882	33,889	7,210	143	54
Portugal	5,078	12	3,650	1,361	21	21	12	1	—
Romania	75,582	4,180	12,057	7,158	6,812	29,798	15,139	322	116
Soviet Union, former	456,884	14,072	30,059	871	31,309	72,306	264,187	30,880	13,200
Russia	46,455	X	X	X	X	X	44,367	6,985	2,225
Ukraine	83,694	X	X	X	X	X	81,263	12,137	3,641
Uzbekistan	16,265	X	X	X	X	X	14,638	2,885	292
Other republics	48,477	X	X	X	X	X	48,336	6,284	1,518
Unknown republic	261,993	14,072	30,059	871	31,309	72,306	75,583	2,589	5,524
Spain	10,791	1	246	4,114	5,317	736	317	29	31
Yugoslavia, former	110,671	9,816	44,755	18,299	11,297	324	13,271	7,597	5,312
Other Europe	10,793	1,082	7,687	778	382	541	260	41	22
Asia	**1,305,901**	**1,106**	**33,422**	**19,895**	**210,683**	**712,092**	**286,125**	**30,835**	**11,743**
Afghanistan	33,047	—	1	—	542	22,946	9,065	356	137
Cambodia	128,116	—	—	—	7,739	114,064	6,088	163	62
China [2]	46,011	319	12,008	5,308	13,760	7,928	5,097	693	898
Hong Kong	9,147	—	1,076	2,128	3,468	1,916	535	19	5
Indonesia	17,704	—	8,253	7,658	222	1,385	174	8	4
Iran	69,832	118	192	58	364	46,773	20,126	1,447	754
Iraq	31,877	—	130	119	6,851	7,540	14,464	1,774	999
Japan	4,545	3	3,803	554	56	110	18	—	1
Korea	4,636	—	3,116	1,316	65	120	14	3	2
Laos	200,828	—	—	—	21,690	142,964	33,701	1,363	1,110
Syria	5,803	4	119	383	1,336	2,145	963	146	707
Thailand	53,097	—	15	13	1,241	30,259	19,323	1,112	1,134
Turkey	7,124	603	1,427	1,489	1,193	1,896	460	35	21
Vietnam	671,506	—	2	7	150,266	324,453	169,560	22,297	4,921
Other Asia	22,628	59	3,280	862	1,890	7,593	6,537	1,419	988
Africa	**78,514**	**20**	**1,768**	**5,486**	**2,991**	**22,149**	**34,224**	**7,651**	**4,225**
Egypt	9,019	8	1,354	5,396	1,473	426	237	71	54
Ethiopia [3]	37,823	—	61	2	1,307	18,542	16,364	1,056	534
Other Africa	31,672	12	353	88	211	3,181	17,623	6,524	3,637
Oceania	**427**	**7**	**75**	**21**	**37**	**22**	**186**	**59**	**20**
North America	**668,549**	**163**	**831**	**132,068**	**252,633**	**121,840**	**111,744**	**32,898**	**16,372**
Cuba	618,109	3	6	131,557	251,514	113,367	76,370	30,377	14,915
El Salvador	5,379	—	—	1	45	1,383	3,623	198	129
Nicaragua	27,865	1	1	3	36	5,590	21,252	666	316
Other North America	17,196	159	824	507	1,038	1,500	10,499	1,657	1,012
South America	**8,086**	**32**	**74**	**123**	**1,244**	**1,986**	**3,025**	**890**	**712**
Chile	1,092	—	5	4	415	532	110	14	12
Colombia	1,363	NA	NA	NA	217	350	471	154	171
Peru	2,495	NA	NA	NA	102	251	1,285	489	368
Venezuela	1,592	NA	NA	NA	83	407	811	173	118
Other South America	1,544	32	69	119	397	446	348	60	73
Unknown or not reported	**2,684**	**36**	**55**	**15**	**1**	**19**	**3**	**30**	**2,525**

[1] Data for fiscal years 1971-90 have been adjusted.   [2] Includes People's Republic of China and Taiwan.   [3] Includes Eritrea.
NOTE: The data no longer include Cuban/Haitian entrants granted immigrant status.
— Represents zero.   NA Not available.   X Not applicable.

SOURCE: "Table 32. Refugees and Asylees Granted Lawful Permanent Resident Status by Region and Selected Country of Birth, Fiscal Years 1946–98," in *1998 Statistical Yearbook of the Immigration and Naturalization Service*. U.S. Department of Justice, Immigration and Naturalization Service: Washington, D.C., November 2000

Hong Kong and Southeast Asia. The camps were closed as the last of the refugees returned to their homeland.

Since 1975, of the more than 3 million people who left Vietnam, Laos, and Cambodia (including nearly 1.8 million Vietnamese boat people and land refugees), over 1.4 million have been resettled in the United States. About 900,000 were from Vietnam. Among them were the estimated 506,000 Vietnamese refugees, immigrants, and parolees in the ODP, including over 80,000 Amerasians and their families, about 166,500 re-education camp prisoners and their families, some 237,000 under the family reunification program, and nearly 15,000 under the ROVR program.

In FY 1999, over 10,200 refugees from East Asia entered the United States. Nearly 97 percent came from Vietnam. A repressive military government in Burma (renamed Myanmar by the present government) has created the largest refugee population in all of Asia east of Pakistan. Until recently only a small number of Burmese refugees have sought admission to the United States—in 1996, just 11 Burmese refugees arrived in this country. However, in 1999, 295 Burmese refugees entered the United States, possibly due to the continuing repression by the Burmese military. Other refugee arrivals to the United States included Indonesians (26) and Laotians (19). (See Table 4.3.)

AFRICAN REFUGEES

Since 1980 about 85,000 African refugees have entered the United States. Most refugees arrived from Ethiopia (over 30,000) and Somalia (over 25,000). In addition, smaller numbers were admitted from Sudan, Liberia, Zaire (renamed Democratic Republic of Congo), Rwanda, Uganda, and Angola.

In 1980, 955 African refugees were admitted to the United States. In 1981 and 1983, the numbers more than doubled and tripled (2,119 and 3,412, respectively). By 1993, the number of African refugees entering the United States reached nearly 7,000, peaking at 7,604 in 1996.

The authorized admissions level for the African region almost tripled in the three years from 1998 to 2001, from 7,000 to 20,000. This higher ceiling allowed about 24 African nationalities to be considered for refugee admissions program. In 1999 about 13,000 African refugees resettled in the United States. (See Table 4.3.)

REFUGEES FROM THE NEAR EAST AND SOUTH ASIA

Although the Near East and South Asian regions have the largest number of the world's refugees, countries within the region have historically taken in refugees from neighboring countries. The majority of refugees have been Iranian, Iraqi, and Afghan nationals. Nearly 2 million Iraqis fled their country during the Persian Gulf War (1991). Although the majority returned to their homes at the end of the war, large numbers stayed in countries of first asylum (first countries where they sought refuge), fearing persecution if they went back.

About 39,000 Iraqis, including ethnic and religious minorities and those who had been involved in rebellion against the Iraqi government, sought refuge in Saudi Arabia. Between 1991 and 1997 the United States, participating in a multi-country resettlement effort led by the United Nations High Commissioner for Refugees, admitted 12,209 Iraqi refugees. Since 1980, 112,500 refugees from Near East and South Asian countries have resettled in the United States. Most have come from Iran (about 47,000), Iraq (31,200), and Afghanistan (28,000).

Members of certain Iranian religious minorities, such as those of the Bahá'í faith, have also left their country due to widespread persecution and discrimination. They are considered persons of special concern to the United States who can apply for refugee status regardless of family ties to the United States. In fiscal year 1999 nearly 4,100 refugees arrived from the Near East and South Asia. The majority came from Iraq (1,962) and Iran (1,737). (See Table 4.3.)

For more than two decades, Afghanistan has been devastated by ongoing conflicts among its different ethnic tribes. In 1996 the ethnic Pushtun Taliban took power, controlling about 90 percent of the country in a few years. Hundreds of Afghans have reportedly been killed. The Taliban, a fundamentalist religious group, advocates and implements a strict interpretation of Islam. Ethnic and religious groups, including Hindus and Shiite Hazaras, have been persecuted. Females are banned from education and employment, and most are confined to their homes, leaving those with no male relatives without means to support or protect themselves. According to the U.S. Department of State *Country Report on Human Rights,* women and girls continue to be victims of such atrocities as murders, beatings, rapes, and forced marriages. As a result of the Taliban's takeover, more than 2 million Afghans have fled to the neighboring countries of Pakistan and Iran.

REFUGEES FROM THE FORMER SOVIET UNION AND EASTERN EUROPE

On December 21, 1991, the Union of Soviet Socialist Republics (USSR, or the Soviet Union) was dissolved. The 15 USSR republics became independent countries. These countries are also referred to as the Newly Independent States (Armenia, Azerbaijan, Belarus, Georgia, Kazakhstan, Kyrgyzstan, Moldova, Russia, Tajikistan, Turkmenistan, Ukraine, and Uzbekistan) and the Baltics (Estonia, Latvia, and Lithuania).

Now that the communist Soviet Union government has collapsed, some persons have questioned whether the

United States still needs to admit so many refugees from this area. Unfortunately, the chaos and turmoil in the new republics have led to ethnic conflict, and anti-Semitism and the persecution of certain Christian groups have increased sharply. Since the Lautenberg Amendment took effect in 1990, over 378,000 persons from the former Soviet Union have been admitted to the United States.

In fiscal year 1999 a total of 16,917 refugees from the former Soviet Union arrived in the United States. However, the flow of refugees from countries that had traditionally sent refugees before the fall of communism (Bulgaria, Czechoslovakia, Hungary, Poland, and Romania) dropped to virtually nothing. In 1999 no refugees arrived from Bulgaria, Czechoslovakia (now the Czech Republic and Slovakia), and Hungary. (See Table 4.3.)

The Former Yugoslavia

Except for the former Soviet Union, the nationals of the countries of the former Yugoslavia continue to make up the greatest number of refugees in Europe. In 2000 the United Nations High Commissioner for Refugees identified over 195,000 refugees from Bosnia and Herzegovina and another 300,000 from the former Yugoslavia.

In 1993 the U.S. State Department expanded its admissions program for Bosnians, adding Bosnia to the list of countries designated as being of special humanitarian concern to the United States. The admissions include former detainees, torture victims, and female victims of violence. Also included are Bosnians in mixed marriages (Muslim-Serb, Serb-Croat, Muslim-Croat) and immediate family members of minor U.S. citizen children who have been displaced as a result of the fighting.

In fiscal year 1999, 38,620 refugees from the former Yugoslavia were admitted to the United States. This was more than twice the allocation of 17,000 for that year. For 2001 the maximum ceiling was set at 20,000.

Kosovo

Between January 1 and late May 1999 Serbian forces and the Yugoslav military, in a campaign of ethnic cleansing, expelled more than 780,000 ethnic Albanians from the Serbian province of Kosovo. Serbia is one of the two republics of the Federal Republic of Yugoslavia (the second is Montenegro). In what is considered Europe's largest refugee exodus since the Bosnian war, the homeless Kosovars fled to Albania (about 442,000), Macedonia (250,000), Montenegro (70,000), and Bosnia-Herzegovina (21,700). The ethnic Albanians had accounted for 90 percent of the Kosovar population.

In April 1999 the U.S. government offered to relocate as many as 20,000 Kosovar refugees to the United States. The priority lists consisted of those with families in America, as well as persons in vulnerable circumstances. About 14,000 Kosovar refugees resettled in the United States.

In June 1999 the Yugoslav government accepted a peace agreement following 78 days of NATO (North Atlantic Treaty Organization) bombing of military installations and other facilities throughout Serbia. To encourage the refugees to return to Kosovo once the crisis was resolved, the State Department funded the trip for those who left the United States before May 1, 2000. About 2,600 returned to their home country.

LATIN AMERICAN AND CARIBBEAN REFUGEES

Since 1975 the United States has offered resettlement to approximately 80,000 refugees from the Latin American and Caribbean countries. Over half have been from Cuba. The remainder were from Haiti, Nicaragua, and El Salvador.

In 2001 all refugee processing in the Latin American and Caribbean region involved Cuba. Admission as refugees was governed by the U.S.-Cuba Bilateral Migration Agreement, in effect since September 9, 1994. The United States agreed that a minimum of 20,000 Cubans could migrate to the United States each year. Cuba, on the other hand, would take measures to prevent its citizens from embarking on unsafe journeys to reach the United States. In fiscal year 1999, 2,020 Cuban and 91 Haitian refugees entered the United States. (See Table 4.3.)

REFUGEE ADJUSTMENT TO THE UNITED STATES

The Refugee Act of 1980 stressed the importance of refugees' participation in the labor force and achieving economic self-sufficiency as soon as possible. The Office of Refugee Resettlement (ORR), an agency of the U.S. Department of Health and Human Services, surveyed refugee adjustments for *Making a Difference: FY 1998 Annual Report to the Congress* (Washington, D.C., 2000). The survey included refugees from all regions of the world who arrived in the United States between May 1, 1993, and April 30, 1998.

Table 4.6 shows the Employment-to-Population Ratio (EPR) as of October 1998 for refugees age 16 and over in the five-year sample population. The EPR, also called the employment rate, is the ratio of the number of individuals age 16 or over who were employed (full- or part-time) to the total number of individuals in the population age 16 or over. The survey found that the overall EPR for all refugees was 56 percent, compared to 64.1 percent for the U.S. population as a whole. The ORR noted that, although the EPR for the newest arrivals (1998) was only 52.5 percent, the EPR for those who arrived in earlier years reached as high as 59.9 percent in 1995. Therefore, refugee employment appeared to increase with each year of U.S. residence.

The difference between the labor force participation rate and the EPR is the proportion of the adult population

TABLE 4.6

Employment status of refugees by year of arrival and sex

Year of Arrival	Employment Rate (EPR)			Labor Force Participation Rate			Unemployment Rate		
	All	Male	Female	All	Male	Female	All	Male	Female
1998	52.5%	59.6%	44.9%	62.3%	70.0%	54.0%	15.0%	13.3%	17.3%
1997	54.5	64.7	45.7	60.1	69.8	51.7	8.8	8.1	10.3
1996	55.3	64.0	46.5	58.2	67.6	48.4	4.1	4.3	3.7
1995	59.9	66.3	53.3	62.9	69.0	56.8	3.5	2.7	4.8
1994	56.4	62.2	50.6	59.4	65.5	53.4	4.4	4.1	4.7
1993	53.0	56.8	49.3	55.5	60.1	50.8	3.3	4.2	2.3
Total Sample	56.0	62.8	49.3	59.1	66.6	52.8	5.2	4.7	5.7
U.S. Rates	64.1	71.6	57.1	67.1	74.9	59.8	4.5	4.4	4.6

Note: As of October 1998. Not seasonally adjusted. Data refer to refugees 16 and over in the five-year sample population consisting of Amerasians, Entrants, and Refugees of all nationalities who arrived in the years 1993–1998. U.S. Rates are for 1998.

SOURCE: "Table 1 - Employment Status of Refugees by Year of Arrival and Sex," in *Making a Difference: FY 1998 Annual Report to the Congress.* U.S. Department of Health and Human Services, Office of Refugee Resettlement: Washington, D.C., 2000

looking for work but unable to find it. Overall, both the refugee-sample population and the U.S. population age 16 and over had the same proportion (3 percent) of persons looking for, but unable to find, work. For all refugees, the proportion seeking employment but failing to find work declined with time—just 2.5 percent of the 1993 arrivals were looking for work but were unable to do so, compared to 9.8 percent of the 1998 arrivals. Similarly, the unemployment rate (the proportion of persons looking for work) decreased with time—3.3 percent for the 1993 arrivals and 15 percent for the 1998 arrivals. (See Table 4.6.)

A breakdown of the refugee groups showed a wide disparity in employment levels. The EPR of Latin Americans (78.7 percent) was much higher than that of the total refugee population (56 percent). The EPR of the Vietnamese refugees (55.8 percent) was about the same as the overall EPR, but the remaining Southeast Asian population had only 26.6 percent of their adult population employed. (See Table 4.7.)

Non-Vietnamese Southeast Asians had the hardest time getting into the labor force—only 28 percent had ever been employed, compared to about 80 percent each for Latin American and Eastern European refugees. Refugees from the former Soviet Union had the highest unemployment rate (14.2 percent), while Vietnamese nationals had the lowest unemployment rate (0.1 percent). (See Table 4.7.)

Education and English language proficiency have a profound effect on a person's ability to get a job in the United States. The average number of years of education for refugees arriving between 1993 and 1998 was 10.6 years, a sharp increase over the past decade, most likely due to the increase in former Soviet refugees who averaged 12.2 years of education. Almost one-third (32.7 percent) of African refugees reported having no education at all. About 56 percent of Vietnam refugees claimed having finished high

school, and about a quarter of Latin American and Soviet refugees reported having a university degree (23.7 percent and 28.6 percent, respectively). (See Table 4.8.)

As for language proficiency, just 4.9 percent of arrivals indicated that they spoke English well or fluently. (Note that this is a self-reported observation.) Nearly one-quarter (23.7 percent) reported not speaking English well, and over two-thirds (69 percent) admitted speaking no English. (See Table 4.8.) For all of the survey respondents, those who reported speaking English well or fluently at the time of the survey had the highest EPR of 59 percent, while those who reported speaking no English had the lowest EPR of 20 percent.

Economic Self-Sufficiency and Welfare

By October 1998 about 60 percent of refugee households who had been in the United States for five years or less had achieved self-sufficiency. Nearly one-fifth (18.7 percent) had reached partial economic independence, depending on both their earnings and public assistance. For another one-fifth (18.8 percent), however, income during the five-year period consisted entirely of public assistance. (See Table 4.9.)

The ORR survey also found that the welfare use varied among the different refugee groups. Nearly 38 percent of refugee households had received some kind of cash assistance in at least one of the 12 months prior to the survey. Southeast Asians, who generally had higher fertility rates (had more children than the average) were more likely to use Aid to Families with Dependent Children (AFDC)/Temporary Assistance for Needy Families (TANF). This service was utilized by 13.7 percent of Vietnamese refugees and 53.8 percent of other Southeast Asians. On the other hand, Soviet refugees who tended to be older than most refugees were proportionally the heaviest users (38.2 percent) of Supplemental Security Income (SSI), a program for the

TABLE 4.7

Employment status of selected refugee groups by sex

Employment Measure	Africa	Latin America	Middle East	Eastern Europe	Former Soviet Union	Vietnam	Other S.E. Asia	All
Employment-to-Population Ratio (EPR)	50.5%	78.7%	49.7%	72.9%	44.3%	55.8%	26.6%	56.0%
Males	55.3%	83.0%	63.3%	79.4%	52.6%	60.0%	29.7%	62.8%
Females	46.1%	73.3%	30.4%	66.7%	37.5%	51.5%	23.5%	49.3%
Worked at any point since arrival	51.1	80.2	52.5	79.5	49.5	55.8	28.0	58.8
Males	56.4	84.4	67.1	85.1	57.1	60.0	30.4	65.3
Females	46.1	74.9	31.8	74.1	43.2	51.5	25.5	52.5
Labor Force Participation Rate	51.5	79.7	53.2	77.0	51.6	55.8	26.8	59.1
Males	56.8	86.3	70.8	84.5	60.8	60.2	35.1	66.6
Females	45.8	75.8	30.6	70.9	45.0	52.1	23.7	52.8
Unemployment Rate	1.4	1.3	6.4	5.3	14.2	0.1	0.0	5.2
Males	2.6	0.0	8.3	5.6	13.0	0.0	0.0	4.7
Females	0.0	3.0	0.0	4.8	15.2	0.3	0.0	5.7

Note: As of October 1998. Not seasonally adjusted. Data refer to refugees 16 and over in the five-year sample population consisting of Amerasians, Entrants, and Refugees of all nationalities who arrived in the years 1993–1998.

SOURCE: "Table 2 - Employment Status of Selected Refugee Groups by Sex," in *Making a Difference: FY 1998 Annual Report to the Congress.* U.S. Department of Health and Human Services, Office of Refugee Resettlement: Washington, D.C., 2000

elderly and disabled. (See Table 4.10.) About 16 percent of refugees from the former Soviet Union were age 65 or over. In comparison, 8 percent of refugees from Latin America and 5 percent or less of all the other refugee groups had members who were age 65 or over.

The proportions of refugees receiving non-cash assistance were greater than those receiving cash aid. Overall, one-third (32.7 percent) of all refugees used food stamps. Food stamp use ranged from a high of 72.9 percent among non-Vietnamese Southeast Asians to a low of 10.9 percent for Latin Americans. Nearly 36 percent of all refugees reported that they received medical coverage through Medicaid or Refugee Medical Assistance (RMA), while 16.2 percent lived in public housing projects. (See Table 4.10.)

SEEKING ASYLUM

An asylee, a person seeking asylum, is like a refugee. The only difference is the location of the alien when he or she applies for refuge. The refugee is outside the United States when applying for refuge, while an asylee is already in the United States or at a port of entry. Just like a refugee applying for entrance into the United States, an asylee seeks the protection of the United States because of persecution or a well-founded fear of persecution.

Asylees include sailors who jump ship while their boat is docked in a U.S. port or athletes who ask for asylum while participating in a sports event in the United States. Any alien physically present in the United States or at a port of entry may request asylum in the United States. It is irrelevant whether the person is a legal or illegal alien. Like refugees, asylum applicants do not count against the worldwide annual U.S. limitation of immigrants.

The Immigration Act of 1990 increased the ceiling for asylum admissions from 5,000 to 10,000 per year. Thousands more people apply for asylum than can be heard or are granted approval. Applications that are received include both newly filed and reopened cases. Cases that have been closed (for example, due to an applicant's failure to show up for his or her interview) are automatically re-opened when the alien applies for a renewal of employment authorization.

Critics charge that many persons seek asylum in the United States to avoid dismal economic conditions at home rather than political or religious persecution or a well-founded fear of death. In addition, some illegal aliens try to obtain the legal right to work by filing for asylum. Unlike illegal aliens, asylees are legally permitted to work under certain circumstances.

Filing of Claims

In the past persons requesting asylum at U.S. ports of entry were referred for exclusion hearings before an immigration judge. Under the provisions of the 1996 Illegal Immigration Reform and Immigrant Responsibility Act (IIRIRA), such aliens are referred to asylum officers who interview them to determine credible fear of persecution. Those who fail to show evidence of fear of persecution are placed in expedited removal proceedings. However, the asylum officer has to refer the asylum seeker to an immigration judge if the person requests it.

Asylees Granted Refugee Assistance Benefits

In June 2000 the Office of Refugee Resettlement (ORR) announced that asylees may participate in

TABLE 4.8

Educational and English proficiency characteristics of selected refugee groups

Education and Language Proficiency	Africa	Latin America	Middle East	Eastern Europe	Former Soviet Union	Vietnam	Other S.E. Asia	All
Average Years of Education before U.S.	7.5	10.9	9.8	10.8	12.2	10.3	2.9	10.6
Highest Degree before U.S.								
None	32.7%	11.8%	19.7%	7.5%	1.4%	19.5%	61.7%	13.9%
Primary School	25.6	18.4	24.3	21.3	10.0	14.5	23.6	16.1
Secondary School	23.7	36.0	26.7	37.8	28.9	56.1	3.4	37.8
Technical School	1.2	4.3	3.3	11.6	20.8	0.3	0.0	8.5
University Degree	5.9	23.7	10.2	13.6	28.6	5.0	0.0	15.6
Medical School	0.0	0.8	1.4	0.3	4.3	0.0	0.0	1.5
Attended School/University (since U.S.)	43.7	7.7	31.1	10.9	17.4	27.0	34.8	20.9
Attended School/University (since U.S.) for degree/certificate	35.3	7.4	21.5	9.4	16.3	24.5	28.9	18.4
High School	16.5	4.0	11.0	6.4	5.6	6.7	23.8	7.4
Associate Degree	63	0.3	1.2	0.4	2.9	8.5	0.0	3.9
Bachelor's Degree	10.0	2.4	5.8	1.3	5.6	8.9	5.1	5.8
Master's/Doctorate	0.0	0.6	0.0	0.0	1.8	0.0	0.0	0.6
Professional Degree	0.0	0.0	0.0	0.5	0.5	0.1	0.0	0.3
Other	0.0	0.0	0.0	0.0	0.2	0.2	0.0	0.1
Degree Received	0.0	0.4	0.3	0.3	1.4	0.3	1.0	0.7
At Time of Arrival								
Percent Speaking no English	44.6	70.0	59.3	74.4	69.8	70.7	75.8	69.0
Percent Not Speaking English Well	38.5	25.8	26.2	15.3	22.1	26.1	15.3	23.7
Percent Speaking English Well or Fluently	15.2	3.1	5.3	8.0	6.9	0.8	2.0	4.9
At Time of Survey								
Percent Speaking no English	4.1	13.4	21.3	13.0	18.4	7.1	26.2	13.5
Percent Not Speaking English Well	20.9	57.9	34.5	39.6	34.8	57.4	30.7	44.3
Percent Speaking English Well or Fluently	74.6	28.4	43.3	42.3	45.1	34.6	40.3	40.7

Note: Data refer to refugees 16 and over in the five-year sample population consisting of Amerasians, Entrants, and Refugees of all nationalities who arrived in the years 1993–1998. These figures refer to self-reported characteristics of refugees. Professional degree refers to a law degree or medical degree.

SOURCE: "Table 3 - Educational and English Proficiency Characteristics of Selected Refugee Groups," in *Making a Difference: FY 1998 Annual Report to the Congress.* U.S. Department of Health and Human Services, Office of Refugee Resettlement: Washington, D.C., 2000

TABLE 4.9

Hourly wages, home ownership, and self-sufficiency by year of arrival

Year of Arrival	Hourly Wages of Employed	Own Home or Apartment	Rent Home or Apartment	Public Assistance Only	Both Public Assistance and Earnings	Earnings Only
1998	$7.21	2.3%	96.0%	24.9%	27.2%	45.6%
1997	7.61	4.9	94.8	21.3	19.5	57.4
1996	7.69	8.4	87.5	15.0	19.5	60.2
1995	7.75	7.8	90.2	15.9	17.4	65.6
1994	8.50	12.6	85.1	19.4	17.0	61.7
1993	8.54	13.9	84.3	22.4	18.8	56.1
Total Sample	7.97	9.2	88.6	18.8	18.7	60.1

Note: Data refer to refugees 16 and over in the five-year sample population consisting of Amerasians, Entrants, and Refugees of all nationalities who arrived in the years 1993–1998. These figures refer to self-reported characteristics of refugees.

SOURCE: "Table 6 - Hourly Wages, Home Ownership, and Self-Sufficiency by Year of Arrival," in *Making a Difference: FY 1998 Annual Report to the Congress.* U.S. Department of Health and Human Services, Office of Refugee Resettlement: Washington, D.C., 2000

---

refugee assistance benefits for eight months, starting on their entry date. Unlike refugees, asylees are not granted asylum at the time they physically enter the United States. They officially "enter" the United States on the date asylum is granted. Under the previous ORR policy, asylees could lose out on some benefits because they "entered" the country well into the eligibility time frame for the public benefits. Because of the new policy, asylees will be able to obtain refugee assistance benefits, including Refugee Cash Assistance (RCA)

TABLE 4.10

Public assistance utilization of selected refugee groups

Type of Public Assistance	Africa	Latin America	Middle East	Eastern Europe	Former Soviet Union	Vietnam	Other S.E. Asia	All
Cash Assistance								
Any Type of Cash Assistance	37.9%	11.8%	24.2%	16.3%	59.9%	38.3%	59.6%	37.5%
AFDC/TANF	31.4	1.5	5.2	1.9	13.5	13.7	53.8	11.7
RCA	0.0	0.0	0.8	0.0	3.3	2.3	3.7	1.7
SSI	8.1	11.0	11.0	7.8	38.2	23.2	8.8	21.8
General Assistance	1.8	0.0	12.4	6.6	18.2	2.3	3.0	8.1
Non-cash Assistance								
Medicaid or RMA	38.3	17.5	34.0	18.8	54.3	28.2	71.6	35.6
Food Stamps	43.5	10.9	21.5	14.3	52.3	27.2	72.9	32.7
Housing	18.9	0.7	7.6	0.5	13.6	37.7	26.7	16.2

Note: Data refer to refugees households in the five-year sample population consisting of Amerasians, Entrants, and Refugees of all nationalities who arrived in the years 1993–1998. Medicaid and RMA data refer to adult refugees age 16 and over. All other data refer to refugee households and not individuals. Many households receive more than one type of assistance.

SOURCE: "Table 9 - Public Assistance Utilization of Selected refugee Groups," in *Making a Difference: FY 1998 Annual Report to the Congress.* U.S. Department of Health and Human Services, Office of Refugee Resettlement: Washington, D.C., 2000

and Refugee Medical Assistance (RMA) for eight months and Refugee Social Services (RSS) for about five years.

ASYLUM REFORM

New asylum regulations designed to speed the process and cut back on deceptive applications went into effect in January 1995. All asylees who show up when scheduled for appearance receive an interview with an asylum officer. Incomplete applications, which in the past were passed on to an immigration judge, are now returned to the applicants. Officers either grant asylum or refer a case to a judge. The provision of Notices of Intent to Deny (NOID), used in the past to give applicants a chance to examine and rebut the information used by the asylum officer to deny a claim, has been eliminated.

Because the process has been reduced to a "grant-refer" procedure (status is granted or the decision is referred to a judge), the INS hopes to schedule all new applicants within 60 days of filing. If the case is passed on to a judge, it is expected to be adjudicated (decided) within 180 days. Based on this timetable, work authorization, which used to be granted with an application for asylum status, is only granted if the asylum process lasts longer than 180 days. The INS believes that the separation of employment authorization from the initial filing of an application discourages people from filing for asylum simply to get permission to work.

In the first four months of 1995, applications were down 18 percent compared to the same period the year before. If Guatemalan and Salvadoran applicants who had filed new applications in response to the class-action lawsuit *American Baptist Churches v. Thornburgh* are excluded, then the number of new applicants during this period dropped 42 percent.

The reform asylum regulations also provided funds for doubling the number of asylum officers and immigration judges. In addition, asylum officers are authorized to reject applicants who have passed through a "safe country of asylum" on their way to the United States. Although refusal is discretionary in the United States, this provision is standard throughout most of Europe.

HOW MANY ASYLEES?

In fiscal year 1998 the INS received 55,428 applications for asylum (newly filed and reopened cases), down 35 percent from 1997 (85,866) and 57 percent from 1996 (128,190). INS district directors and asylum officers granted asylum to 12,951 applicants. The former Soviet Union had the highest approvals (1,317), followed by Somalia (1,308), Iran (708), and the People's Republic of China (668). (See Table 4.11.)

In fiscal year 2000, the INS received 49,462 applications for asylum. A total of 16,810 applications were approved. Nearly 14,000 applications were referred to immigration judges for review. Due to the backlog of cases, about 329,000 applications were pending.

Cuban Asylees

In the past, the few Cubans who managed to escape their island nation were nearly automatically given asylum in the United States. For Americans, they represented a condemnation of Fidel Castro's communist government

TABLE 4.11

Persons granted asylum by INS district directors and asylum offices by nationality, fiscal years 1992–98

Nationality	1992 [1]	1993	1994	1995	1996	1997	1998
All nationalities	**3,959**	**7,464**	**11,764**	**17,493**	**18,556**	**15,896**	**12,951**
Afghanistan	90	70	159	335	216	262	283
Albania	23	30	47	147	433	378	539
Bangladesh	2	33	87	349	247	118	101
Bulgaria	44	75	40	59	45	64	74
Burma	22	42	87	215	151	176	271
Burundi	—	—	19	98	91	58	44
Cameroon	19	26	74	160	95	77	154
China, People's Republic	277	336	414	535	433	497	668
Colombia	16	36	69	104	92	48	107
Congo, Democratic Republic [2]	22	45	93	214	137	141	205
Cuba	214	319	494	524	634	312	196
Czechoslovakia, former	—	2	2	6	1	5	4
Czech Republic	—	—	—	—	—	—	—
Slovak Republic	—	—	—	4	—	2	3
Unknown republic	—	2	2	2	1	3	1
Egypt	11	28	54	196	136	126	355
El Salvador	110	74	187	237	195	172	385
Eritrea	7	2	2	2	—	4	101
Estonia	—	—	5	12	34	44	7
Ethiopia	347	352	667	1,096	818	444	543
Fiji	18	70	29	51	35	8	2
Guatemala	94	172	373	1,065	889	344	472
Haiti	120	636	1,060	749	1,491	694	389
Honduras	19	32	92	194	140	52	49
Hungary	1	2	13	27	13	4	2
India	78	357	584	1,108	1,709	886	396
Iran	231	347	638	785	607	408	708
Iraq	70	101	214	204	918	5,540	176
Jordan	31	35	38	55	20	19	23
Laos	56	79	85	33	17	15	15
Latvia	5	5	15	7	18	7	3
Lebanon	81	65	91	91	76	37	62
Liberia	209	247	305	615	694	471	491
Libya	14	22	20	20	6	7	10
Lithuania	1	5	5	6	—	—	3
Mauritania	1	10	17	275	407	101	141
Mexico	—	—	9	83	43	34	40
Nicaragua	341	291	520	484	418	129	147
Pakistan	83	176	219	512	442	264	275
Panama	3	6	1	2	7	1	1
Peru	113	241	470	688	464	243	224
Philippines	16	58	76	54	37	15	19
Poland	2	58	3	10	13	1	6
Romania	156	258	184	181	80	55	44
Rwanda	—	13	43	148	69	101	81
Sierra Leone	2	22	48	71	59	25	157
Somalia	122	121	150	286	529	708	1,308
Soviet Union, former [3]	442	923	1,175	1,556	1,440	1,108	1,317
Armenia	2	28	75	409	334	241	312
Azerbaijan	1	4	25	78	127	80	160
Belarus	—	1	2	14	10	19	26
Georgia	—	5	36	81	70	60	67
Kazakhstan	—	3	1	17	15	17	27

and were encouraged to leave Cuba. In 1980 the Cuban government permitted people to exit the country from the port of Mariel in boats bound for the United States. Thousands of boats exited the port and almost 125,000 people fled the country.

The asylum seekers included several thousand criminals and psychiatric patients. Unlike the earlier white, middle-class refugees from Cuba, the "Marielitos" were mainly working-class, racially diverse individuals who were raised under communist rule. Many of the asylees resettled in Miami. They did not assimilate easily into the existing Cuban-American community in Miami, although tensions did ease after a few years.

In the early 1990s the U.S. Coast Guard picked up thousands of Cubans arriving in Florida by boats and rafts. The Castro government had encouraged recalcitrant Cubans to board patched-together boats and set sail for Florida. The United States responded to this threat by insisting that it would not permit another mass Cuban refugee flow like the Mariel boatlift.

TABLE 4.11

Persons granted asylum by INS district directors and asylum offices by nationality, fiscal years 1992–98 [CONTINUED]

Nationality	1992 [1]	1993	1994	1995	1996	1997	1998
Kyrgyzstan	—	—	—	6	5	12	4
Moldova	—	3	8	15	12	6	3
Russia	51	233	565	578	477	371	433
Tajikistan	—	1	7	10	11	6	15
Turkmenistan	—	—	1	—	3	17	12
Ukraine	7	54	191	218	215	190	142
Uzbekistan	—	3	22	62	43	39	53
Unknown republic	381	588	242	68	118	50	63
Sri Lanka	44	16	62	69	32	45	53
Sudan	73	133	248	397	343	266	400
Syria	16	638	1,032	680	304	35	44
Yugoslavia, former[4]	72	521	906	1,414	2,470	629	527
Bosnia—Herzegovina	4	15	164	289	192	4	20
Croatia	4	9	52	59	62	47	38
Macedonia	4	—	—	11	10	33	22
Slovenia	4	1	6	—	1	—	—
Unknown	72	496	684	1,055	2,205	509	447
Other	241	334	539	1,284	1,008	718	1,329

[1] The 3,959 individuals known to have been granted asylum were in the 2,740 cases in the data system. An additional 1,179 cases were granted asylum, but the number of individuals covered and their nationalities are unknown.
[2] In May 1997 Zaire was formally recognized as the Democratic Republic of the Congo.
[3] Beginning in 1992, some claims filed by persons from the former Soviet Union were recoded under the separate former Soviet republics.
[4] Data for the independent states of the former Yugoslavia are not available separately from Yugoslavia prior to fiscal year 1993. Yugoslavia was officially dissolved as an independent republic in 1992.
— Represents zero.   X Not applicable.

SOURCE: "Table 28. Number of Individuals Granted Asylum by INS District Directors and Asylum Officers by Selected Nationality, Fiscal Years 1992–98," in *1998 Statistical Yearbook of the Immigration and Naturalization Service*. U.S. Department of Justice, Immigration and Naturalization Service: Washington, D.C., November 2000

In August 1994 the U.S. government announced that the U.S. Coast Guard and Navy would transfer Cubans rescued at sea to the U.S. naval base at Guantánamo Bay in Cuba, for detention. This policy shift did not deter the flow of fleeing Cubans. Consequently, on September 9, 1994, the United States signed an agreement with the Cuban government, known as the U.S.-Cuba Bilateral Migration Agreement. In addition, the United States would cease granting parole to Cubans seeking asylum in the United States.

In May 1995 the two governments reached another accord by which the United States would parole about 30,000 Cubans being detained at Guantánamo Bay into the United States. Cubans intercepted by the Coast Guard at sea would be sent back no matter how close they were to shore. Since then over 3,500 Cubans have been sent back. However, those who reach shore and turn themselves in are paroled for a year and then allowed to apply for permanent resident status. Only Cuban asylees have this privilege.

By January 1996 the last of the Guantánamo refugees arrived in the United States as "Special Guantánamo Entrants," bringing to about 32,000 the number of Cubans admitted since 1994. The only ones not admitted were persons with criminal records; those with medical, physical, or mental conditions; or persons who committed acts of violence while at Guantánamo.

OTHER CRITERIA FOR GRANTING ASYLUM

Since 1994 the number of asylum cases approved has exceeded the 10,000 ceiling. Some persons charge that the United States constantly changes its definition of what constitutes "membership in a particular social group" to accommodate the growing number of asylum-seekers. The Refugee Act of 1980 defines a social group as composed of persons "all of whom share a common characteristic that is either immutable [not susceptible to change], or should not be required to change because it is fundamental to their individual identities and consciences."

For example, Somali clan membership has been defined as social group membership, although the INS noted that "mere membership in a clan will not be sufficient to establish refugee status unless the applicant can establish special circumstances that would justify the conclusion that all members of the clan are threatened with persecution."

Those who believe the term should be interpreted broadly argue that the intent of the law was to provide a catch-all to include all the types of persecution that can occur. Those with a narrow view see the law as a means of identifying and protecting individuals from known forms of harm, not in anticipation of future types of abuse.

Persecution Based on Gender and Sexual Orientation

As the United States and the world have become more aware of persecution based on gender and sexual orientation, these criteria are being considered as persecution of a "social group." The United Nations High Commissioner for Refugees issued a formal "Conclusion" that "women asylum-seekers who face harsh or inhumane treatment due to their having transgressed the social mores of the society in which they live may be considered as a 'particular social group' within the meaning of the Refugee Convention."

The INS, however, has rarely granted asylum on the basis of gender-based persecution. A 1993 case denied asylum to an Iranian who claimed that if she did not wear the traditional chador (veil and robe that cover women from head to toe), she would be subjected to harsh penalties. Iran punishes uncovered women with 74 lashes and a year's imprisonment, in addition to risking rape and abuse within the community. The court found against the woman because she had not shown either that she would disobey the rules and risk the consequences or that obeying the rules would be so "profoundly abhorrent" as to amount to persecution.

The INS has recognized homosexuals as belonging to a "social group" for purposes of asylum. In Colombia, Romania, and Brazil, gay men and transvestites have been targeted and killed by death squads. In Iran, Mauritania, and Yemen, Muslims convicted of homosexuality face the death penalty.

In 1996, an immigration judge in New York granted asylum on the basis of membership in a particular social group to an HIV-positive Togolese man who said he would be persecuted if he returned to Togo. The Presidential Advisory Council on HIV/AIDS policy recommended that the INS should "grant stays of deportation ... and asylum based on the social group of HIV-positive individuals."

GAY MEN WITH FEMALE SEXUAL IDENTITIES. Geovanni Hernandez-Montiel, a Mexican national, fled to the United States in 1994. The following year he applied for asylum and withholding of deportation. At his hearing Hernandez-Montiel testified that he was gay and that he behaved and dressed as a woman. He left Mexico because of fear of repeated persecution by the Mexican police who raped him twice. He also presented testimony from a Latin American history and culture expert who had lived in Mexico and who testified that in Mexico gay men with female sexual identities are a "separate social entity" and are brutalized and persecuted.

Although the immigration judge found the petitioner's claim to be credible, the petitioner's membership in the social group the judge categorized as "homosexual males who wish to dress as a woman" does not fall within the law's definition of "refugee." Upon appeal the Board of Immigration Appeals also ruled that the Mexican national was credible but had failed to demonstrate that his dressing as a female was "an immutable characteristic." Hernandez-Montiel petitioned for a federal review of his case.

On August 24, 2000, the U.S. Court of Appeals for the Ninth Circuit, in *Hernandez-Montiel v. INS* (No. 98-70582), ruled that "gay men with female sexual identities" constitute a "particular social group" eligible for asylum and withholding of deportation. The court held that the petitioner had demonstrated his membership in this group and his persecution due to that membership. The court rendered its own interpretation of a "particular social group" as one "united by a voluntary association, including a former association, or by an innate characteristic that is so fundamental to the identities or consciences of its members that members either cannot or should not be required to change it."

FEMALE GENITAL MUTILATION. Another area of concern for asylum is the ritual circumcision of females. In 1996 the INS asked for a ruling that would consider female genital mutilation (FGM) as grounds for asylum, but narrowed it to cover only those women who could establish that they would be forced to undergo FGM upon their return to their country and not merely subjected to social pressure to have it done.

In 1994, 19-year-old Fauziya Kasinga fled her native Togo to escape genital mutilation. When she arrived in the United States, she asked for asylum and was held in a detention center for 16 months waiting for her case to be heard by the Board of Immigration Appeals. In June 1996 (*In re Fauziya Kasinga, A 73 479 695*), she became the first individual granted asylum on the basis of gender persecution.

OTHER LEGAL DECISIONS

INS v. Cardoza-Fonseca

In 1987 a 6-to-3 divided U.S. Supreme Court, in *Immigration and Naturalization Service v. Cardoza-Fonseca* (480 U.S. 421), ruled that the government must relax its standards for deciding whether aliens who insist that they would be persecuted if they returned to their home countries are eligible for political asylum.

Luiz Marina Cardoza-Fonseca, a Nicaraguan citizen, came to the United States in 1979 as a visitor and remained longer than her visa allowed. She did not accept the INS's offer of voluntary departure, and so the INS began deportation proceedings. Cardoza-Fonseca applied for asylum and testified that her brother, with whom she had fled Nicaragua, had been tortured and imprisoned there because of his political beliefs. Although she had not been politically active herself, her brother's situation and her opposition to the Sandinista government would cause her to be tortured if she were forced to return. The immi-

TABLE 4.12

Asylum applications filed with the INS by Central Americans, fiscal years 1992–98

Area of citizenship	1992	1993	1994	1995	1996	1997	1998
Central America	**53,966**	**54,898**	**62,310**	**104,228**	**83,410**	**21,599**	**13,904**
Nicaragua	2,075	3,180	4,682	1,908	2,034	1,674	819
El Salvador	6,781	14,616	18,600	75,860	65,588	8,156	6,345
Guatemala	43,915	34,198	34,433	23,202	13,892	9,811	5,896
Honduras	1,127	2,805	4,385	3,163	1,836	1,851	809
Other	68	99	209	95	60	107	35

Note: Includes applications received and reopened during year.

SOURCE: "Table E: Asylum Applications Filed with the INS by Central Americans, Fiscal Years 1992–98," in *1998 Statistical Yearbook of the Immigration and Naturalization Service*. U.S. Department of Justice, Immigration and Naturalization Service: Washington, D.C., November 2000

gration judge ruled against her, claiming she had failed to establish a "clear probability of persecution."

The Board of Immigration Appeals also denied her appeal, but the U.S. Court of Appeals for the Ninth Circuit reversed the decision, and the U.S. Supreme Court upheld the reversal. The High Court ruled that the Reagan Administration's interpretation did not comply with Congress's "more generous intent" in the Refugee Act of 1980. The "well-founded fear" standard of proof was not to be interpreted as requiring a "more likely than not" chance of being persecuted.

American Baptist Churches v. Thornburgh

In the 1980s there were strong protests that the INS regularly admitted asylees from some countries while routinely denying applicants from others. Aliens who fled communist countries and countries considered U.S. adversaries had higher asylee approval rates than U.S. allies, such as El Salvador and Guatemala. For example, between 1983 and 1988 the approval rates for Salvadorans and Guatemalans were less than 3 percent compared to approval rates ranging from 30 to 62 percent for Iran, Syria, and several communist countries.

In 1985 Salvadoran and Guatemalan nationals filed a class-action suit against the INS, the Executive Office for Immigration Review (EOIR), and the U.S. Department of State, charging bias against them in the resolution of asylum claims. In 1991 in *American Baptist Churches v. Thornburgh* (the *ABC Case*; 760 F. Supp. 796 [N.D. Cal. 1991]), the three government agencies settled the lawsuit.

The settlement barred deportation for all Salvadorans present in the United States as of September 19, 1990, and for all Guatemalans who were here as of October 1, 1990. In addition, nationals of the two countries, who were in the United States by the specified dates and had not applied for asylum, were allowed to stay. They had until January 31, 1996, to apply for asylum. In fiscal year 1996, 65,588 Salvadorans and 13,892 Guatemalans had filed for asylum.

In fiscal year 1998, over 6,300 Salvadorans and nearly 5,900 Guatemalans filed for asylum. (See Table 4.12.) Between fiscal years 1989 and 1998, about 2,900 Salvadorans and 3,800 Guatemalans were approved for asylum.

INS v. Aguirre-Aguirre

Juan Anibal Aguirre-Aguirre (referred to as Aguirre), a Guatemalan native, illegally entered the United States in 1993. In 1994 the INS began deportation proceedings against him. Appearing before an immigration judge, Aguirre requested that the judge not only withhold his deportation but also grant him asylum. He testified that, as a politically active student leader in Guatemala, he had demonstrated against the government's indifference to the disappearances and murders of students and other political activists, as well as against its raising of students' bus fares. Aguirre had forced passengers off buses, then burned the empty buses. He had also vandalized stores. Agreeing that Aguirre might suffer persecution for his past political opinions and activities if returned to Guatemala, the immigration judge withheld his deportation and granted him asylum.

Upon appeal from the INS, the Board of Immigration Appeals (BIA) reversed the immigration judge's decision and ordered Aguirre deported. The BIA claimed that "the criminal nature of the respondent's acts outweigh [its] political nature." The BIA further argued that his acts against innocent Guatemalans who got caught in the middle of the protests precluded his being considered for asylum. Under the Immigration and Nationality Act (PL 82-414), an alien who has committed a serious nonpolitical crime abroad cannot be granted asylum. Aguirre petitioned the U.S. Court of Appeals for the Ninth Circuit to review his case. In a 2-1 decision, in *Aguirre-Aguirre v. INS* (121 F.3d 521 [9th Cir. 1997]), the appeals court remanded the case (sent it back to the BIA for further proceedings).

The INS asked the U.S. Supreme Court to determine whether the federal appeals court erred in reversing the

BIA's ruling. In 1999 a unanimous Supreme Court, in *Immigration and Naturalization Service v. Aguirre-Aguirre* (67 U.S.L.W 4270), ruled that aliens who have committed serious nonpolitical crimes in their home countries are ineligible to seek asylum in the United States regardless of the risk of persecution when returned to their countries.

According to the Supreme Court, the appeals court should have deferred to the attorney general, who is authorized to administer and enforce all INS laws. "The attorney general, while retaining ultimate authority, has vested the BIA with power to exercise the 'discretion conferred upon the attorney general by law' in the course of considering and determining cases before it."

Justice Anthony M. Kennedy, delivering the opinion of the Supreme Court, added that the United Nations High Commissioner for Refugees's *Handbook on Procedures and Criteria for Determining Refugee Status* (Geneva, Switzerland, 1979), which the federal appeals court relied on, while useful as an "interpretative aid, is not binding on the attorney general, the BIA, or United States courts."

NACARA AMENDS THE IIRIRA

Under the 1991 *American Baptist Churches v. Thornburgh* settlement, the government allowed a great number of Salvadorans and Guatemalans to reside and work in the United States until they were granted asylum. The Illegal Immigration Reform and Immigrant Responsibility Act (IIRIRA) of 1996, among its provisions, revised the regulations for deporting aliens in violation of immigration law. Under IIRIRA, long-term undocumented aliens were subject to stricter standards for obtaining hardship relief for suspension of deportation. Before IIRIRA, suspension of deportation was granted to an alien who had been physically present in the United States for seven years, was of good moral character, and whose deportation would result in extreme hardship to the alien or to the alien's permanent resident or citizen spouse, child, or parent.

The Nicaraguan Adjustment and Central American Relief Act (NACARA; Public Law 105-100) was enacted on November 19, 1997, to amend IIRIRA. Under NACARA, approximately 200,000 Salvadorans, 50,000 Guatemalans, and about 10,000 nationals of the former Soviet Union are allowed to apply for suspension of deportation under more lenient standards used before the enactment of IIRIRA. The law also allowed 150,000 Nicaraguans and 5,000 Cubans to adjust to permanent resident status without having to make any hardship showing. The attorney general designated the period from January 16, 1998, until September 11, 1998, for eligible aliens to file a motion to reopen under NACARA. Applications under NACARA ended on March 31, 2000. The processing of applications continues, with 5,000 visas annually coming from those previously allotted to the Diversity Program of the Immigration Act of 1990 (IMMACT; see chapter 3).

CHAPTER 5
ILLEGAL ALIENS

WHAT IS AN ILLEGAL ALIEN?

Illegal aliens are also known as illegal immigrants, illegal migrants, undocumented immigrants, or undocumented aliens. People often assume that illegal aliens refer to Mexicans who cross the U.S.-Mexico border illegally to work in the United States. Although Mexicans make up the majority (54 percent in 1996) of illegal aliens in this country, illegal aliens come from all over the world.

An illegal alien is a person who is not a U.S. citizen and who is in the United States in violation of U.S. immigration laws. An illegal alien may be one of the following:

• An undocumented alien, also known as an EWI (Entry Without INS [Immigration and Naturalization Service] Inspection), who has entered the United States without a visa, often between land ports of entry.

• A person who has entered the United States using fraudulent documentation.

• A person who entered the country legally with a temporary visa and then stayed beyond the time allowed. This person is referred to as a nonimmigrant overstay or a visa overstay.

• A legal permanent resident who commits a crime after entry and becomes subject to an order of deportation but fails to depart.

HOW MANY ILLEGAL ALIENS ARE THERE?

Because illegal aliens do not readily identify themselves for fear of deportation, it is almost impossible to determine how many illegal aliens are in the United States. Various sources have estimated between 2 and 12 million, but most estimates are little more than educated guesses and are often politically influenced. (The wide variance among the estimates is an indication of their unreliability.) The actual figure may be somewhat less during the winter months, when less agricultural work is available, and more during the summer months.

In 1972 the Immigration and Naturalization Service (INS) estimated about 1 million illegal aliens were in the United States. By 1975 the INS estimated figures were between 4 and 12 million; however, no indication was ever given regarding the methodology used to reach these wide-ranging figures. In 1976 the INS estimated that 6 million illegal aliens were in the country. During a congressional testimony in 1978, the INS commissioner reported that 3 to 6 million illegal aliens resided in the United States, although he referred to the figures as "soft."

In the early 1980s the INS was reluctant to cite any figure or even a numerical range as to the number of illegal aliens. A few older studies and several new ones were beginning to show that the past estimates were considerably smaller than had originally been reported by the INS. Immigration experts Jeffrey Passel and Robert Warren, using the Census Bureau's *Current Population Survey*, estimated that from 1980 to 1986, the number of illegal aliens increased by 100,000 to 300,000 annually. This would put the count of illegal aliens in this country in 1990 at between 3 million and 6 million people. In 1992 the Bureau of the Census estimated that the population increase due to illegal immigration was about 200,000 persons per year, or 2 million over the previous decade.

The U.S. General Accounting Office (GAO), the investigative arm of Congress, periodically studies matters pertaining to the illegal alien population. In its report to Congress in August 1993, the GAO estimated that the illegal alien population numbered a maximum of 3.4 million.

1996 Illegal Alien Estimates

In 1992 the INS estimated that 3.4 million illegal aliens lived in the United States, but later revised that number to 3.9 million. Robert Bach, then INS executive associate commissioner, observed that "the problem was greater than we believed in 1992." In 1997 the INS estimated that, as of October 1996, the United States was home to approximately 5 million (with a range of 4.6 to 5.4 million) illegal aliens. About 60 percent entered illegally, while 40 percent overstayed temporary nonimmigrant visas. California had the largest illegal alien population (2 million, or 40 percent of the nation's illegal alien population), followed by Texas (700,000), New York (540,000), Florida (350,000), Illinois (290,000), New Jersey (135,000), and Arizona (115,000). These seven states accounted for nearly 83 percent of all illegal aliens in the United States. (See Table 5.1.)

According to the INS, the estimated total illegal immigrant population grew by about 275,000 annually during the 1992–1996 period, about the same as the annual growth of 281,000 estimated for 1988–1992. Part of the 1996 increase reflects a change in the 1992 estimate rather than an increase in the number of undocumented immigrants.

Nonimmigrant Overstays

Each year millions of legal nonimmigrants enter the United States. Most are tourists who enter by air. In fiscal year 1998 a record 30.1 million nonimmigrants were admitted to the United States. Although the INS has a system for tracking the dates when foreign visitors arrive in the country, the agency has no effective system to determine that those individuals not recorded as having left the country have actually overstayed their authorized period of visit.

The INS is responsible for collecting documents from incoming travelers, but airlines and shipping lines are responsible for collecting departure forms when visitors leave and for sending those forms to the INS. However, departure forms may go unrecorded because they are not turned in or collected, they are collected by the airline but not sent to the INS, or the forms are returned to the INS but incorrectly recorded. Therefore, the number of visa overstays, people who enter the United States legally as nonimmigrant visitors but do not leave under the terms of their admission, is also difficult to estimate.

The INS estimates that, in 1996, nonimmigrant overstays made up about 2.1 million, or 41 percent, of the illegal alien population residing in the United States. About 16 percent (432,000) of Mexican illegal aliens were nonimmigrant overstayers, compared to 26 percent (171,600) of those from Central America (El Salvador, Guatemala, Honduras, and Nicaragua). About 91 percent (1,492,400) of illegal aliens from other countries were nonimmigrant overstayers.

Section 110 of the Illegal Immigration Reform and Immigrant Responsibility Act of 1996 (IIRIRA) mandated that the INS develop an automated system to track the entry and exit of all noncitizens—nonimmigrants and immigrant residents entering or leaving all ports of entry, including land borders and sea ports. Those who opposed Section 110 included the INS, the Canadian government, and the airline industry. According to the INS, it lacked the resources to put in place such an integrated system and asked that studies be made on how the system would work at seaports and land borders. The Canadian government claimed that filling out the entry form (Form I-94) and having it checked by INS inspectors would cause large backups at the border. Airlines who had not been required by the INS to supply computerized information considered the Section 110 as an additional reporting mandate.

On June 15, 2000, Congress passed the Immigration and Naturalization Service Data Management Improvement Act to amend Section 110 of the IIRIRA. Public Law 106-215 requires the INS to develop an electronic system that "provides access to, and integrates, alien arrival and departure data," using available data to identify lawfully admitted nonimmigrants who may have overstayed their visits. The law does not require additional documentation, nor that all ports of entry be monitored. A deadline of December 31, 2003, was set for all airports and seaports to have the system in place. Fifty land border ports determined by the U.S. attorney general to have the highest number of arrivals and departures were given until December 31, 2004, to have the system operating.

Newest INS Illegal Alien Estimates

In October 2000 Representative Lamar Smith (R-TX), Chairman of the Subcommittee on Immigration and Claims of the House Judiciary Committee, announced that his committee had subpoenaed new INS estimates of the illegal alien population. The INS claimed that the report was just a draft revision and that the official report would be released at a later date.

INS estimates of the illegal alien population during the 1988–92 and 1992–1996 periods showed little difference in the average annual levels. However, the new draft report showed that illegal immigration rose rapidly in the years immediately following the amnesty granted by the Immigration Reform and Control Act of 1986 (IRCA). Representative Smith reported,

> The INS now estimates that the net increase in the number of illegal aliens residing in the United States averaged 457,000 in each of the five years immediately following the [1986] amnesty (1987–1991), rising to a peak of 585,000 three years after the amnesty....

The INS draft report stated that, since annual estimates of the illegal alien population are not available before IRCA, the population trends before and after IRCA cannot be compared. "Nonetheless," according to the

TABLE 5.1

Estimated resident undocumented population by state, October 1992 and October 1996

| State | Estimated Resident Undocumented Population | | | | Average Annual |
	October 1996	Range (+/–)	Pct of Total	October 1992	Change: 1992–1996
TOTAL	**5,000,000**	**400,000**	**100.0%**	**3,900,000**	**275,000**
Alabama	4,000	300	0.1%	3,200	—
Alaska	3,700	300	0.1%	2,400	—
Arizona	115,000	10,000	2.3%	95,000	6,000
Arkansas	5,400	400	0.1%	4,400	—
California	2,000,000	170,000	40.0%	1,600,000	99,000
Colorado	45,000	4,000	0.9%	35,000	3,000
Connecticut	29,000	2,000	0.6%	22,000	2,000
Delaware	2,500	200	—	2,000	—
D.C.	30,000	2,000	0.6%	21,000	2,000
Florida	350,000	25,000	7.0%	270,000	20,000
Georgia	32,000	2,000	0.6%	26,000	1,000
Hawaii	9,000	500	0.2%	6,400	1,000
Idaho	16,000	1,000	0.3%	12,000	1,000
Illinois	290,000	20,000	5.8%	220,000	16,000
Indiana	14,000	1,000	0.3%	11,000	1,000
Iowa	6,400	400	0.1%	5,000	—
Kansas	20,000	1,000	0.4%	15,000	1,000
Kentucky	6,000	400	0.1%	4,600	—
Louisiana	22,000	2,000	0.4%	18,000	1,000
Maine	3,300	200	0.1%	2,200	—
Maryland	44,000	3,000	0.9%	33,000	3,000
Massachusetts	85,000	5,000	1.7%	65,000	6,000
Michigan	37,000	3,000	0.7%	28,000	2,000
Minnesota	7,200	500	0.1%	5,800	—
Mississippi	3,700	200	0.1%	2,800	—
Missouri	16,000	1,000	0.3%	12,000	1,000
Montana	1,200	100	—	1,100	—
Nebraska	7,600	600	0.2%	5,800	—
Nevada	24,000	2,000	0.5%	19,000	1,000
New Hampshire	2,000	100	—	1,500	—
New Jersey	135,000	10,000	2.7%	105,000	8,000
New Mexico	37,000	3,000	0.7%	29,000	2,000
New York	540,000	30,000	10.8%	410,000	33,000
North Carolina	22,000	2,000	0.4%	20,000	1,000
North Dakota	800	—	—	600	—
Ohio	23,000	2,000	0.5%	18,000	1,000
Oklahoma	21,000	2,000	0.4%	17,000	1,000
Oregon	33,000	3,000	0.7%	27,000	1,000
Pennsylvania	37,000	3,000	0.7%	27,000	2,000
Rhode Island	12,000	1,000	0.2%	9,000	1,000
South Carolina	4,800	300	0.1%	4,100	—
South Dakota	800	100	—	600	—
Tennessee	13,000	1,000	0.3%	9,500	1,000
Texas	700,000	70,000	14.1%	530,000	43,000
Utah	15,000	1,000	0.3%	13,000	1,000
Vermont	2,700	100	0.1%	2,400	—
Virginia	55,000	4,000	1.1%	42,000	3,000
Washington	52,000	4,000	1.0%	42,000	3,000
West Virginia	2,000	100	—	1,600	—
Wisconsin	7,700	500	0.2%	6,100	—
Wyoming	1,700	100	—	1,400	—
Guam	6,500	500	0.1%	4,100	1,000
Puerto Rico	34,000	3,000	0.7%	21,000	3,000
Virgin Islands	11,000	1,000	0.2%	8,100	1,000
Unknown	2,000	100	—	2,300	—

— Rounds to zero.

SOURCE: *Estimates of the Unauthorized Immigrant Population Residing in the United States: October 1996,* U.S. Immigration and Naturalization Service, Washington, D.C., 1997

TABLE 5.2

Estimated illegal immigrant population for top twenty countries of origin, 1996

Country of origin	Population
All countries	5,000,000
1. Mexico	2,700,000
2. El Salvador	335,000
3. Guatemala	165,000
4. Canada	210,000
5. Haiti	105,000
6. Philippines	95,000
7. Honduras	90,000
8. Poland	70,000
9. Nicaragua	70,000
10. Bahamas	70,000
11. Colombia	65,000
12. Ecuador	55,000
13. Dominican Republic	50,000
14. Trinidad & Tobago	50,000
15. Jamaica	50,000
16. Pakistan	41,000
17. India	33,000
18. Dominica	32,000
19. Peru	30,000
20. Korea	30,000
Other	744,000

SOURCE: *Illegal Alien Resident Population,* U.S. Immigration and Naturalization Service, Washington, D.C., 1999

report, "the estimates do show a large increase in unauthorized immigration in 1988 and 1989 and a steep decline after 1990. Much of the increase after IRCA could have been the result of relatives coming illegally to join newly legalized aliens."

WHERE DO ILLEGAL ALIENS COME FROM?

In 1996 Mexico was the leading country of origin of illegal aliens to the United States, accounting for 54 percent (2.7 million) of the total undocumented population. Fifteen countries were each the source of 50,000 or more illegal aliens. Of these 15 countries, only Poland and the Philippines were not within the Western Hemisphere. (See Table 5.2.)

WHO ENFORCES IMMIGRATION LAWS?

The INS determines who may enter the United States. The INS is also responsible for enforcing immigration laws within the United States and along the 8,000 miles of U.S. land and water boundaries. INS officials locate and arrest aliens attempting to illegally enter the United States, aliens who have illegally entered the country, and those who were admitted legally but have since lost their legal status.

INS Inspectors and U.S. Customs Inspectors

The INS Inspections and the U.S. Customs Service share responsibility for inspection of all applicants seeking admission at approximately 300 U.S. ports of entry. To prevent the entry of illegal aliens, they detect fraudulent documents, including claims of U.S. citizenship or permanent resident status. They also seize conveyances used for illegal entry.

Southwest border inspectors apprehend an increasing number of persons attempting illegal entry into the United States using fraudulent documents and falsely claiming U.S. citizenship. Between 1994 and 1998 the use of fraudulent documents increased 12 percent, from 73,260 to 82,101. False claims to U.S. citizenship numbered over 20,000 in 1998. (See Table 5.3.)

The U.S. Border Patrol

The U.S. Border Patrol is responsible for maintaining the inviolability of the American border—a difficult, sometimes dangerous, and often frustrating task. The main task of Border Patrol agents is to secure the 8,000 miles of U.S. borders between ports of entry. The United States is divided into 21 Border Patrol Sectors. (See Figure 5.1.) Nine of the Border Patrol sectors are along the southwest border.

THE SOUTHWEST BORDER. The biggest illegal entry problem occurs along the 1,956-mile border between the United States and Mexico. The four states bordering Mexico—Texas, New Mexico, Arizona, and California—have 39 ports of entry. About 5 million Mexican nationals reside in the Mexican municipalities (municipios) along the southwest border. (See Table 5.4.)

RECRUITING BORDER PATROL AGENTS. The IIRIRA of 1996 mandated that the Immigration and Naturalization Service add 1,000 Border Patrol agents each year starting fiscal year 1997 through 2001. In 1997 and 1998 the INS fulfilled the law's mandate but fell short in 1999, when just 369 agents were added. (See Figure 5.2.) In March 1999 the Clinton Administration announced it would not request more funding for Border Patrol positions, citing the problems that could result from having too many inexperienced agents. Over the years, the rate of attrition (reduction of agents due to resignations, retirements, or career changes) among Border Patrol agents had grown, increasing from 5 percent in 1994 to 13 percent in 1998.

The low pay and benefits offered to Border Patrol agents make it difficult to attract new personnel. Border Patrol agents with one year's experience receive about $33,000 in salary. They earn an additional 10 to 15 percent pay for hazardous duty and overtime. According to the INS, an agent can expect to be making over $50,000 per year (including over-time, holiday, and night pay) by the fifth or sixth year of service.

In 2000 the INS strengthened its recruiting efforts by training Border Patrol agents as recruiters and offering

TABLE 5.3

Immigration and Naturalization Service (INS) inspections, selected workload and enforcement data by southwest border district offices, fiscal years 1994–1998

INS District Office	FY 94	FY 95	FY 96	FY 97	FY 98
San Diego					
U.S. citizens inspected[a]	28,808,845	26,776,081	26,342,930	28,952,299	28,644,148
Aliens inspected[a]	63,152,638	59,387,840	57,278,208	61,149,254	63,620,553
Total persons inspected[a]	91,961,483	86,163,921	83,621,138	90,101,553	92,264,701
Pedestrians inspected	[b]	16,744,829	19,420,202	19,013,607	17,871,910
Vehicles inspected	[b]	28,094,028	26,152,680	29,495,749	30,180,317
Fraudulent documents intercepted	41,974	46,515	41,221	35,719	44,751
Oral false claims to U.S. citizenship	15,403	19,368	12,633	8,603	8,928
Individuals smuggled	6,565	5,377	6,581	7,976	11,656
Phoenix					
U.S. citizens inspected[a]	11,717,738	8,299,518	8,313,959	8,317,647	8,480,693
Aliens inspected[a]	23,268,288	23,072,110	23,035,160	23,716,873	24,577,651
Total persons inspected[a]	34,986,026	31,371,628	31,349,119	32,034,520	33,058,344
Pedestrians inspected	[b]	7,806,361	7,657,480	7,651,290	7,209,033
Vehicles inspected	[b]	8,951,615	8,984,091	9,311,850	9,752,364
Fraudulent documents intercepted	7,599	6,367	5,338	4,461	5,503
Oral false claims to U.S. citizenship	825	686	772	916	1,073
Individuals smuggled	279	253	427	408	355
El Paso					
U.S. citizens inspected[a]	27,230,751	24,975,450	22,481,928	22,178,758	22,729,667
Aliens inspected[a]	42,033,208	39,821,598	36,339,994	36,178,016	38,316,842
Total persons inspected[a]	69,263,959	64,797,048	58,821,922	58,356,774	61,046,509
Pedestrians inspected	[b]	4,578,798	4,571,073	4,578,644	6,982,414
Vehicles inspected	[b]	18,143,401	17,529,375	17,534,880	17,741,105
Fraudulent documents intercepted	8,173	8,754	11,034	11,777	11,309
Oral false claims to U.S. citizenship	4,567	5,887	6,725	6,980	5,429
Individuals smuggled	751	599	611	578	602
San Antonio					
U.S. citizens inspected[a]	18,668,021	13,979,554	14,355,119	14,998,041	15,935,580
Aliens inspected[a]	39,567,895	41,165,203	39,708,171	46,218,306	46,931,023
Total persons inspected[a]	58,235,916	55,144,757	54,063,290	61,216,347	62,866,603
Pedestrians inspected	[b]	7,289,530	5,219,599	7,003,458	7,782,173
Vehicles inspected	[b]	11,454,275	13,026,781	13,432,433	14,274,699
Fraudulent documents intercepted	6,338	6,100	7,636	8,899	10,046
Oral false claims to U.S. citizenship	1,467	1,284	1,541	1,897	2,619
Individuals smuggled	1,559	1,224	1,349	1,228	1,601
Harlingen					
U.S. citizens inspected[a]	20,831,853	12,920,985	12,849,749	13,740,688	14,534,702
Aliens inspected[a]	40,564,252	39,536,870	40,258,253	41,632,438	40,022,402
Total persons inspected[a]	61,396,105	52,457,855	53,108,002	55,373,126	54,557,104
Pedestrians inspected	[b]	7,348,097	7,943,636	7,798,241	7,551,773
Vehicles inspected	[b]	14,412,630	15,195,266	16,059,800	16,896,525
Fraudulent documents intercepted	9,176	7,100	9,681	9,299	10,492
Oral false claims to U.S. citizenship	1,264	1,549	1,702	1,271	2,447
Individuals smuggled	1,394	897	1,299	1,256	1,703
Total Southwest border					
U.S. citizens inspected[a]	107,257,208	86,951,588	84,343,685	88,187,433	90,324,790
Aliens inspected[a]	208,586,281	202,983,621	196,619,786	208,894,887	213,468,471
Total persons inspected[a]	315,843,489	289,935,209	280,963,471	297,082,320	303,793,261
Pedestrians inspected	[b]	43,767,615	44,811,990	46,045,240	47,397,303
Vehicles inspected	[b]	81,055,949	80,888,193	85,834,712	88,845,010
Fraudulent documents intercepted	73,260	74,836	74,910	70,155	82,101
Oral false claims to U.S. citizenship	23,526	28,774	23,373	19,667	20,496
Individuals smuggled	10,548	8,350	10,267	11,446	15,917

[a]Estimate based on periodic sampling of the number of occupants per vehicle entering the port of entry.
[b]INS did not collect data on these categories in fiscal year 1994.

SOURCE: "INS Inspections, Selected Workload and Enforcement Data by Southwest Border District Offices, Fiscal Years 1994 Through 1998" in *Illegal Immigration: Status of Southwest Border Strategy Implementation*, U.S. General Accounting Office, Washington, D.C., 1999

entrance exams all over the country. It advertised in movie theaters, on television, and on the Internet. About 80 percent of those interested applied over the Internet. In addition, the INS offered a $2,000 recruitment bonus to each recruit. As a result, more than 1,700 new agents were hired, bringing the total number of agents to 9,212. (See Figure 5.2.) The Bush Administration's 2002 budget called for adding a total of 1,140 Border Patrol agents during 2002 and 2003 to fulfill the 5,000 additional agents mandated by IIRIRA.

FIGURE 5.1

Border patrol sectors

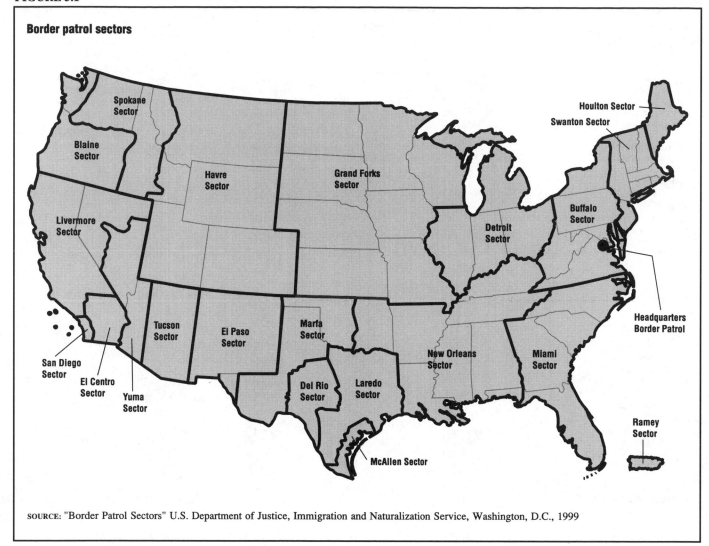

SOURCE: "Border Patrol Sectors" U.S. Department of Justice, Immigration and Naturalization Service, Washington, D.C., 1999

TABLE 5.4

Border statistics by state

State	County Border Population	Border Length	Ports-of-Entry	*Municipio* Population
Texas (15 Counties)	2 million	1,100 miles	23	2.6 million
New Mexico (3 Counties)	200,000	225 miles	3	32,000
Arizona (4 Counties)	1.1 million	481 miles	7	515,000
California (2 Counties)	3 million	150 miles	6	2 million
Totals (24 Counties)	6.3 million	1,956 miles	39	5.1 million

SOURCE: Tanis J. Salant et al., "Border Statistics by State" in *Illegal Immigrants in U.S.–Mexico Border Counties: The Costs of Law Enforcement, Criminal Justice, and Emergency Medical Services,* University of Arizona, Institute for Local Government, Tucson, AZ, 2001

FIGURE 5.2

Border patrol agents on-board (including aircraft pilots)

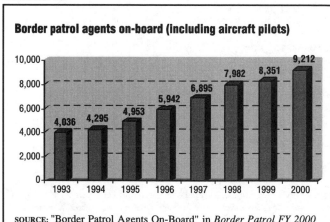

SOURCE: "Border Patrol Agents On-Board" in *Border Patrol FY 2000 Recruiting and Hiring Report,* U.S. Department of Justice, Immigration and Naturalization Service, Washington, D.C., 2000

APPREHENSION OF ILLEGAL ALIENS

In 1998 the INS apprehended nearly 1.7 million illegal aliens, up from about 1.5 million in 1997 and a 76 percent increase from the 954,243 apprehended in 1989. (See Table 5.5 and Figure 5.3.) The large drop between 1986 (the highest recorded number of apprehended illegal aliens) and 1989 was a result of the passage of the 1986 Immigration and Reform Control Act (IRCA). Of the total number of illegal aliens apprehended, about 1.6 million were made by the Border Patrol; 97 percent of these were made along the southwest border.

In 1998 about 73 percent of Border Patrol agents were assigned to the southwest border. In 1994 the Border Patrol allocated additional personnel to sectors of the country (San Diego, California, and El Paso, Texas) where most illegal entries had historically occurred. Consequently, the number of illegal-alien apprehensions in these areas declined. As anticipated by the INS, the illegal alien traffic moved to other locations along the border. In the first half of fiscal year (FY) 1993 San Diego and El Paso accounted for 67 percent of all southwest-border apprehensions. In FY 1998 the proportion of apprehensions in these areas was about 25 percent. In 1998 Tucson, Arizona, and El Centro and Del Rio, Texas, accounted for nearly half (49 percent) of the apprehensions along the southwest border. (See Table 5.6.)

Source Countries of Aliens Apprehended

In 1998 nationals of 186 countries were apprehended by the INS. Almost all of those arrested were from Mexico (96 percent). The next largest source countries were El Salvador, Honduras, Guatemala, the Dominican Republic, Canada, Cuba, Jamaica, Colombia, Haiti, and Ecuador. In 1999 the INS indicated that for every illegal alien it apprehends, it believes 2 to 3 actually make it through. It is important to remember, however, that the INS counts apprehensions, not individuals. Many of those apprehended and returned to Mexico will return to the border to attempt to cross again.

Removal of Illegal Aliens

Noncriminal aliens apprehended while attempting illegal entry into the United States may be offered voluntary departure. If they accept, they waive their right to a hearing and leave the country under supervision. Aliens who are apprehended after entering the United States may

TABLE 5.5

Deportable aliens located, fiscal years 1892–1998

Year	Deportable aliens located [1]	Year	Deportable aliens located [1]
1892-1998	**38,204,117**	1977	1,042,215
1892-1900	NA	1978	1,057,977
1901-10	NA	1979	1,076,418
1911-20	NA	1980	910,361
1921-30	128,484	**1981-90**	**11,883,328**
1931-40	147,457	1981	975,780
1941-50	1,377,210	1982	970,246
1951-60	3,598,949	1983	1,251,357
1961-70	**1,608,356**	1984	1,246,981
1961	88,823	1985	1,348,749
1962	92,758	1986	1,767,400
1963	88,712	1987	1,190,488
1964	86,597	1988	1,008,145
1965	110,371	1989	954,243
1966	138,520	1990	1,169,939
1967	161,608	**1991-98**	**11,138,835**
1968	212,057	1991	1,197,875
1969	283,557	1992	1,258,481
1970	345,353	1993	1,327,261
1971-80	**8,321,498**	1994	1,094,719
1971	420,126	1995	1,394,554
1972	505,949	1996	1,649,986
1973	655,968	1997	1,536,520
1974	788,145	1998	1,679,439
1975	766,600		
1976	875,915		
1976, TQ [2]	221,824		

[1] Aliens apprehended were first recorded in 1925. Prior to 1960, data represent total aliens actually apprehended. Since 1960, figures are for total deportable aliens located, including nonwillful crewman violators.
[2] The three-month period—July 1 through September 30, 1976—between fiscal year 1976 and fiscal year 1977.
NA Not available.

SOURCE: "Table 57. Deportable Aliens Located: Fiscal Years 1892–1998," in *1998 Statistical Yearbook of the Immigration and Naturalization Service.* U.S. Department of Justice, Immigration and Naturalization Service: Washington, D.C., November 2000

TABLE 5.6

Apprehensions by southwest border patrol sector, fiscal years 1993–1998

Border Patrol sector	FY 93	FY 94	FY 95	FY 96	FY 97	FY 98
San Diego	531,689	450,152	524,231	483,815	283,889	248,092
El Centro	30,058	27,654	37,317	66,873	146,210	226,695
Yuma	23,548	21,211	20,894	28,310	30,177	76,195
Tucson	92,639	139,473	227,529	305,348	272,397	387,406
El Paso	285,781	79,688	110,971	145,929	124,376	125,035
Marfa	15,486	13,494	11,552	13,214	12,692	14,509
Del Rio	42,289	50,036	76,490	121,137	113,280	131,058
Laredo	82,348	73,142	93,305	131,841	141,893	103,433
McAllen	109,048	124,251	169,101	210,553	243,793	204,257
Total Southwest border	**1,212,886**	**979,101**	**1,271,390**	**1,507,020**	**1,368,707**	**1,516,680**

SOURCE: "Apprehensions by Southwest Border Patrol Sector, Fiscal Years 1993 Through 1998" in *Illegal Immigration: Status of Southwest Border Strategy Implementation,* U.S. General Accounting Office, Washington, D.C., 1999

FIGURE 5.3

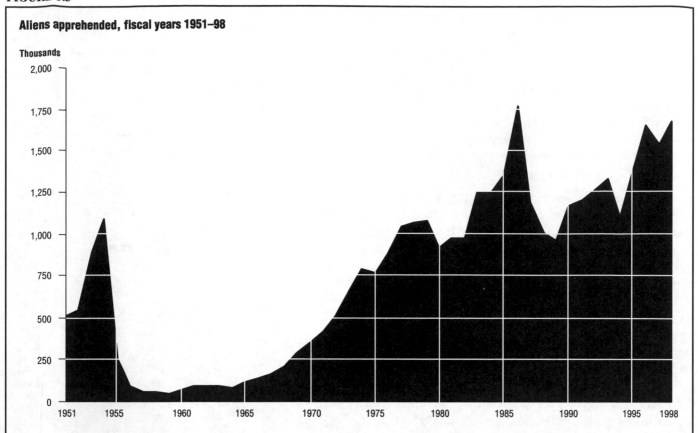

Aliens apprehended, fiscal years 1951–98

SOURCE: "Chart R: Aliens Apprehended: Fiscal years 1951–98," in *1998 Statistical Yearbook of the Immigration and Naturalization Service*. U.S. Department of Justice, Immigration and Naturalization Service: Washington, D.C., November 2000

FIGURE 5.4

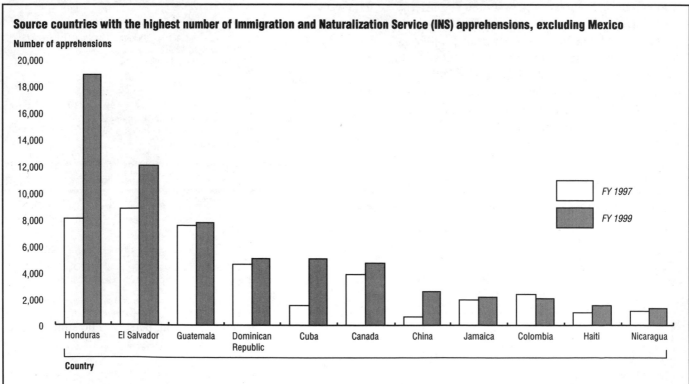

Source countries with the highest number of Immigration and Naturalization Service (INS) apprehensions, excluding Mexico

SOURCE: "Source Countries With the Highest Number of INS Apprehensions, Excluding Mexico" in *Alien Smuggling: Management and Operational Improvements Needed to Address Growing Problem*, U.S. General Accounting Office, Washington, D.C., 2000

Immigration and Illegal Aliens: Burden or Blessing?

also be allowed to depart voluntarily. In both cases, an immigration judge or an INS District Director grants the permission to depart. The INS reports that most voluntary departures (97 percent) generally involve aliens apprehended by the Border Patrol.

Prior to the passage of IIRIRA in 1996, the INS used the term "exclusion" to mean denial of an alien's entry into the United States. "Deportation" referred to the formal removal of an alien from the United States after being found in violation of immigration laws. IIRIRA consolidated the two procedures into "removals."

The administrative reason for removal refers to the main charge cited by the judge in ordering an alien's deportation or exclusion. In 1998, 172,547 aliens were ordered formally removed from the United States. Aliens who tried to enter the country without proper documents or through fraud or misrepresentation accounted for 46 percent of formal removals. Those found residing in the United States after an illegal entry represented 28 percent of removals. Another 21 percent of aliens were cited for criminal charges. (See Table 5.7.) Orders of formal removal include penalties, such as fines, imprisonment for up to 10 years, or barring future legal entry. Felonies entail a permanent bar to legal entry into the United States, while less serious crimes bar the aliens from legally entering the country for up to 20 years.

ALIEN SMUGGLING

Illegal aliens are increasingly using alien smugglers to enter the United State illegally. In *Alien Smuggling: Management and Operational Improvements Needed to Address Growing Problem* (Washington, D.C., May 2000), the General Accounting Office reported that, between 1997 and 1999, the number of smuggled aliens apprehended while attempting to enter the United States rose almost 80 percent, from approximately 138,000 to about 247,000.

According to the GAO, the INS believes that aliens from countries other than Mexico are more likely to use the services of smugglers. The INS, therefore, has concluded that the increasing numbers of apprehended aliens from those countries mean an increase in alien smuggling. The INS reported to the GAO that in 1997 almost 4 percent (58,000) of INS apprehensions were illegal aliens from countries other than Mexico. By 1999 that proportion had risen to nearly 5 percent (81,000) of total apprehensions. Figure 5.4 shows the 11 countries, excluding Mexico, which made up the greatest number of INS apprehensions in FYs 1997 and 1999.

Smuggling Organizations are on the Rise

The INS identifies two types of smuggling organizations. "Blue-collar" operations smuggle mostly Mexican

TABLE 5.7

Aliens removed by administrative reason for removal, fiscal years 1991–98

Year	Total	Attempted entry without proper documents or through fraud or misrepresentation	Criminal	Failed to maintain status	Previously removed, ineligible for reentry
1991	33,189	3,058	14,475	1,135	735
1992	43,671	3,630	20,098	1,076	1,008
1993	42,469	3,031	22,435	781	929
1994	45,621	2,840	23,695	502	1,005
1995	50,873	5,335	24,989	494	1,392
1996	69,588	14,757	27,133	598	1,954
1997	114,292	35,910	34,056	1,024	3,109
1998	172,547	79,141	35,783	968	7,055

Year	Present without authorization[1]	Security	Smuggling or aiding illegal entry	Other	Unknown
1991	13,347	7	28	191	213
1992	17,403	31	177	57	191
1993	14,977	54	208	30	24
1994	14,944	57	209	25	2,344
1995	16,730	34	196	31	1,672
1996	23,213	36	274	47	1,576
1997	39,228	30	384	530	21
1998	48,257	15	489	820	19

[1] Includes those aliens charged under the statutes previous to April 1, 1997 as "entered without inspection".

NOTE: The administrative reason for formal removal is the legal basis for removal. Some aliens who are criminals may be removed under a different administrative reason (or charge) for the convenience of the government. Removals include those actions known as deportation and exclusion prior to the revision of law that was effective April 1, 1997.

SOURCE: "Table 64. Aliens Removed by Administrative Reason for Removal, Fiscal Years 1991–98," in *1998 Statistical Yearbook of the Immigration and Naturalization Service.* U.S. Department of Justice, Immigration and Naturalization Service: Washington, D.C., November 2000

nationals and run their businesses out of a border area. "White-collar" organizations are international operations that deal with aliens from countries other than Mexico. They usually charge higher fees. According to the INS, smugglers charge anywhere from several hundred dollars for border crossing up to $50,000 to smuggle nationals from the People's Republic of China. The international smuggling trade is highly organized. It consists of a sophisticated network of persons who set up smuggling transactions, forge documents, transport aliens, and handle aliens at the destination.

A Dangerous Journey

In order to avoid detection, persons who smuggle illegal aliens into the United States may use transporting methods that are not necessarily safe. Aliens who cross the U.S.-Mexico or U.S.-Canadian borders may travel in enclosed, packed trucks with little ventilation. Others, who travel by sea for thousands of miles from such countries as the People's Republic of China and India, may be stowed on cargo ships and subjected to extreme conditions, including lack of comfort facilities and stifling heat.

In May 2001, 14 Mexican nationals died during one of the deadliest illegal border-crossings in recent years. The men died of exposure to temperatures exceeding a hundred degrees in the Arizona deserts. They had been abandoned by smugglers who promised to accompany them into the United States. Another 13 men who survived the ordeal suffered severe dehydration. Even before this incident, in an effort to save the lives of aliens attempting border-crossings, the Border Patrol had added extra personnel to patrol desert regions and dispatched helicopters to fly over the deserts. The INS reports that, in 2000, about 400 people died crossing the U.S.-Mexico border.

Some illegal aliens have drowned while trying to swim across the Rio Grande that forms the border between Texas and Mexico. Others have fallen prey to border bandits who steal from them and injure or kill them. Some illegal aliens who bring in drugs as payment for their entry into the United States put themselves in harm's way because of the dangerous nature of their undertakings.

Multinational Anti-Smuggling Efforts

In October 2000, 38 alien smugglers were arrested in a multinational anti-smuggling operation, the largest ever conducted in the Western Hemisphere. This coordinated effort of the United States and six countries in Latin America (Belize, El Salvador, Guatemala, Honduras, Mexico, and Panama) also resulted in the arrest of 3,500 illegal aliens headed for the United States.

In early 2000 the INS, with the help of other U.S. agencies and the Canadian government, broke up the largest international alien smuggling operation on the northern border. The organization had smuggled in about 3,600 Chinese nationals through Canada and the St. Regis Mohawk Territory, earning $170 million in fees. At around the same time, the INS and foreign law enforcement agencies arrested 24 individuals belonging to an alien smuggling conglomeration that had brought into the United States about 10,000 illegal aliens from Ecuador, India, Pakistan, Syria, and Afghanistan. The organization had made upwards of $22 million.

MEXICO'S SPECIAL RELATIONSHIP WITH THE UNITED STATES

In no other place in the world does a rich nation like the U.S. border such a poor nation as Mexico. Within Mexico, huge disparities exist between rich and poor, and it is no wonder that the proximity of one of the world's richest industrial nations attracts Mexico's poor.

An Open Border

Before the twentieth century, the Southwest had little demand for Mexican labor even though Mexicans moved easily back and forth across completely open borders to work in the mines, on the ranches, and on the railroad. The Southwest, however, had yet to begin its development, and most labor was supplied by European and Asian laborers and settlers from the other states.

Increased demand for Mexican labor began with the Southwest's development combined with the gradual effect of the Chinese Exclusion Act and the "Gentleman's Agreement" with Japan, which slowed Asian immigration. While less than 1,000 Mexicans immigrated between 1891 and 1900, almost 50,000 came during the period 1901 to 1910. The flow from Mexico soared to almost 220,000 between 1911 and 1921 and reached nearly 460,000 between 1921 and 1930. (See Table 1.2, Chapter 1.)

This increase in Mexican immigration was spurred by the decline in overall American immigration caused by the growing tension and eventual war (World War I) in Europe. It was further fueled by the growing need for labor as America prepared to supply the Allies and sent many thousands of its young men off to fight the war. While legal immigration rose after the war, a large amount of illegal immigration also occurred. Exact statistics are unavailable, though some historians estimate that during the 1920s there might have been more illegal Mexican aliens than legal immigrants. The need for Mexican labor was so great that in 1918 the commissioner-general of immigration exempted Mexicans from meeting most immigration conditions, such as head taxes (small amounts paid to come into the country) and literacy requirements.

The First Illegal Alien "Problem"

The increase in the number of illegal aliens from Mexico led to the creation of the U.S. Border Patrol in 1924. The United States had maintained a small force of mounted guards to deter alien smuggling, but this force was inadequate to stop large numbers of illegal aliens. The efforts of the Border Patrol contributed to a sharp increase in the number of aliens deported during the 1920s and 1930s.

In 1929 administrative control along the Mexican border was significantly tightened as the Great Depression led many Americans to blame the nation's unemployment on the illegal aliens. Consequently, thousands of Mexicans were repatriated (sent back to Mexico)—legal immigrants along with illegal aliens. To force them to leave, the United States denied many Mexicans government benefits to which they were entitled. Stranded in the United States, many Mexicans had to be helped by the Mexican government to return to Mexico. Thousands of others left voluntarily. The Mexican-born population in the United States declined from 639,000 in 1930 to 377,000 in 1940.

The Bracero Program (1942 to 1964)

World War II brought the country out of the Great Depression as the United States again became supplier to the Allies. Industry expanded, drawing rural laborers into the cities. Other workers were drafted and went off to war. Once more, the United States needed laborers, especially farm workers, and the nation again turned to Mexico. The Bracero Program was a negotiated treaty between Mexico and the United States, permitting the entry of Mexican farm workers on a temporary basis under contract to U.S. employers. (The term *bracero* literally means a pair of arms, or *brazos*; in this case, it means a laborer.)

The Bracero Program, initially authorized by the 78th Congress as Public Law 45 (1943), included agricultural workers not only from Mexico but also from what were then the British West Indies, most notably Jamaica and the Bahamas. After 1951, Public Law 48 limited the program to Mexicans, although a few British West Indians were admitted under other laws. The Mexican government, wary after the repatriation of Mexican immigrants in the 1930s, demanded the braceros receive humane care, including adequate pay, housing, food, and transportation both ways. The entire program lasted 22 years and involved approximately 4.8 million Mexican workers.

Although the program offered an alternative to illegal immigration, it probably contributed to it. Far more Mexican workers wanted to participate in the program than there were openings. Many who had traveled to the U.S.-Mexico border to find contract labor simply continued across the border illegally when they could not enter the program. Others found it easier to avoid government red tape, which might involve a bribe, and entered the United States illegally.

Many American farmers, who disliked the protection the Bracero Program offered the Mexicans, actually preferred the illegal immigrants. This was especially true in Texas since the Mexican government, aware of that state's long history of discrimination toward Mexicans, refused to permit the Bracero Program to include Texas. Consequently, Texas farmers sought out illegal immigrants. Often called "wetbacks" (because the Mexicans allegedly swam across the Rio Grande River to enter the United States), the number of these illegal immigrants apprehended from the mid-1940s to the mid-1950s reached numbers equaled only in recent years.

The U.S.-Mexico relationship over the Bracero Program could best be described as strained. Working standards required by the program deteriorated as the program continued, and the Mexican government felt uncomfortable with an agreement that implied Mexican inferiority. American labor organizations complained that the braceros kept wages low and conditions deplorable for domestic workers. With a docile alien workforce available, American farmers and the nation as a whole did not have to face the problems of low wages, poor education, and appalling living conditions of American migrant workers.

The Bracero Program continued until 1964, when it was dropped after a sharp conflict between southwestern farmers, who wanted the cheap labor program, and labor advocates, who stressed the program's negative effects on domestic workers. Congressional investigations found that braceros were exploited by their employers, who paid them low wages and maintained poor working conditions.

The ending of the Bracero Program, however, did not end illegal immigration but further contributed to its increase. Many Mexicans had become accustomed to working in the United States and earning higher wages than they could get in Mexico. They had told friends and relatives that, while conditions were not always satisfactory, the pay was better than in Mexico. The pattern, begun over a century ago and reinforced by the Bracero Program, continued as Mexican workers migrated north in search of work. In 1997 the U.S. General Accounting Office estimated that about 600,000 farm workers (37 percent of the agricultural labor force) employed in the United States had no legal authorization. The U.S. Department of Labor, in *Findings from the National Agricultural Workers Survey (NAWS) 1997–1998* (Washington, D.C., March 2000), reported that as of 1998 this proportion of undocumented workers rose to 52 percent.

Missing Money

Between 1942 to 1950 American employers deducted 10 percent from the braceros' weekly wages. The U.S. government then transferred the money to savings banks in Mexico. However, when the braceros went back to their country, no money could be found. It is estimated that, with interest, the savings accounts should have yielded $500 million or more. Many former braceros had pay stubs showing the deductions made. In April 2001 braceros filed a class-action lawsuit seeking reparations for the money deducted from their salaries. The lawsuit, filed in California, was brought against the U.S. and Mexican governments.

Immigrant rights organizations are using the Bracero "problems" to warn leaders of both countries who are considering another guest worker program. Mexican president Vicente Fox has proposed a guest worker arrangement not unlike the Bracero Program.

NORTH AMERICAN FREE TRADE AGREEMENT (NAFTA)

In December 1993 the North American Free Trade Agreement (NAFTA) (Public Law 103–182) was passed to eliminate trade and investment barriers among the United States, Canada, and Mexico over a 15-year period. NAFTA is intended to promote economic growth in each country so that, in the long run, the number of illegal immigrants seeking to enter the United States for work would diminish. NAFTA, among its provisions, facilitated temporary entry on a reciprocal basis among the three countries and established procedures for the temporary entry into the United States of Canadian— and Mexican—citizen professional business persons to render services for pay. President Bill Clinton claimed that more jobs on both sides of the southwest border meant more income for Mexican nationals, which would help reduce the number of undocumented aliens entering the United States.

K. Larry Storrs, in *Mexico-U.S. Relations: Issues for the 107th Congress* (The Library of Congress, Congressional Research Service, Washington, D.C., May 4, 2001),

reported that total U.S. trade with Mexico grew from $100 billion to $248 billion between 1994 and 2000. However, due partly to the devaluation of the peso (Mexican money) in 1994, the U.S. trade balance with Mexico had gone from a surplus of $1.3 billion in 1994 to a deficit of $24.2 billion in 2000.

Some experts point to the increasing number of Mexicans migrating to the United States as evidence that NAFTA is not working. In 1996, three years after the enactment of NAFTA, an estimated 5 million illegal aliens were residing in the country. The majority (54 percent) were Mexican nationals.

CHAPTER 6

THE COST OF IMMIGRATION

Much public concern about immigrants (legal and illegal) has focused on their use of public benefits and their overall cost to the nation's taxpayers. Some people believe that too many immigrants come to the United States to take advantage of taxpayer-funded education, health care, and other social services without ever contributing to the system. In opposition, others believe that the revenues immigrants help produce far outweigh the initial cost of their immigration.

Many of the immigration issues presented in this chapter are hotly contested. Researchers on both sides of the issues conduct studies supporting their views. Immigration supporters, such as the Urban Institute, suggest that calculating the costs of immigration to the United States should take into consideration the revenues contributed by immigrants. George J. Borjas, an immigrant who left Cuba at age 12 and became a professor of public policy at the John F. Kennedy School of Government at Harvard University, believes immigration is harming the country. He argues that, since immigration accounts for the continuing growth in U.S. population, immigrants play an increasing role in determining America's demographic and economic trends. Borjas claims that the lower educational levels of the more recent immigrants will keep them at an economic disadvantage, which in the long run will result in the greater use of welfare.

The National Research Council, in *The New Americans: Economic, Demographic, and Fiscal Effects of Immigration* (National Academy Press, Washington, D.C., 1997), concluded that immigration has little negative effect on the wages and job opportunities of most native-born Americans. The council further claimed that the annual estimates of immigrants' costs to state and local taxpayers may be inflated.

Economist Donald Huddle, in *The Costs of Immigration* (Carrying Capacity Network [CCN], Washington, D.C., 1993), initially brought the cost debate to the

nation's attention. He completed the study for the CCN, an environmental group that warns against rapid population growth. Huddle reported that for every 100 unskilled immigrants who were working, 25 or more unskilled American-born workers were displaced from jobs. The cost for these 2.1 million displaced American workers was $11.9 billion. For 1992, Huddle placed the net costs of immigration at $42.5 billion. In 1997, he reported that the net costs of immigration had risen to $68 billion.

Jeffrey S. Passel, in *Immigrants and Taxes: A Reappraisal of Huddle's "The Costs of Immigration"* (The Urban Institute, Washington, D.C., 1994), contested Huddle's findings. Passel charged that Huddle neglected to take into account any positive economic impact of immigrant businesses or consumer spending. The author also claimed Huddle overstated costs and displacement effects (loss of employment by American-born citizens) and massively understated the revenues collected from immigrants. According to Passel, the correct calculations show that *"Immigrants pay over $70 billion in taxes—or over $50 billion more than Huddle estimates"* (italics by Passel).

ONE VIEW OF THE FISCAL IMPACT OF LEGAL IMMIGRANTS

In *A Fiscal Portrait of the Newest Americans* (National Immigration Forum and the Cato Institute, Washington, D.C., 1998), Stephen Moore, an economist at the libertarian think tank called the Cato Institute, notes that a great majority of the foreign-born population in the United States are legal immigrants.

Moore notes that, unfortunately, the Census Bureau generally does not distinguish between legal and illegal immigrants. Consequently, studies using the Bureau's data might be biased against the legal immigrant population because illegal aliens generally do not do as well as legal immigrants, especially those who become naturalized citizens.

TABLE 6.1

Age profile of native born versus foreign born, 1996

Age:	Native Born	All Foreign Born	Recent Arrivals (1990–1996)
Under 18	28.5%	11.2%	25.4%
18–34	24.9%	33.9%	47.6%
Over 65	12.1%	11.2%	3.3%

SOURCE: "Table B: Selected Characteristics of Natives and the Foreign-Born Population," in *Current Population Survey*, U.S. Bureau of the Census, Washington, D.C., 1996, cited in Stephen Moore, *A Fiscal Portrait of the Newest Americans*, National Immigration Forum and the Cato Institute, Washington, D.C., 1998

Age Characteristics of Legal Immigrants

In 1996, according to the Census Bureau, 1 of 4 immigrants (25.4 percent) entered the United States when younger than age 18. (See Table 6.1.) Therefore, the source countries (where they were born and/or raised) of 3 of 4 immigrant children (74.6 percent), and not U.S. taxpayers, bore the public costs of child rearing—education and, in some cases, day care and health care. The author estimated that, in 1998, it cost the U.S. government about $6,500 per year to educate an American child. The typical immigrant generally receives about 10 years of education in his or her country of origin, saving the U.S. government $65,000 per immigrant who entered the country with a high school degree.

In 1996 nearly 3 out of 10 (28.7 percent) immigrants came to the United States when they were children or after age 65. (See Table 6.1) This means 7 of 10 immigrants (71.3 percent) arrived in their prime working years and therefore paid their share of income and payroll taxes. In comparison, 6 of 10 native-born Americans are in their working years at any point in time.

Legal Immigrants' Role in Social Security and Medicare

To illustrate the principal fiscal benefit of immigrants, Stephen Moore explains that through a "pay-as-you-go mechanism" current workers, through their taxes, fund the previous generation's Medicare and Social Security benefits. Moore pointed out that while legal immigrants working in the United States pay into the Social Security and Medicare programs, their parents are not collecting benefits since they are, in most cases, not in the United States. According to Moore, "That creates a huge one-generation windfall to the Social Security system." In addition, immigrants will help ease the financial hardship that is projected to begin in 2011, when the first Baby Boomers (persons born between 1946 and 1964; about 40 million retirees) will start collecting retirement benefits.

TABLE 6.2

Projected impact of immigration on Social Security finances, 1991–2065

	25 Years (1998–2022)	50 Years (1991–2040)	75 Years (1991–2065)
800,000 Net Immigration Per Year			
Average Annual Increase in Net Trust Fund Balance	$19.3	$22.3	$25.8
Total Increase in Net Trust Fund Balance	$484	$1,117	$1,934
1,000,000 Net Immigration Per Year			
Average Annual Increase in Net Trust Fund Balance	$24.2	$27.9	$32.2
Total Increase in Net Trust Fund Balance	$604	$1,396	$2,418

Note: Figures in billions of 1998 dollars.

SOURCE: Stephen Moore, *A Fiscal Portrait of the Newest Americans*, National Immigration Forum and the Cato Institute, Washington, D.C., 1998

The 1998 *Social Security Board of Trustees Report* (Washington, D.C., 1998) analyzed the impact of immigration on the Social Security trust fund balance. If net immigration (immigration minus emigration) remains at 800,000 over the next 25, 50, and 75 years, working immigrants would contribute an average of $19.3 billion, $22.3 billion, and $25.8 billion, respectively, to the Social Security trust fund balance. (See Table 6.2.) The table also shows the results of increasing legal immigration by another 200,000 admissions annually.

Taxes Paid by Legal Immigrants

Based on Census Bureau information, Moore estimated that in 1997 the total immigrant income was $390 billion. Using data from the Tax Foundation (a public policy research group that monitors fiscal issues at the federal, state, and local levels), the author estimated that median-income immigrant households paid 34 percent, or nearly $133 billion, of their income in taxes that year. (See Table 6.3.) In addition, according to the Census Bureau's 1996 *Current Population Survey*, families with an adult, foreign-born, naturalized citizen had higher adjusted gross incomes, an average of $40,502 a year compared to $35,249 a year for families with all American-born members. Families with a naturalized-citizen member paid an average of $6,580 in federal taxes, while those with U.S. citizen members paid an average of $5,070.

WELFARE PARTICIPATION

Recently Naturalized Citizens and Public Assistance

Between 1945 and 1995 the annual number of immigrants who became naturalized citizens never exceeded

400,000. After that period the naturalization numbers increased, with 1996 showing 1,044,689 naturalizations, followed by 598,225 in 1997 and 463,060 in 1998.

Congress, concerned that some immigrants might have been applying for naturalization so as not to lose the public assistance they were receiving prior to the 1996 welfare reform law, asked the U.S. General Accounting Office (GAO) to look into the matter. The GAO, in *Welfare Reform: Public Assistance Benefits Provided to Recently Naturalized Citizens* (Washington, D.C., June 1999), reported that recently naturalized immigrants used public benefits at a higher rate in 1997 than the native-born population.

The Supplemental Security Income (SSI) is a cash assistance for the aged, blind, and disabled. The GAO reported that, nationally, out of the approximately 927,000 recently naturalized immigrants, 8.3 percent received SSI benefits in 1997, about three and one-half times higher than the rate (2.4 percent) for native-born citizens. These naturalized recipients represent about 1.2 percent of all 6.6 million recipients that year.

Unlike SSI, which is administered by the federal government, Medicaid, TANF, and the food stamp program are administered by the states. Medicaid is a joint federal-state health insurance program for certain low-income and needy people, and Temporary Assistance for Needy Families (TANF) is a federal block grant program for poor families with dependent children.

The GAO obtained data for these three programs from the five states (California, Florida, Illinois, New York, and Texas) that represented about 76 percent of recently naturalized immigrants in 1997. About 19 percent (135,681) of the 702,560 recently naturalized citizens in the five states were Medicaid recipients. The proportion of recipients in these states ranged from a low of 7.5 percent in Illinois to a high of 23.7 percent in California. In comparison, the proportion of native-born citizens receiving Medicaid in these states ranged from 6.1 percent in Texas to 9.6 percent in New York.

The GAO found that 11 percent (77,351) of recently naturalized citizens in the five states received food stamp benefits. Florida had the highest percentage of food stamp recipients (17.6 percent), followed by New York (14.6 percent), Texas (13.1 percent), California (7.9 percent), and Illinois (5.7 percent). For the purpose of the study, the GAO obtained a list of the naturalized citizen recipients of food stamps in each of the five states. However, it could not use the food stamp information on native-born citizens collected by the Census Bureau for comparison, since the Census Bureau counted food stamp receipt by households, not individuals.

About 30,050 recently naturalized citizens were receiving TANF benefits in four states—California (5.8

percent), Florida (1.8 percent), New York (4.7 percent), and Texas (1.5 percent). These four states represented 71 percent of all recently naturalized citizens in GAO's study. The TANF beneficiaries comprised about 4.6 percent of all recently naturalized citizens residing in those states. In comparison, about 1 to 2 percent of native-born citizens received TANF benefits in those same states.

HOW MUCH DOES IT COST? The GAO estimated that, in 1997, federal and state governments spent about $735 million on public assistance—SSI, Medicaid, TANF, and food stamp benefits—to recently naturalized citizens. SSI benefits paid to recently naturalized citizens totaled $331 million, or 1.3 percent of the benefits to all recipients that year. Medicaid claims cost $317 million, accounting for 0.6 percent of all Medicaid benefits in the five states the GAO investigated. For the same five states, food stamp benefits cost about $45 million, or 0.7 percent of all food stamp benefits paid by those states. Data on four states showed a total of $42 million paid for TANF benefits, or 0.5 percent of all TANF benefits paid in those states. (See Table 6.4.)

Benefit Use by IRCA-Naturalized Citizens

The U.S. General Accounting Office also analyzed the IRCA-naturalized citizens to determine their use of public benefits. Under the Immigration Reform and Control Act (IRCA) of 1986, nearly 2.8 million undocumented immigrants were legalized. The first of these immigrants became eligible for naturalization in 1994.

The GAO identified about 927,000 recently naturalized citizens in 1997. Nearly 3 of 10 (29.6 percent) of this number were IRCA-naturalized citizens, but of the 76,823 recently naturalized citizens who were receiving SSI, only 5,181 (6.7 percent) were IRCA-naturalized. Of the total $331 million paid for SSI benefits in 1997, $20.8 million (6.3 percent) went to IRCA-naturalized citizens. (See Table 6.5.)

IRCA-naturalized citizens made up 21.3 percent (28,884) of all recently naturalized citizens receiving Medicaid benefits in California, Florida, Illinois, New York, and Texas in 1997. About three-quarters of IRCA-naturalized

TABLE 6.3

Estimated total taxes paid directly by immigrants, 1997

1995 Income of Immigrant Households	$330 billion
Total Immigrant Income Updated for 1997	$390 billion
Immigrant Household Average Tax Rate	34%
1997 Taxes Paid by Immigrants	$133 billion

SOURCE: Stephen Moore, *A Fiscal Portrait of the Newest Americans*, National Immigration Forum and the Cato Institute, Washington, D.C., 1998

TABLE 6.4

TABLE 6.5

Recently naturalized citizens receiving Medicaid, Temporary Assistance for Needy Families (TANF), and Food Stamp benefits by state in calendar year 1997

State		Medicaid	TANF	Food stamps
California	Recipients	81,686	20,079	27,349
	Benefits	$125,442,072	$27,758,412	$15,324,541
Florida	Recipients	17,591	1,737	16,537
	Benefits	$42,925,584	$2,691,765	$10,598,000
Illinois	Recipients	3,311	a	2,493
	Benefits	$10,572,484	a	$1,478,937
New York	Recipients	27,226	7,342	22,962
	Benefits	$121,601,682	$11,178,877	$13,254,328
Texas	Recipients	5,867	894	8,010
	Benefits	$16,676,456	$362,828	$4,126,632

Note: The number of recipients should not be totaled across programs because some recipients may have received benefits from more than one program.
aNo data on TANF were usable because of formatting problems.

SOURCE: "Recently Naturalized Citizens Receiving Medicaid, TANF, and Food Stamp Benefits by State in Calendar Year 1997" in *Welfare Reform: Public Assistance Benefits Provided to Recently Naturalized Citizens,* U.S. General Accounting Office, Washington, D.C., 1999

Benefits received by Immigration Reform and Control Act (IRCA)-naturalized citizens in 1997

Program	Source of data	Number of recipients	Total benefits (millions of dollars)[a]	Percentage of all recently naturalized recipients	Percentage of all recently naturalized recipient benefits
SSI	National	5,181	$20.8	6.7	6.3
Medicaid	Calif.[b]	21,737	22.5	26.6	17.8
	Fla.[b]	1,704	3.1	9.7	7.2
	Ill.	789	2.0	23.8	18.6
	N.Y.[c]	3,176	11.7	11.7	9.6
	Tex.	1,478	4.1	25.2	24.6
Subtotal		28,884	43.4	21.3[d]	13.6[d]
TANF[e]	Calif.	6,371	8.2	31.7	29.6
	Fla.	442	0.6	25.4	24.0
	N.Y.	991	1.5	13.5	13.2
	Tex.	429	0.2	48.0	46.5
Subtotal		8,233	10.5	27.4[d]	25.0[d]
Food stamps[e]	Calif.	9,837	5.1	36.0	33.4
	Fla.	1,935	1.0	11.7	9.3
	Ill.	696	0.3	27.9	23.5
	N.Y.	2,480	1.3	10.8	9.9
	Tex.	3,230	1.4	40.3	34.0
Subtotal		18,178	9.2	23.5[c]	20.5[c]
Total			**$83.9**		

[a] Sum of entries may not total because of rounding.
[b] Medicaid data for California and Florida were obtained from HCFA's Medicaid Statistical Information System.
[c] Medicaid data for New York are for fiscal year 1997.
[d] Average across the states that provided data for this program.
[e] Food Stamp and TANF data are estimates based on average payment per recipient, per month.

SOURCE: "Benefits Received by IRCA-Naturalized Citizens in 1997" in *Welfare Reform: Public Assistance Benefits Provided to Recently Naturalized Citizens,* U.S. General Accounting Office, Washington, D.C., 1999

citizens resided in California, while the smallest group (nearly 3 percent) resided in Illinois. IRCA-naturalized citizens received $43.4 million (13.6 percent) of the total Medicaid benefits paid for all recently naturalized citizens. (See Table 6.5.)

Of the recently naturalized citizens receiving food stamp benefits in the same five states, 23.5 percent (18,178) were IRCA-naturalized citizens. Most (54 percent) lived in California, and the smallest proportion (4 percent) lived in Illinois. IRCA-naturalized citizens obtained 20.5 percent ($9.2 million) of the total food stamp benefits. (See Table 6.5.)

Nearly 28 percent (8,233) of recently naturalized citizens receiving TANF benefits in California, Florida, Texas, and New York were IRCA-naturalized citizens. The majority (77 percent) lived in California, and the smallest number (5 percent) lived in Texas. IRCA recipients were granted 25 percent ($10.5 million) of the total $42 million spent on all recently naturalized citizens who were TANF recipients. (See Table 6.5.)

Noncitizen Recipients of Supplemental Security Income (SSI)

Over the years, provisions of the SSI program that involve noncitizens have been changed. As of 1998, SSI-eligible noncitizens include those who were legally in the United States on August 22, 1996 (the day the welfare reform legislation was enacted), refugees, persons in refugee-like circumstances, and persons who have contributed to the country through their military service or extended periods of work.

Between 1982 and 1995 the proportion of noncitizens receiving SSI rose steadily. In December 1982, 127,900 noncitizens accounted for 3.3 percent of the 3.9 million SSI recipients. By 1995 the proportion of noncitizens receiving SSI payments reached a high of 12.1 percent (785,410) of all SSI recipients. At the end of 1999 the proportion of noncitizen SSI recipients (684,930) declined to 10.4 percent. (See Table 6.6.)

Over two-thirds (66.7 percent) of noncitizen SSI recipients were age 65 and over. Among citizen recipients, 23.9 percent were ages 18 to 39 and 20.4 percent were ages 50 to 64. Most SSI recipients (citizens and noncitizens) were female. The majority of recipients lived in their own households. Almost twice as many citizens (37.9 percent) than noncitizens (21.7 percent) were receiving social security benefits, while nearly twice as many noncitizens (61.9 percent) than citizens (29.6 percent) were receiving both federal SSI and state supplements. (See Table 6.7.)

TABLE 6.6

Number and percent of noncitizens receiving SSI payments, by eligibility category, 1982–99

December	Total Noncitizens	Total Percent of total SSI	Aged Noncitizens	Aged Percent of total SSI	Blind and disabled Noncitizens	Blind and disabled Percent of total SSI
1982	127,900	3.3	91,900	5.9	36,000	1.6
1983	151,200	3.9	106,600	7.0	44,600	1.9
1984	181,100	4.5	127,600	8.3	53,500	2.1
1985	210,800	5.1	146,500	9.7	64,300	2.4
1986	244,300	5.7	165,300	11.2	79,000	2.8
1987	282,500	6.4	188,000	12.9	94,500	3.2
1988	320,300	7.2	213,900	14.9	106,400	3.5
1989	370,300	8.1	245,700	17.1	124,600	4.0
1990	435,600	9.0	282,400	19.4	153,200	4.6
1991	519,660	10.2	329,690	22.5	189,970	5.2
1992	601,430	10.8	372,930	25.4	228,500	5.6
1993	683,150	11.4	416,420	28.2	266,730	5.9
1994	738,140	11.7	440,000	30.0	298,140	6.2
1995	785,410	12.1	459,220	31.8	326,190	6.3
1996	724,990	11.0	417,360	29.5	307,630	5.9
1997	650,830	10.0	367,200	27.0	283,630	5.5
1998	669,630	10.2	364,980	27.4	304,650	5.8
1999	684,930	10.4	368,330	28.2	316,600	6.0

SOURCE: Alfreda M. Brooks, "Number and percent of noncitizens receiving SSI payments, by eligibility category, 1982–99" in *SSI Annual Statistical Report, 1999,* Social Security Administration, Office of Research, Evaluation, and Statistics, Baltimore, 2000

Noncitizen Recipients under the TANF Program

In fiscal year 1999 (October 1, 1998 to September 30, 1999) noncitizens accounted for a small proportion of TANF recipients. Of the over 2 million adults who received TANF benefits, nearly 9 of 10 (87.9 percent) were U.S. citizens, while 11.7 percent were noncitizens. California (28 percent, or 141,667 recipients) had the largest proportion of TANF adult noncitizen recipients, followed by Guam (a U.S. territory; 19.8 percent, or 528), New York (16.1 percent, or 43,487), Washington (14.6 percent, or 8,726) and Rhode Island (14.6 percent, or 2,335), and Florida (14.5 percent, or 6,847). (See Table 6.8.)

In fiscal year 1999 about 5.3 million children received TANF benefits; 96.1 percent were U.S. citizens and just 2.6 percent were noncitizens. The states with the highest percentages of noncitizen children receiving TANF benefits were Arkansas (9.7 percent, or 2,088 noncitizen children), Washington (8.2 percent, or 9,888), Minnesota (7.3 percent, or 6,497), California (5.1 percent, or 70,451), Massachusetts (4.7 percent, or 4,502), and Nebraska (1.1 percent, or 1,017). (See Table 6.9.)

COST OF ILLEGAL IMMIGRATION TO SOUTHWEST BORDER COUNTIES

About 97 percent of apprehensions by the U.S. Border Patrol are made along the southwest border, the 1,956-mile border between the United States and Mexico. Tanis J. Salant et al., in *Illegal Immigrants in U.S.-Mexico Border Counties: The Costs of Law Enforcement, Criminal Justice, and Emergency Medical Services* (University of

TABLE 6.7

Number and percentage distribution of citizens and noncitizens receiving SSI payments, by selected characteristics, December 1999

Characteristics	Citizens Number	Citizens Percent	Noncitizens Number	Noncitizens Percent
Total	5,857,540	100.0	684,930	100.0
Age				
Under 18	839,970	14.3	5,750	0.8
18–39	1,400,620	23.9	45,730	6.7
40–49	858,070	14.6	43,050	6.3
50–64	1,197,520	20.4	133,690	19.5
65–74	806,100	13.8	245,070	35.8
75 or older	755,260	12.9	211,640	30.9
Sex				
Male	2,450,220	41.8	257,470	37.6
Female	3,407,320	58.2	427,460	62.4
Living Arrangements				
Own household	4,831,320	82.5	593,950	86.7
Another's household	196,880	3.4	74,450	10.9
Parents household	696,780	11.9	5,570	0.8
Medicaid institution	132,560	2.3	10,960	1.6
Income				
Social security	2,222,830	37.9	148,930	21.7
Worker	1,447,870	24.7	109,200	15.9
Auxiliary	774,960	13.2	39,730	5.8
Earnings	284,600	4.9	9,790	1.4
SSI Payment				
Federal SSI only	3,871,700	66.1	232,440	33.9
State supplement only	252,620	4.3	28,610	4.2
Both	1,733,220	29.6	423,880	61.9

SOURCE: Alfreda M. Brooks, "Number and percentage distribution of citizens and noncitizens receiving SSI payments, by selected characteristics, December 1999" in *SSI Annual Statistical Report, 1999,* Social Security Administration, Office of Research, Evaluation, and Statistics, Baltimore, 2000

TABLE 6.8

Percent distribution of Temporary Assistance for Needy Families (TANF) adult recipients by citizenship status, October 1998–September 1999

State	Total Adults	U.S. Citizen	Noncitizen	Unknown
U.S. Total	2,068,024	87.9	11.7	0.4
Alabama	9,960	100.0	0.0	0.0
Alaska	8,663	88.3	4.9	6.9
Arizona	23,030	93.6	6.3	0.1
Arkansas	6,574	87.2	11.4	1.4
California	505,957	71.9	28.0	0.1
Colorado	10,345	99.4	0.6	0.0
Connecticut	25,770	96.3	3.7	0.0
Delaware	4,091	99.2	0.8	0.0
Dist. of Col.	15,142	99.9	0.1	0.0
Florida	47,222	85.5	14.5	0.0
Georgia	36,431	99.3	0.7	0.0
Guam	2,667	80.2	19.8	0.0
Hawaii	14,629	97.5	2.5	0.0
Idaho	613	94.9	5.1	0.0
Illinois	100,384	98.1	1.8	0.2
Indiana	33,749	99.4	0.6	0.0
Iowa	18,947	99.9	0.1	0.0
Kansas	9,207	97.7	2.3	0.0
Kentucky	28,219	98.9	1.1	0.0
Louisiana	27,438	99.6	0.4	0.0
Maine	11,676	98.8	1.2	0.0
Maryland	28,503	97.1	2.9	0.0
Massachusetts	39,484	86.1	13.9	0.0
Michigan	68,702	97.5	2.5	0.0
Minnesota	36,131	86.0	11.9	2.1
Mississippi	8,656	99.8	0.2	0.0
Missouri	36,309	98.9	1.0	0.2
Montana	4,731	99.4	0.6	0.0
Nebraska	9,811	92.3	7.7	0.0
Nevada	5,216	96.1	3.9	0.0
New Hampshire	5,085	93.6	3.2	3.2
New Jersey	44,944	98.0	0.0	2.0
New Mexico	26,160	93.7	6.2	0.0
New York	270,105	82.0	16.1	1.8
North Carolina	32,513	99.6	0.3	0.2
North Dakota	2,379	97.4	2.6	0.0
Ohio	81,195	98.6	1.4	0.0
Oklahoma	13,590	98.7	0.7	0.6
Oregon a/	14,048			
Pennsylvania	87,233	96.1	3.9	0.0
Puerto Rico	39,254	99.1	0.3	0.6
Rhode Island b/	15,994	85.4	14.6	0.0
South Carolina	10,197	99.5	0.3	0.2
South Dakota	1,692	100.0	0.0	0.0
Tennessee	41,590	99.5	0.5	0.0
Texas	84,085	91.3	8.7	0.0
Utah	7,499	97.1	2.9	0.0
Vermont	6,576	98.8	1.2	0.0
Virgin Islands	968	91.2	7.0	1.7
Virginia	24,028	96.0	4.0	0.0
Washington	59,769	85.4	14.6	0.0
West Virginia	11,949	98.8	0.5	0.7
Wisconsin	8,510	100.0	0.0	0.0
Wyoming	407	99.7	0.3	0.0

Note: 'a/' = Data not reported.
     'b/' = Data reported but not reliable.

SOURCE: "Percent Distribution of TANF Adult Recipients by Citizenship Status, October 1998–September 1999" in *Temporary Assistance for Needy Families (TANF) Program: Third Annual Report to Congress*, U.S. Department of Health and Human Services, Administration for Children and Families, Office of Planning, Research and Evaluation, Washington, D.C., 2000

TABLE 6.9

Percent distribution of Temporary Assistance for Needy Families (TANF) recipient children by citizenship status, October 1998–September 1999

State	Total Children	U.S. Citizen	Noncitizen	Unknown
U.S. Total	5,318,722	96.1	2.6	1.3
Alabama	38,428	100.0	0.0	0.0
Alaska	17,260	97.2	2.5	0.3
Arizona	42,615	96.9	1.4	1.7
Arkansas	21,524	88.9	9.7	1.4
California	1,381,384	94.3	5.1	0.5
Colorado	29,855	99.1	0.2	0.7
Connecticut	59,991	96.9	0.8	2.3
Delaware	12,639	95.0	0.2	4.8
Dist. of Col.	40,080	99.4	0.2	0.4
Florida	155,337	97.3	1.6	1.1
Georgia	115,620	99.2	0.4	0.4
Guam	6,611	96.5	3.0	0.5
Hawaii	31,477	98.8	0.6	0.6
Idaho	2,148	98.3	1.4	0.3
Illinois	277,314	99.6	0.4	0.0
Indiana	77,627	100.0	0.0	0.0
Iowa	40,006	99.3	0.1	0.5
Kansas	23,910	96.7	0.8	2.5
Kentucky	71,792	98.6	0.3	1.0
Louisiana	104,742	99.5	0.1	0.5
Maine	24,381	97.5	0.9	1.6
Maryland	64,493	97.7	1.1	1.2
Massachusetts	96,441	94.0	4.7	1.3
Michigan	200,661	98.3	0.7	1.0
Minnesota	89,002	86.1	7.3	6.6
Mississippi	33,164	99.2	0.1	0.7
Missouri	102,356	99.5	0.4	0.1
Montana	9,182	97.9	0.3	1.7
Nebraska	23,118	95.6	4.4	0.0
Nevada	15,287	98.2	0.1	1.7
New Hampshire	10,697	95.1	1.2	3.7
New Jersey	124,835	97.8	0.0	2.2
New Mexico	53,120	99.1	0.2	0.7
New York	568,349	92.2	3.8	4.0
North Carolina	102,166	94.9	0.2	4.9
North Dakota	6,202	96.1	2.7	1.2
Ohio	210,464	97.6	0.8	1.6
Oklahoma	36,984	98.9	0.0	1.1
Oregon a/	30,703			
Pennsylvania	212,041	96.3	1.5	2.2
Puerto Rico	78,465	99.1	0.6	0.4
Rhode Island b/	28,711			
South Carolina	33,724	98.8	0.5	0.7
South Dakota	6,266	99.8	0.0	0.2
Tennessee	111,387	98.9	0.2	0.9
Texas	220,374	98.9	0.6	0.6
Utah	18,541	97.9	1.4	0.7
Vermont	11,746	98.5	0.3	1.2
Virgin Islands	2,714	98.7	0.8	0.5
Virginia	64,483	97.1	2.2	0.7
Washington	120,585	90.8	8.2	1.0
West Virginia	20,545	98.7	0.2	1.1
Wisconsin a/	35,859			
Wyoming	1,317	99.1	0.0	0.9

Note: 'a/' = Data not reported.
     'b/' = Data reported but not reliable.

SOURCE: "Percent Distribution of TANF Recipient Children by Citizenship Status, October 1998–September 1999" in *Temporary Assistance for Needy Families (TANF) Program: Third Annual Report to Congress*, U.S. Department of Health and Human Services, Administration for Children and Families, Office of Planning, Research and Evaluation, Washington, D.C., 2000

Arizona, Institute for Local Government, Tucson, AZ, February 2001), reported that in fiscal year 1999 the Border Patrol arrested 1.35 million illegal aliens. That number is expected to increase in coming years.

Dr. Salant noted that illegal aliens and legal border-crossers caught committing a state felony, or two or more misdemeanors, are processed in the enforcement and criminal justice system of county governments in the same manner as U.S. citizens or legal visitors to the United States. Illegal aliens who give birth in the United States, get hurt, or die receive medical services. In a study conducted for the United States/Mexico Border Counties Coalition (USMBCC), Dr. Salant and researchers from the University of Texas at El Paso, New Mexico State University, and San Diego State University found that the 24 border counties along the U.S.-Mexico border spent about $108.2 million providing law enforcement, criminal justice, and emergency healthcare services to illegal aliens apprehended in fiscal year 1999. (See Table 6.10.) USMBCC is made up of the county judges, commissioners, and supervisors of the U.S. counties located on the border with Mexico.

California's two border counties paid more than half ($55.7 million) of the total costs of providing criminal justice and medical services to illegal aliens due to the size of San Diego County and the 2 million Mexican nationals in the neighboring municipalities. Arizona's four border counties (comprising just 17 percent of the border county population) paid over 22 percent ($24.2 million) of the total costs. Texas's 15 border counties incurred over 21 percent of the costs ($23.3 million), while New Mexico's three border counties spent $5 million. States helped fund some of the costs. (See Table 6.10.)

State Criminal Alien Assistance Program (SCAAP)

The State Criminal Alien Assistance Program (SCAAP) is administered by the Bureau of Justice Assistance (BJA) of the U.S. Department of Justice in cooperation with the INS. SCAAP provides federal funding to states and localities that are incurring costs of incarcerating criminal illegal aliens convicted of state and local offenses. SCAAP is neither an entitlement nor a reimbursement program.

For fiscal year 1999 the border counties received $12.4 million from SCAAP. Law enforcement and criminal justice services accounted for 82 percent ($89.1 million) of the total costs to the border states. The $12.4-million SCAAP award represented just 13.9 percent of incarceration costs and just 11.5 percent of the total $108.2 million cost. The amount received by each border state pays for just a minimal portion of its total expenses for the year—15 percent for California, 9 percent for Texas, 8 percent for New Mexico, and 5 percent for Arizona. (See Figure 6.1 and Table 6.11.)

TABLE 6.10

Total costs of services provided to illegal immigrants, in millions, by county function and state, 1999

Function	Texas	New Mexico	Arizona	California	Total
Sheriff	$7	$2	$7	$10.8	$26.8
Detention	$6.6	$1.8	$7.3	$10.4	$26.1
Prosecution	$2	—*	$1	$5.2	$8.2
Defense	$1.5	—*	$1.1	$2.2	$4.8
Lower Court	$.7	—*	$.5	—**	$1.2
Trial Courts	$2	$.06	$1.1	$5.8	$9
Court Clerks	$1.4	—*	$.3	—**	$1.7
Probation	$.1	—*	$.4	$7.1	$7.6
Juveniles	$1	$.03	$.5	$2.1	$3.6
Medical	$1	$1.1	$5	$12.1	$19.2
TOTALS	**$23.3**	**$5**	**$24.2**	**$55.7**	**$108.2**

*state function ** unified with trial courts

SOURCE: Tanis J. Salant et al., "Total Costs by County Function and State" in *Illegal Immigrants in U.S.–Mexico Border Counties: The Costs of Law Enforcement, Criminal Justice, and Emergency Medical Services,* University of Arizona, Institute for Local Government, Tucson, 2001

FIGURE 6.1

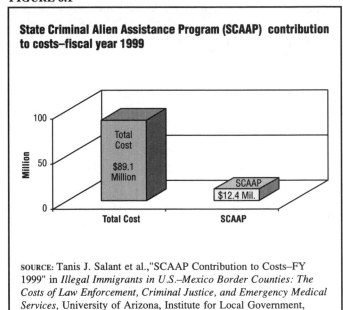

State Criminal Alien Assistance Program (SCAAP) contribution to costs–fiscal year 1999

SOURCE: Tanis J. Salant et al.,"SCAAP Contribution to Costs–FY 1999" in *Illegal Immigrants in U.S.–Mexico Border Counties: The Costs of Law Enforcement, Criminal Justice, and Emergency Medical Services,* University of Arizona, Institute for Local Government, Tucson, 2001

Just 19 of the 24 border counties received monetary assistance.

The Federation for American Immigration Reform, in *The Costs of Immigration* (Washington, D.C., May 2000), reported that in 1999 states submitted expenses totaling nearly $1.5 billion to SCAAP. However, state and local jurisdictions were awarded only 39 percent of their costs for incarcerating criminal illegal aliens. About $573 million was distributed among states, with state and local taxpayers bearing almost $911 million of the cost. In 1999 border counties were awarded just 2 percent of the SCAAP allocation.

CALIFORNIA

California's Role in Immigration

It would be too simple to say that California is the helpless victim of illegal aliens and the federal government. Some policies promoted in the 1980s actively encouraged illegal immigration. For example, in 1984 and 1985 city councils in Los Angeles, San Francisco, and many other California cities passed resolutions making their cities sanctuaries for illegal aliens from Central American countries regarded as having repressive governments supported by the United States.

Furthermore, many California homeowners and businesses have never been averse to hiring illegal aliens to maintain their homes; care for their children; or work in stores, factories, and farms. Illegal aliens go to California because other refugees from similar areas of the world might be there and have set up local, culturally rich communities. Finally, refugees, like many other Americans, are attracted to California's pleasant climate. The INS warned the cities that the word would spread everywhere and illegal aliens from all over would flock to California. The INS estimated that, in 1996, about 2 million illegal aliens, or 40 percent of the total number of illegal residents, lived in California.

TABLE 6.11

State Criminal Alien Assistance Program (SCAAP) compensation to border counties by state

State	SCAAP	% total costs
Texas	$2,168,255	9%
New Mexico	$397,162	8%
Arizona	$1,287,624	5%
California	$8,416,979	15%
Total	**$12.4 million**	**11.5% (ave)**

SOURCE: Tanis J. Salant et al., "SCAAP Compensation to Border Counties by State–$12.4 million" in *Illegal Immigrants in U.S.–Mexico Border Counties: The Costs of Law Enforcement, Criminal Justice, and Emergency Medical Services,* University of Arizona, Institute for Local Government, Tucson, 2001

Governor Pete Wilson's Role

Former governor Pete Wilson has also been charged with complicity in California's illegal alien problem. When the Immigration Reform and Control Act of 1986 was being debated in the Senate, Wilson (a senator at the time) supported a special amnesty for illegal aliens (the Special Agricultural Worker [SAW] program) who could prove that they worked as farm laborers for at least 90 days between May 1985 and May 1986.

When the INS demanded proof that the applicants for legalization under IRCA's SAW program had indeed fulfilled their employment requirement, Wilson opposed it. He wrote President Ronald Reagan, complaining that the

TABLE 6.12

Percentage of adults reporting receiving public assistance income by gender, age, and immigration status in California, 1970–90

	Men			Women		
	1970	1980	1990	1970	1980	1990
Adults age 64 or less						
Recent immigrants[a]	2.0	2.5	3.6	3.0	4.0	5.6
Earlier immigrants[b]	3.1	2.7	2.3	3.9	5.1	4.7
All immigrants	2.7	2.6	2.9	3.5	4.6	5.1
Native-born population	2.7	2.5	2.5	4.6	6.1	6.0
Adults age 65 or more						
Recent immigrants[a]	38.4	35.5	33.4	40.9	36.8	35.5
Earlier immigrants[b]	11.4	13.1	15.0	18.2	19.6	21.0
All immigrants	11.8	15.4	18.4	18.9	21.7	23.7
Native-born population	11.3	9.1	6.7	13.7	14.9	11.4

SOURCE: U.S. Department of Commerce, 1970, 1980, and 1990.

Note: These rates are based on responses of individuals to the question of whether they personally had received income from a public assistance program. Also, the Census does not distinguish among the various public assistance programs. Generally adults age 64 or less would primarily benefit from the AFDC, AFDC-U and General Relief programs, although some may also benefit from the SSI Disabled, Blind, and Aged Program. Adults age 65 or more would primarily benefit from the SSI program.

[a] Recent immigrants are immigrants who entered the country in the 10 years preceding the Census year.

[b] Earlier immigrants are immigrants who entered the country 10 years or more prior to the Census year.

SOURCE: Kevin F. McCarthy and Georges Vernez, *Immigration in a Changing Economy: California's Experience,* MR-854, Santa Monica, California: RAND, 1997. Copyright © RAND 1997. Reprinted by permission.

TABLE 6.13

Number of children by age and immigration status in California, 1970–90

	Immigrants			Native-Born Population			All		
Age Group	1970	1980	1990	1970	1980	1990	1970	1980	1990
0–11	115,900	300,530	410,744	4,265,350	3,875,200	5,024,416	4,381,250	4,175,730	5,435,160
12–18	128,600	319,320	548,595	2,504,500	2,427,800	2,162,402	2,633,100	2,747,120	2,710,997
Total	**244,500**	**620,020**	**959,339**	**6,769,850**	**6,303,000**	**7,186,818**	**7,014,350**	**6,923,020**	**8,146,157**

SOURCE: Kevin F. McCarthy and Georges Vernez, *Immigration in a Changing Economy: California's Experience,* MR-854, Santa Monica, California: RAND, 1997. Copyright © RAND 1997. Reprinted by permission.

crops were rotting in the fields while the INS carried out "burdensome SAW application procedures."

Some experts believe that many undocumented aliens legalized under the SAW program were admitted under fraudulent circumstances. Although the program was supposed to grant amnesty to about 350,000 workers, nearly 1.3 million illegal immigrants gained permanent resident status through the program; most settled in California. Since families were not legalized through the SAW program, hundreds of thousands of family members entered the United States illegally. Most were women and children—those most likely to use medical and educational services.

Immigrants' Use of Cash Assistance in California

Kevin F. McCarthy and Georges Vernez, in *Immigration in a Changing Economy: California's Experience* (RAND, Santa Monica, CA, 1997), reported that the decennial (occurring every 10 years) censuses showed that welfare use by adult immigrants in California rose between 1970 and 1990. In 1970, 2.7 percent of all male immigrants age 64 and under reported receiving cash assistance. By the 1990 census, that proportion had risen slightly to 2.9 percent. The proportion of female immigrants age 64 and under who reported receiving cash assistance rose at a greater rate, from 3.5 percent in 1970 to 5.1 percent in 1990. (See Table 6.12.)

The authors noted that the dependence on cash assistance by male immigrants age 64 and under declined the longer they lived in the United States. In 1970, 3.1 percent of those immigrants who entered the country 10 or more years prior to the census year indicated that they received cash assistance; by 1990, just 2.3 percent received cash assistance. However, their female counterparts reported increased dependence on cash assistance, from 3.9 percent in 1970 to 4.7 percent in 1990. It should be noted that, for the overall male population age 64 and under, the proportion of immigrants receiving cash assistance was close to that of native-born persons (2.7 percent each in 1970, 2.6 percent versus 2.5 percent in 1980, and 2.9 percent versus 2.5 percent in 1990). (See Table 6.12.)

Among the elderly population age 65 and over, immigrants were much more likely to use public assistance than their native-born counterparts. In 1970, 11.8 percent of male immigrants age 65 and over reported receiving cash assistance, compared to 11.3 percent of native-born persons. In 1980 the proportion of elderly male immigrants receiving cash assistance rose to 15.4 percent. The proportion for the native-born population that year declined to 9.1 percent. In 1990 more than two and one-half times as many elderly male immigrants as elderly native-born men (18.4 percent versus 6.7 percent) reported relying on cash assistance. Reliance on cash assistance among elderly female immigrants was consistently higher

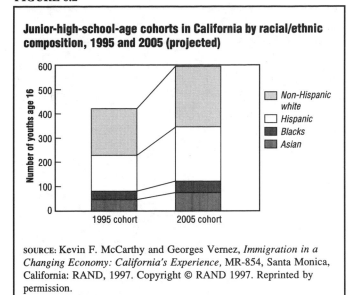

FIGURE 6.2

Junior-high-school-age cohorts in California by racial/ethnic composition, 1995 and 2005 (projected)

SOURCE: Kevin F. McCarthy and Georges Vernez, *Immigration in a Changing Economy: California's Experience*, MR-854, Santa Monica, California: RAND, 1997. Copyright © RAND 1997. Reprinted by permission.

than among their male counterparts and the elderly female native-born population during the three census years. (See Table 6.12.)

Public Education and California's Immigrant Children

In California education has been the public service most affected by both legal and illegal immigration. Since the early 1970s enrollments in California's primary and secondary schools have continued to rise as a result of the steady influx of school-age immigrants and the growing numbers of American-born children of immigrants. (See Table 6.13.) Strains are expected on the resources of state community colleges and universities.

The number of 16-year-olds is projected to increase markedly by the year 2005. According to McCarthy and Vernez, about two-thirds of the increase in this age group is projected to be made up of Asian (17 percent) and Hispanic (45 percent) children born in the United States. Non-Hispanic white (32 percent) and black (6 percent) children will account for the remaining increase. (See Figure 6.2.)

Proposition 187

In November 1994 increasing concern about the effects of a large number of illegal aliens culminated in California voters approving Proposition 187 by a margin of 59 to 41 percent. The ballot initiative prohibits illegal aliens and their children from receiving any welfare services, education, or emergency health care. It further requires local law-enforcement authorities, educators, medical professionals, and social-service workers to report suspected illegal aliens to state and federal authorities. It also considers the manufacture, distribution, and sale of fraudulent documents a state felony punishable by up to five years in prison.

TABLE 6.14

Aggregated estimates of the number of native-born workers whose job opportunities were affected by immigrants, in California, 1990

Years of Education and Gender	Estimate I	Estimate II
Men		
< 12	−14,600	−47,800
= 12	−13,900	−53,200
13–15	−55,300	−300
16 +	+23,700	0
Subtotal	**−60,100**	**−101,300**
Women		
< 12	−2,800	−44,800
= 12	−57,500	−4,200
13–15	−50,200	−44,400
16 +	+42,400	0
Subtotal	**−68,100**	**−93,400**
Total	**−128,200**	**−194,700**

SOURCE: Kevin F. McCarthy and Georges Vernez, *Immigration in a Changing Economy: California's Experience,* MR-854, Santa Monica, California: RAND, 1997. Copyright © RAND 1997. Reprinted by permission.

TABLE 6.15

Comparison of foreign-born residents by legal status, in California and the rest of the U.S., 1995

	California		Rest of the Nation	
	Number	Percentage	Number	Percentage
Naturalized	2,300	29	6,700	41
Legal residents	4,100	51	7,400	45
Refugees[a]	700	9	900	6
Amnesty	1,500	19	1,150	7
Other	1,900	23	5,350	32
Illegal	1,600	20	2,400	14
EWI[b]	1,200	15	1,200	7
Visa abusers	400	5	1,200	7
Total	**8,000**	**100**	**16,500**	**100**

[a]Includes refugee admission since 1980 only.
[b]Entered without inspection.

SOURCE: Kevin F. McCarthy and Georges Vernez, *Immigration in a Changing Economy: California's Experience,* MR-854, Santa Monica, California: RAND, 1997. Copyright © RAND 1997. Reprinted by permission.

The day after California voters approved Proposition 187, civil rights groups filed a lawsuit in federal district court to block the implementation of the ballot initiative. One week later U.S. District Court Judge Matthew Byrne issued a temporary restraining order.

In November 1995 U.S. District Court Judge Mariana Pfaelzer ruled unconstitutional Proposition 187's provision involving elementary and secondary education for undocumented children. The judge cited the U.S. Supreme Court decision on the Texas case *Plyler v. Doe* (457 U.S. 202, 1982), which held that the equal protection clause of the Fourteenth Amendment prohibits states from denying education to illegal immigrants. Civil rights and education groups had argued that states have no legal rights to regulate immigration, which is a federal responsibility.

In March 1998 Judge Pfaelzer permanently barred Proposition 187's restrictions on benefits, citing the federal welfare reform law, the Personal Responsibility and Work Opportunity Reconciliation Act, as "preempting all state regulation of benefits for aliens except as allowed under Public Law 104-193 provisions." Pfaelzer allowed the criminal provisions requiring state authorities to investigate arrestees suspected of being illegal immigrants, to report illegal aliens, and to consider as a felony the manufacture, distribution, and use of false documents. Pfaelzer ruled that these provisions may be enforced because they had not been preempted by federal law.

Former governor Pete Wilson appealed Pfaelzer's decision. In April 1999 Wilson's successor, Governor Gray Davis, announced that the state of California would ask a federal appeals court to mediate the legal disputes over Proposition 187. Although Davis opposed the ballot initiative, he claimed he had no authority to disregard the voters' wishes or to rule on Proposition 187's constitutionality. Some individuals on both sides of the issue charged that the new governor had taken the easy way out.

In July 1999 Governor Davis and the civil rights groups agreed to end the litigation, in effect nulling the public votes banning public education and social services to illegal aliens. Only the two criminal provisions would be implemented.

Effect of Immigration on Native-Born Workers

McCarthy and Vernez, in *Immigration in a Changing Economy: California's Experience*, found that immigration in California in 1990 had a negative effect on native-born workers who did not finish high school and workers with just a high school degree. The researchers estimated that between 128,200 and 194,700 native-born workers were displaced (were unemployed or had withdrawn from the labor force) by immigrants. This number accounted for 1 to 1.3 percent of California's adult native-born population ages 16 to 64. (See Table 6.14.)

California Does Not Necessarily Mirror the Whole Nation

McCarthy and Vernez noted that California's immigrants differ greatly from immigrants in other parts of the country—they are younger, have lived in the United States for shorter periods of time, and have somewhat less education. In addition, their immigration statuses differ from those of immigrants in other states. In 1995 there were higher proportions of refugees (9 percent), amnesty recipients (19 percent), and illegal aliens (20 percent) in

California compared to the rest of the nation—6 percent, 7 percent, and 14 percent, respectively. (See Table 6.15.) Consequently, it does not necessarily mean that areas of the country with increasing numbers of immigrants would face the same difficulties confronting California.

LABOR FORCE PARTICIPATION

In 1890 about 5 million foreign-born persons were working in the United States, accounting for one-quarter (26.1 percent) of the labor force. In the following century the number of working immigrants changed little. However, because of the dramatic increase in the native-born population, the proportion of immigrants in the U.S. labor force fell until it bottomed out in 1970. That year 4.2 million foreign-born persons made up only 5.1 percent of the labor force. By 1990, 11.6 million foreign-born individuals were in the labor force, comprising 9.3 percent of the total labor force. (See Table 6.16.)

In 1998, immigrants accounted for 9.8 percent of the total U.S. population (26.3 million out of 243.1 million) and 11.7 percent of the total labor force. (See Table 6.16.) Out of the total immigrant population, 61 percent of immigrants were in the labor force; the proportion of native-born persons in the labor force was 45 percent. (About 120.7 million native-born persons were in the labor force that year.) One explanation for this discrepancy is that immigrants are more likely to be of working age.

According to the Census Bureau, in March 2000 the foreign-born population was more likely than the native population to be unemployed, 4.9 percent versus 4.3 percent. Foreign-born and native males had similar unemployment rates—4.5 percent and 4.4 percent, respectively. However, foreign-born females had a higher unemployment rate (5.5 percent) than native females (4.2 percent). Foreign-born persons who arrived in the United States before 1970 had the lowest unemployment rate (3.6 percent) compared to those who came most recently in the 1990s (6.1 percent). (See Table 6.17.)

Income and Poverty

In 1999 more than one-third (36.3 percent) of foreign-born full-time, year-round workers earned less than $20,000 compared to one fifth (21.3 percent) of their native counterparts. Native workers (nearly 25 percent) were more likely to earn $50,000 or more than foreign-born workers (19 percent). Among foreign-born workers, those from Central America (57 percent) were more likely than those from Asia (22.4 percent) and Europe (16.2 percent) to earn less than $20,000.

The Census Bureau uses "a set of money income thresholds that vary by family size and composition to determine who is poor." If a family's total income is less than that family's threshold, then all family members are

TABLE 6.16

Foreign-born U.S. population and labor force, 1850–1998

Year	Foreign-Born Population (millions)	Percentage of Total Population	Foreign-Born Labor Force (millions)	Percentage of Total Labor Force
1850	2.2	9.7	—	—
1860	4.1	13.2	—	—
1870	5.6	14.0	2.7	21.6
1880	6.7	13.3	3.5	20.1
1890	9.2	14.6	5.1	26.1
1990	10.3	13.6	5.8	23.0
1910	13.5	14.7	7.8	24.0
1920	13.9	13.2	7.7	21.2
1930	14.2	11.6	7.4	17.4
1940	11.5	8.8	5.8	12.3
1950	10.3	6.9	4.8	9.2
1960	9.7	5.4	4.2	6.3
1970	9.6	4.7	4.2	5.1
1980	14.1	6.2	7.1	6.7
1990	19.8	7.9	11.6	9.3
1994	22.6	8.7	12.9	9.8
1995	23.0	8.8	12.9	9.7
1996	24.6	9.3	14.4	10.7
1997	25.8	9.7	15.4	11.3
1998	26.3	9.8	16.1	11.7

Note: Labor force data for 1850–1990 refer to the noninstitutional labor force, including the armed forces. Labor force data for 1994–98 refer to the civilian population.

SOURCE: Roger G. Kramer, "Table 16: Foreign-born U.S. Population and Labor Force: 1850–1998," in *Developments in International Migration to the United States: 1999*. U.S. Department of Labor, Bureau of International Labor Affairs, Washington, DC, 1999

considered poor. For example, in 1999 a family of three people had an average poverty threshold of $13,290. A family of three with an income below that amount is considered poor.

In 1999 a higher proportion of foreign-born persons (16.8 percent) than natives (11.2 percent) were living below the poverty level. Among the foreign-born residents, Latin Americans had the highest poverty rate (21.9 percent) compared to Asians (12.8 percent) and Europeans (9.3 percent). Among Latin Americans, South Americans had the lowest poverty rate (11.5 percent). (See Figure 6.3.)

THE COST OF THE IRCA LEGALIZATION 10 YEARS LATER

David Simcox, in *Measuring the Fallout: The Cost of the IRCA Amnesty After 10 Years* (Center for Immigration Studies, Washington, D.C., 1997), reported that in 1996, 10 years after legalization, the illegal aliens amnestied under the Immigration Reform and Control Act of 1986 (IRCA) had cost the government, in terms of 20 public assistance programs, a total of $102.1 billion, while paying taxes of only $78 billion. In addition, indirect costs related to the legalized population—including aid to displaced native workers ($9.9 billion), aid to American-born

TABLE 6.17

Labor force status of foreign-born civilian population by sex and year of entry, March 2000[1]

| Employment Status | Total | | Year of Entry | | | | | | | |
| | | | 1990-2000 | | 1980-1989 | | 1970-1979 | | Before 1970 | |
	Number	Percent	Number	Percent	Number	Percent	Number	Percent	Number	Percent
Total										
Civilian labor force	17,385	66.6	6,112	65.9	5,625	73.2	3,436	74.7	2,212	48.7
Employed	16,532	95.1	5,737	93.9	5,361	95.3	3,302	96.1	2,133	96.4
Unemployed	852	4.9	375	6.1	264	4.7	134	3.9	79	3.6
Not in civilian labor force	8,714	33.4	3,165	34.1	2,056	26.8	1,161	25.3	2,332	51.3
Not employed	8,714	100.0	3,165	100.0	2,056	100.0	1,161	100.0	2,332	100.0
Male										
Civilian labor force	10,334	79.6	3,843	82.4	3,387	84.6	1,907	85.3	1,198	57.7
Employed	9,873	95.5	3,633	94.5	3,246	95.9	1,842	96.6	1,152	96.1
Unemployed	461	4.5	210	5.5	140	4.1	65	3.4	46	3.9
Not in civilian labor force	2,646	20.4	821	17.6	618	15.4	329	14.7	878	42.3
Not employed	2,646	100.0	821	100.0	618	100.0	329	100.0	878	100.0
Female										
Civilian labor force	7,050	53.7	2,269	49.2	2,238	60.9	1,529	64.8	1,014	41.1
Employed	6,659	94.5	2,104	92.7	2,115	94.5	1,460	95.4	981	96.8
Unemployed	391	5.5	166	7.3	123	5.5	70	4.6	32	3.2
Not in civilian labor force	6,068	46.3	2,343	50.8	1,439	39.1	832	35.2	1,454	58.9
Not employed	6,068	100.0	2,343	100.0	1,439	100.0	832	100.0	1,454	100.0

[1]Numbers in thousands; age 16 years and over.

SOURCE: Lisa Lollock, "Labor Force Status of the Foreign-Born Civilian Population by Sex and Year of Entry: March 2000" in *The Foreign-Born Population in the United States, March 2000, Current Population Reports, Series P20-534*, U.S. Bureau of the Census, Washington, D.C., 2001

FIGURE 6.3

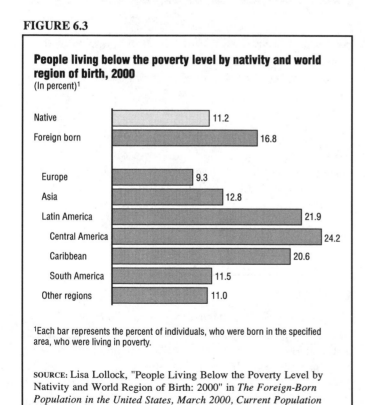

People living below the poverty level by nativity and world region of birth, 2000
(In percent)[1]

Native — 11.2
Foreign born — 16.8

Europe — 9.3
Asia — 12.8
Latin America — 21.9
Central America — 24.2
Caribbean — 20.6
South America — 11.5
Other regions — 11.0

[1]Each bar represents the percent of individuals, who were born in the specified area, who were living in poverty.

SOURCE: Lisa Lollock, "People Living Below the Poverty Level by Nativity and World Region of Birth: 2000" in *The Foreign-Born Population in the United States, March 2000, Current Population Reports, Series P20-534*, U.S. Bureau of the Census, Washington, D.C., 2001

children of legalized women ($36.1 billion), and public education costs for the undocumented children of legalized aliens ($8.6 billion)—totaled $54.6 billion. (See Table 6.18.)

PUBLIC OPINION—CHANGING VIEWS ON IMMIGRATION

The results of the 2000 Census have added to the continuing debate on the effect of immigration on the population growth in the United States. Between 1990 and 2000 the U.S. population grew over 13 percent, from 248.7 million to 281.4 million—7 million more people than the Census Bureau had projected. At the same time, March 2000 data on the foreign-born population showed that it had grown 30 percent during the last decade—from 19.8 million to 28.4 million. In March 2001 the Gallup Poll asked the American public what they thought about the increasing number of foreign-born persons in the United States. Forty-four percent thought it was "a good thing" for the country that the foreign-born population has increased during the past decade, while a slightly lower proportion (39 percent) indicated it was "a bad thing." (See Table 6.19.)

In March 2001 the Gallup Poll found that half (51 percent) of the American public supported keeping immigration at the current level or increasing it, while 44

TABLE 6.18

Summary table of costs of the IRCA amnesty, 1987–96

Direct costs of the legalized population
Population: 1987: 2.67 million
              1996: 2.03 million
Total 10-year costs of 20 assistance programs: $102.1 billion

Revenues from the legalized population
Total 10-year tax contributions: $78 billion

Total 10-year revenue deficit on direct costs   **$24.1 billion**

Indirect costs
  1. Aid to displaced resident workers $9.9 billion

  2. Citizen children 18 and under:
     Population: 1987: 679,200
                  1996: 1.16 million
     Total 10-year costs of four programs $36.1 billion

  3. Illegal alien dependents 18 and under:
     Population: 1987: 177,100
                  1996: 401,000
     Total 10-year education costs $8.6 billion

Total indirect costs   **$54.6 billion**

Total 10-year deficit on all costs   **$78.7 billion**

SOURCE: David Simcox, *Measuring the Fallout: The Cost of the IRCA Amnesty after 10 Years,* Center for Immigration Studies, Washington D.C., 1997

FIGURE 6.4

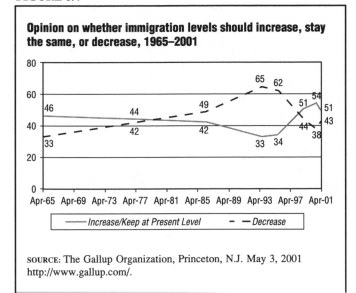

Opinion on whether immigration levels should increase, stay the same, or decrease, 1965–2001

SOURCE: The Gallup Organization, Princeton, N.J. May 3, 2001
http://www.gallup.com/.

TABLE 6.19

Opinion on growth in number of foreign-born residents in the U.S., March 2001
The new U.S. census results show that the percentage of people now living in the United States but who were born in another country has increased significantly during the past 10 years. Just your opinion, is this a good thing or a bad thing for the country?

	Good thing %	Bad thing %	Both/Neither (vol.) %	No opinion %
2001 Mar 26-28	44	39	11	6

(vol.) = Volunteered response

SOURCE: The Gallup Organization, Princeton, N.J. May 3, 2001
http://www.gallup.com/.

FIGURE 6.5

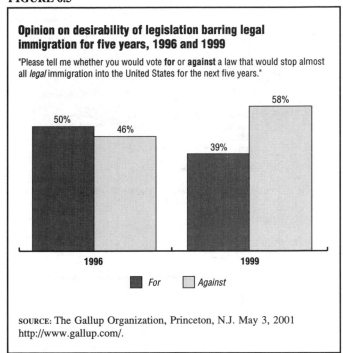

Opinion on desirability of legislation barring legal immigration for five years, 1996 and 1999

"Please tell me whether you would vote **for** or **against** a law that would stop almost all *legal* immigration into the United States for the next five years."

SOURCE: The Gallup Organization, Princeton, N.J. May 3, 2001
http://www.gallup.com/.

percent favored lowering the level of immigration admissions. (See Figure 6.4.) According to the Gallup Organization, the state of the economy appears to influence Americans' attitude toward immigration. In 1993 and 1995, following the economic recession, two-thirds (65 percent) of Americans wanted immigration decreased; just one-third wanted it kept at the same level or increased. During generally good economic times, almost the reverse is true. In 1965 one third of Americans thought immigrant admissions should be reduced, while nearly half (46 percent) said admissions should be increased or kept at the current level.

A 1999 Gallup Poll asked the American public if it would support or oppose a law that would ban all legal immigration to the United States for the next five years. Nearly 6 of 10 (58 percent) respondents opposed such a law, compared to about 4 of 10 (39 percent) in favor of it. Three years earlier, in 1996, half of Americans (50 percent) supported a law closing America's doors to all legal immigration. (See Figure 6.5.)

In September 2000 more Americans believed that immigrants in the long run "become productive citizens and pay their fair share of taxes" (48 percent) than "cost the taxpayers too much by using government services like public education and medical services" (40 percent). In

TABLE 6.20

Opinion on whether immigrants ultimately contribute to or cost society, 1993–2000

Which comes closer to your point of view — [ROTATED: immigrants in the long run become productive citizens and pay their fair share of taxes, (or) immigrants cost the taxpayers too much by using government services like public education and medical services?]

	Pay their fair share of taxes	Cost taxpayers too much	No opinion
2000 Sep 11-13	48%	40	12
1999 Feb 26-28	47%	45	8
1994 Dec 16-18	36%	57	7
1993 Jul 9-11	37%	56	7

SOURCE: The Gallup Organization, Princeton, N.J. May 8, 2001 http://www.gallup.com/.

TABLE 6.21

Opinion on whether immigrants help or hurt the economy, 1993–2000

Do you think immigrants — [ROTATED: mostly help the economy by providing low cost labor, (or) mostly hurt the economy by driving wages down for many Americans?

	Mostly help %	Mostly hurt %	Neither (vol.) %	Both (vol.) %	No opinion %
2000 Sep 11-13	44%	40	7	3	6
1999 Feb 26-28	42%	48	3	1	6
1993 Jul 9-11	28%	64	2	2	4

(vol.) = Volunteered response

SOURCE: The Gallup Organization, Princeton, N.J. May 8, 2001 http://www.gallup.com/.

TABLE 6.22

Attitude towards increasing diversity in the U.S. due to immigration, 1993 and 2001

In your view, does the increasing diversity in the United States that is created by immigrants **mostly improve** American culture or **mostly threaten** American culture?

	Mostly improve %	Mostly threaten %	Both (vol.) %	Neither (vol.) %	No opinion %
2001 Mar 26-28	45	38	4	5	8
1993 Jul 9-11 ^	35	55	3	3	4

^In your view, does the increasing diversity that immigrants bring to this country **mostly improve** American culture or **mostly threaten** American culture?

(vol.) = Volunteered response

SOURCE: The Gallup Organization, Princeton, N.J. May 3, 2001 http://www.gallup.com/.

1999 Americans were equally split on these two issues. (See Table 6.20.) Forty-four percent of the respondents thought immigrants help the U.S. economy by providing low-cost labor, compared to 28 percent who thought so in 1993. At that time 64 percent of the public believed immi-

grants hurt the economy by driving wages down for many workers; however, the share of those who indicated immigration hurt the economy dropped to 40 percent in 2000. (See Table 6.21.) In 1999, when the Gallup Organization asked the same question, it found that Americans with lower incomes were more likely to say that immigration hurts the economy—more than half (58 percent) of those earning less than $30,000 annually believed so. An equal proportion (58 percent) of those making over $50,000 yearly thought immigration helps the economy.

Some Americans feel threatened by immigrants who they believe are unable or unwilling to assimilate into American culture. Others feel that, just as previous waves of immigrants added richness and a distinctive quality to American life, future influxes of foreign-born people will contribute more than just their numbers to the American society. In March 2001, 45 percent of Gallup Poll respondents believed that the increased diversity in the country, resulting from the coming of immigrants, mostly improves American culture; 38 percent thought such diversity threatens American culture. In 1993, 55 percent said that the increasing diversity brought by immigrants threatens the United States. (See Table 6.22.)

CHAPTER 7

THE GOVERNMENT SHOULD RAISE THE ANNUAL CAP ON H-1B VISAS TO MEET THE WORKFORCE NEEDS OF THE INFORMATION TECHNOLOGY INDUSTRY

STATEMENT OF SENATOR SPENCER ABRAHAM (R -MI), SUBCOMMITTEE CHAIRMAN, BEFORE THE SUBCOMMITTEE ON IMMIGRATION OF THE SENATE JUDICIARY COMMITTEE, OCTOBER 21, 1999

...Since the passage of the legislation [American Competitiveness and Workforce Improvement Act of 1998; Public Law 105-277], the case for maintaining an adequate supply of H-1B visas has grown stronger.

First, despite the H-1B cap having been raised to 115,000 in FY [fiscal year] 1999 and 2000, and 107,500 in 2001, the increase has proven insufficient due to the tight labor market, increasing globalization, the rapid pace of the high-tech sector, and the backlog of visas that developed from the prior year. With the cap reached by June this year, employers were again left wondering why government restrictions are causing them to shelve projects and draw up plans to place key personnel overseas.

Second, foreign countries are stepping up their own recruitment efforts, including a pitch by the Canadian government for U.S. high-tech companies to move to Canada so as to avoid the problem of hitting the H-1B visa cap year after year here in America. The CEO of Lucent Technologies stated this summer at a Capitol Hill technology forum that it has placed hundreds of engineers and other technical people in the United Kingdom in response to an insufficient supply of U.S.-based workers—keeping many related jobs from being created in America.

...[W]e have seen more studies and more individuals reach the same conclusion embodied in last year's legislation.

A study by Joint Venture: Silicon Valley found that a lack of skilled workers is costing Silicon Valley companies $3 to $4 billion a year.

A study by the Computer Technology Industry Association concluded that a shortage of information technolo-gy professionals is costing the U.S. economy as a whole $105 billion a year.

In a study for the Public Policy Institute of California, U.C.-Berkeley, Professor Annalee Saxenian found that immigrants are a major source of job creation. Her research showed that Chinese and Indian immigrant entrepreneurs in northern California alone were responsible for employing 58,000 people, with annual sales of nearly $17 billion.

And most notably, Laura D'Andrea Tyson, former chief economic adviser to President Clinton, wrote recently in *Business Week* : "Conditions in the information technology sector indicate that it's time to raise the cap on H-1B visas yet again and to provide room for further increases as warranted. Silicon Valley's experience reveals that the results will be more jobs and higher incomes for both Americans and immigrant workers."

In closing, I'd like to note that although this hearing is in the immigration subcommittee, I don't think anyone here thinks the issues we address today are solely immigration issues. Our long-term goal should be to make sure American workers have the skills to fill the high-tech jobs of the future....

TESTIMONY BY SUSAN WILLIAMS DEFIFE, CEO, WOMENCONNECT.COM, BEFORE THE SUB COMMITTEE ON IMMIGRATION OF THE SENATE JUDICIARY COMMITTEE, OCTOBER 21, 1999

...[T]he H1-B visa issue...is an issue that is becoming critical to the future growth of the technology industry.

To give you a little background on my company, womenCONNECT.com is the leading Internet site for women in business—providing original daily content, interactive tools, online discussion groups, and e-commerce. When I started the company in 1994, the Internet was not yet a part of most people's lives, the InfoComm industry in Northern Virginia was in its infancy, and skilled technical workers or those who had the knowledge base to learn new technologies were fairly easy to come by.

In the past five years, the growth in the industry has exceeded even our own aggressive predictions. The Internet has become an integral part of people's everyday lives, changing how we communicate, how we gather information, how we shop, and how we do business. In Northern Virginia, you only have to drive from Tysons to Dulles to see the impact of the industry on the economy. You can see the size, the strength, and the wealth of the new technology companies in the many buildings cropping up. Those new buildings also represent an extraordinary increase in new jobs and the demand for more and more skilled workers to fill those positions.

From industry giants like AOL to the emerging growth companies like womenCONNECT.com, the shortage of skilled workers has become one of the highest priority issues facing us. For emerging companies like mine with a smaller employee base—we have 25 employees—one unfilled tech position can severely impact our ability to grow.

These emerging companies are fueling the technology revolution and making significant contributions to the strong economy we now enjoy. Among them will be the next AOL or Amazon.com. We are the companies that are innovating and growing fast. At womenCONNECT.com we've doubled in size in each of the past two years and we expect to double again within the next six months. There are many stories like ours. As investment capital flows into start-ups and puts them on a fast growth track, the demand for workers will continue to far exceed the supply. And the workforce shortage isn't limited to our region. Similar concerns are expressed across the country.

What happens when companies like mine can't hire the workers we need? We have to delay projects and in the Internet industry where change occurs daily and competitors are springing up all around you, waiting to execute on a project can be lethal.... As we've entered into new partnerships with industry heavyweights such as Lycos, CNN, CompuServe, and USA Today, we have had to carefully space those projects to ensure we can meet scheduled delivery dates and hold off on new projects until the appropriate staff people can come on board.

In order to fill these positions, the options for tech companies are not particularly attractive: we can limit our growth, but then we lose the ability to compete; we can "steal" employees from other companies, which makes none of us stronger and forces us to constantly look over our shoulders; or, in the case of larger companies I know, move operations offshore.

I understand the desire to provide jobs to American citizens; but, in an economy where unemployment is at record lows, it is unrealistic to believe we can fill all of the new jobs being created within the technology industry with the workers we have. I agree with those who call for increased educational programs. We should be developing new workers who can fully participate in the new economy and maintain our competitiveness.

Many business leaders like me are willing to step up to fully participate and support those programs. But they are long-term solutions. In the short term, limiting our ability to recruit skilled workers from a larger labor pool around the world only limits the growth of emerging companies and ultimately slows the economy. I hope Congress will give strong consideration to the importance of the H-1B program and support an increase in the annual cap on these visas.

STATEMENT OF CHARLES FOSTER, TINDALL & FOSTER, PC, BEFORE THE SUBCOMMITTEE ON IMMIGRATION AND CLAIMS OF THE HOUSE JUDICIARY COMMITTEE, AUGUST 5, 1999

...H-1B visas...today constitute one of the very few viable options for U.S. companies to recruit highly skilled professional employees for work in the United States. That is, given the lengthy process and extraordinary long delays in obtaining lawful permanent residency which result from meltdowns in both the Immigration and Naturalization Service (INS) and the Department of Labor (DOL), the only viable option for a U.S. company to legally hire a foreign national in a reasonable period of time has been to qualify professionals for temporary H-1B visas. You can be sure that U.S. companies would not seek foreign professionals if Americans were available. Their first choice and option has been and always will be the U.S. labor force....

H-1B Professionals are Used Throughout the U.S. Economy to Contribute Needed Skills and Talent That Otherwise Would be Unavailable in the United States.

...This hearing gives us the opportunity to highlight U.S. employers that are using and benefiting from the talents and skills of H-1B workers. For example:

A government contractor in Colorado has hired several H-1B engineers with expertise in the decommissioning and decontaminating of former nuclear weapons facilities. Their expertise is being used in the cleanup of several Department of Energy facilities that formerly were used in this nation's nuclear weapons complex.

A school in California devoted to teaching children with cerebral palsy has used the H-1B category to bring in several teachers from Hungary trained in a special technique (called "conductive therapy") that currently is unavailable in the United States. Parents of U.S. children helped by these teachers call their children's progress "miraculous."

Many of this country's leading pharmaceutical and biotechnology research companies and institutions hire H-1B scientists to work on projects ranging from cures for cancer and AIDS to developing safer and more effective drug delivery systems and surgical techniques.

...Manufacturing companies bring H-1B engineers to this country to introduce and train U.S. workers in technologies and manufacturing techniques currently not yet in use here, including the development of more environmentally friendly thin-film coating techniques for locking products,...better catalytic converter systems for automobile exhaust, and many other important areas.

One H-1B visa holder sponsored by a local university, trains teachers in inner city schools to utilize the Internet in the classroom. He developed learning Web sites for teachers and students and works with La Escuela Rice, which teaches primarily from Web-based curriculum. Through his efforts, he, the students, and teachers of Rice University have gone on to develop learning Web sites that have won awards ranging from *Texas Monthly's* "100 Best Web sites in Texas" to a very prestigious award from the Smithsonian Institution.

The Continued Availability of H-1B Workers Is Essential to the Growth of the U.S. Economy

...In fact, H-1B professionals often already are here. They are graduates of our colleges and universities who are undergoing periods of "practical training" in their specialties in the U.S. If unable to get H-1B visas, these individuals would be required to go abroad and would be unable to contribute their talents to U.S. companies. Instead, they would be hired by those companies' competitors outside of the U.S. Or, the U.S. companies that need their skills will move their operations or projects abroad, including the jobs that go with them, to where the individual can work.

Far from taking jobs away from U.S. workers, H-1B professionals actually *spur* job creation in this country, allowing U.S. companies to expand into new areas, both geographically and in terms of new products and services, and fill critical positions upon which many other jobs depend that are filled by Americans.... [T]he only thorough congressional study to date done on H-1B nonimmigrants in the U.S. was published by the General Accounting Office (GAO) in April 1992.... The GAO study, *Immigration and the Labor Market: Nonimmigrant Alien Workers in the United States,* stated: "One of the major purposes of the nonimmigrant work-related visas is to enable U.S. businesses to compete in a global economy. Increasingly, U.S. business[es] find themselves competing for international talent and for the 'best and brightest' around the world. **The nonimmigrant visa can be a bridge or a barrier to successful international competition by U.S. companies, depending on how the non-**immigrant visa categories are interpreted and administered" (emphasis added by Mr. Foster).

Challenges for the H-1B Program

Opponents of the H-1B visa...allege that there is a great deal of fraud in the program.... But allegations of widespread fraud are not backed up by fact....

Fraud and misrepresentation are real issues that must be addressed in order to maintain the integrity of the H-1B program. Yet [these issues] must be addressed in proportion to the scope of the problem.... Given limited resources, agencies should investigate only the most likely targets.... Referral for a full-fledged investigation should be undertaken only where there are multiple indicators of possible fraud in a case. This is especially true since most cases turn out to be bona fide.

STATEMENT OF CRYSTAL NEISWONGER, IMMIGRATION SPECIALIST FOR TRW INC., CLEVELAND, OHIO, BEFORE THE SUBCOMMITTEE ON IMMIGRATION AND CLAIMS OF THE HOUSE JUDICIARY COMMITTEE, AUGUST 15, 1999.

...I am pleased to appear before this subcommittee on behalf of the National Association of Manufacturers (NAM). NAM is the nation's largest and oldest multi-industry trade association. NAM represents 14,000 members including 10,000 small and mid-sized companies and 350 member associations serving manufacturers and employees in every industrial sector and all fifty states.

TRW Inc. is a global company focused on supplying advanced technology products and services to the automotive, aerospace, and information services marketplace. We are in the process of merging our recently acquired group of LucasVarityCompanies into TRW to become a $19 billion company with 130,000 employees by year end. I am honored to appear as a member of this panel to talk about the H-1B program and its importance to our company.

Since the inception of the H-1B program in 1952, TRW has selectively used H-1B visas. These visas are used to hire foreign nationals for specialty positions in our businesses, and also for shortage occupations for which we cannot find U.S. workers with equivalent experience and academic qualifications. In 1998, we used 36 H-1B visas, and up until July 1999, we had used 28....

...[S]ince 1995, it has become increasingly difficult for us to find U.S. candidates for positions requiring degrees in electrical, mechanical, industrial, and software engineering. U.S. colleges and universities lack American-born students who choose these majors and students who choose to pursue advanced degrees in these areas.

TRW recruiters who visit college campuses estimate that only three in ten resumes for our positions come from

U.S. persons. Consequently, the labor pool TRW and other global companies need to draw from is comprised overwhelmingly of foreign-born students attending American universities. On August 3, 1999, TRW listed 1,023 career opportunities on its website, www.trw.com. Using traditional recruitment methods such as newspaper advertisements and professional journals, and now the Internet, TRW recruiters are receiving no response to many of the ads placed, or are receiving resumes from individuals whose skills and education do not match the job requirements. We received only three resumes for an ad we ran in the Sunday *New York Times* for a chemical engineer with expertise in injection molding. Unfortunately, none of the applicants met the job requirements. In addition, we use "headhunters," open houses at our facilities and recruitment fairs to attract potential new hires. Even with this outreach, we continue to have hundreds of openings at TRW....

TRW has used the financial resources of the TRW Foundation and corporate resources to train and retrain its current workforce, and to finance a variety of educational initiatives to attract young people to the academic programs where workers are in short supply. Internally, we have a generous tuition reimbursement program, we offer fellowships to current employees, and we provide scholarships to children of TRW employees.

Since 1955, TRW's Foundation has donated approximately $100 million to non-profit organizations. For the last several years, Foundation support has been directed towards enhancing math and science curricula at the elementary and high school levels....

For the past five years, TRW has sent over 300 disadvantaged children from its plant communities, who have the potential to be high achievers, to a week of Space Camp at the U.S. Space and Rocket Center in Huntsville, Alabama. This program has documented that students who have experienced Space Camp improve their grades in math and science....

TRW has financially supported MATHCOUNTS, a unique nationwide program for middle school students since 1986. This program involves the on-site participation of TRW engineers who coach students in developing an appreciation for the critical need for mathematics in the workplace....

We have also sponsored high school teams to participate in the FIRST Competition, an international engineering competition designed to inspire young people to excel in math and science. This program partners high school math and science students with engineers to design and build a robot to perform particular objectives and compete against other teams in Orlando, Florida....

However, it will take several years to develop a pipeline of American students who pursue degrees in the engineering and math sciences that are now in short supply. In the meantime, the H-1B visa program is needed until we have an adequate supply of American workers.

REMARKS BY HARRIS N. MILLER, PRESIDENT, INFORMATION TECHNOLOGY ASSOCIATION OF AMERICA (ITAA), BEFORE THE SUBCOMMITTEE ON IMMIGRATION AND CLAIMS OF THE HOUSE JUDICIARY COMMITTEE, APRIL 21, 1998

...Responding to the short-term best interests of the U.S. economy, as well as U.S. companies, shareholders, and workers, is not a bad, immoral or evil thing. Rather, business immigration should be viewed as one important component of a much longer-term solution, a step complementing—not replacing—the need to help more Americans acquire the skills needed to compete in the information economy. It is also important to note that these skilled foreign workers create more economic opportunities for American workers. This is not a zero-sum game.

So let's begin with the good news: there has never been a better time to be an IT professional in America. The marketplace is confronted with a major shortage of appropriately skilled technical workers, and this gap between supply and demand has driven up wages, benefits, and opportunities for computer programmers, systems analysts, computer scientists and similarly skilled individuals. A recent study prepared for ITAA by Virginia Tech found that 346,000 slots for professionals in these categories are now unfilled. That equates to 1 out of 10 positions across the country—obviously a seller's market.

...Nice work if you can get it. But many Americans do not have the background, education, or skills to qualify for these assignments. Training is an important response to this unfortunate situation, and the high tech industry in the U.S. invests three times the national average in training per employee, according to the American Society for Training and Development (ASTD). ASTD finds high tech spending $911 per employee versus $300 to $500 for other industry categories. Last year, the IT industry spent $210 billion to field its work force, with much of this total going to investments in training and retraining. But even that monumental number is at best a partial answer. Newly trained people do not hit the ground running on Day 1. On the contrary, many assignments may take months or even years to master.

Companies do not have months or years to be productive. Product development cycles in the information technology industry can be as little as 12 months. We do not ask medical residents to conduct brain surgery or flight engineers to pilot the plane. We expect fully qualified professionals to fill these roles. Why expect any less from the people who design our information systems?...

100   The Government Should Raise the Annual Cap on H-1B...

Immigration and Illegal Aliens: Burden or Blessing?

...Software metrics expert Howard Rubin, chairman of the Computer Science Department at Hunter College, estimates that the talent shortage could be responsible for as much as $500 billion in lost corporate revenue every year. Rubin computes that total by calculating that every IT salary dollar can be expected to generate $43 in revenue. At an average wage of $55,000 per year, that equates to $2.4 million in lost revenue per employee or $500 billion nationwide.

Companies that cannot get the help they need will look at other options. In Texas, where as many as 15,000 high-tech jobs go unfilled, a Texas A&M University survey found that 40 percent of firms polled would consider locating or expanding outside the state if the work force shortage situation continues....

...While the flat-earth chorus drones on about an industry discriminating against its older workers, the data in the Labor Department's bi-annual studies of displaced workers say that the displacement rate for employees ages 45–54 is the same as employees ages 25–44. And when IT workers do lose their jobs, studies show that they find new jobs faster and with more money than their non-IT counterparts. And as for training, BLS [Bureau of Labor Statistics] statistics of company-provided formal and non-formal training show that workers in the 45 to 54 age group receive more training than their younger colleagues.

...The truth of the situation is that in 1996, the economy generated 135,000 new positions in the software industry alone—while universities produced only 36,000 computer science graduates. Simple math tells us that the new graduates could fill only 27 percent of available openings. So where did the remaining 73 percent come from? Many from the existing base of seasoned IT professionals.

The myth merchants have at least one part of their story correct. In 1997, the number of students enrolling in computer science programs rose, as did the number of new computer science graduates. The Computer Research Association's *Taulbee Survey,* measuring trends within universities offering doctoral degrees in computer science education, found 16,197 new enrollments and 7,586 undergraduate degrees granted in the 1996–1997 school year. That's up from 11,972 and 7,293 the previous year. Far from trying to suppress or hide this data, we say it is fantastic news—one indicator that our message is getting through. But we must also remember that this is one data point and that the number of degrees awarded between 1986 and 1994 dropped 43 percent.

...I understand it may be easier to point fingers and berate IT companies as greedy corporate pirates. But I also remember, even if others would rather forget that, in creating the H-1B program, Congress put in place the kind of controls that prevent employer abuses. In electing to hire a foreign worker, the employer must pay the higher of two wage rates: either the prevailing wage in the geographic area or the wage paid to other company employees performing the same work. Those wages must be posted on the company premises and the H-1B visa applications themselves are available for public inspection at the Department of Labor....

TESTIMONY OF DR. DANIEL L. SULLIVAN, SENIOR VICE PRESIDENT, HUMAN RESOURCES, QUALCOMM, INCORPORATED, BEFORE THE SUBCOMMITTEE ON IMMIGRATION AND CLAIMS OF THE HOUSE JUDICIARY COMMITTEE, APRIL 21, 1998

...Founded and headquartered in San Diego, California, QUALCOMM is recognized around the world as a leader in digital wireless telecommunications, with over $2.1 billion in annual sales, 500 patents (issued or pending), and 10,400 employees worldwide. The company develops, manufactures, markets, licenses, and operates advanced communications systems based on its wireless technologies....

...Much of QUALCOMM's success can be credited to the contributions of employees who came to the company as foreign nationals....

...They and others like them came to this country for opportunity—both in education, and in the workplace. America has long housed the world's preeminent technology companies and research universities, which are natural magnets for top international students. These engineers stayed because America gave them H-1B visas that allowed them to contribute to our economy before they became U.S. citizens.

...While legal immigrants make up only 5.5 percent of QUALCOMM's workforce, they are vital contributors to our success. Over the past several years, immigrants have become the bedrock of industry's technical workforce. Today the facts are unmistakable—American technology companies cannot compete globally without access to the top engineering and scientific talent, and that includes engineers and scientists drawn from an international pool of talent.

...QUALCOMM currently employs 476 H-1B workers, and a total of 572 workers on visas of all types. These workers, rather than taking jobs from American labor pools, are creating more jobs for U.S. workers through the application of their specialized skills.

...National trends reflect our experience. According to a 1994 report of the American Association of Engineering Societies, 33 percent of all Master of Science and 52 percent of all Ph.D. degrees conferred by U.S. institutions in the 1993/94 school year went to foreign nationals. Specific to the engineering field, this same report found that 824 of 1,597, or 52 percent, of Ph.D. degrees in electrical engineering went to foreign nationals.

To solve this problem over the long term, we must recognize that our educational system needs to fundamentally change in order to be globally competitive. To that end, QUALCOMM is actively involved in providing enhanced educational opportunities in math and science at all levels, to create highly skilled future U.S. engineers.

The troubling statistics about America's substandard student performance are predictors of the skill level of our graduates. U.S.-educated children don't learn math or science as quickly or as well as their counterparts around the globe. The last round of standardized tests for eighth graders places the U.S. seventeenth among all countries in science and twenty-eighth in mathematics proficiency—far behind countries like Singapore, South Korea, and Japan. Test scores of the very best U.S. students are competitive with "average" students in Asia and parts of Europe.

QUALCOMM is concerned with these trends—that's why our corporate philanthropy program is focused on K–12 education and why we regularly consult with our county's school districts on the future of educational policy and the needs of local industry....

...In addition to focusing on students, QUALCOMM is active in providing retraining for many of the engineers who were displaced when the defense industry fled San Diego. Forty percent of our total workforce is comprised of employees who previously worked in the military or aerospace industrial sector....

All of these efforts, however, do not mitigate our need to hire a relatively small, but critically important group of foreign nationals with advanced skills and education. Limiting the number of H-1B visas granted each year will only force U.S. companies to hire these students and settle them in their countries of origin, or in another country that doesn't have the same restrictions on incorporating highly skilled workers in its labor force.

TESTIMONY OF DR. RICHARD W. LARIVIERE, ASSOCIATE VICE PRESIDENT OF INTERNATIONAL PROGRAMS, UNIVERSITY OF TEXAS AT AUSTIN, BEFORE THE SUBCOMMITTEE ON IMMIGRATION AND CLAIMS OF THE HOUSE JUDICIARY COMMITTEE, APRIL 21, 1998

...I would like to tell the Subcommittee the importance of the H-1B program as it relates to colleges and universities, and to outline some difficulties in the implementation of the program. First, I want to emphasize that the role of H-1B workers on college and university campuses is essential. U.S. universities are the best in the world and, therefore, they draw both students and scholars from around the world. This is clearly beneficial for the students, in that they receive the best education the world can offer, and for scholars, who join a remarkably productive community of colleagues....

The presence of H-1B professionals in academia is an integral part of training and educating the American workforce.... Increasingly, U.S. students find themselves entering a global workforce, and exposure to foreign nationals while still in college is extremely beneficial to them and their employers. On campuses across the country, multinational teams of researchers perform cutting edge research in engineering, medicine, physics, economics, and many other fields....

The contributions of H-1B professionals at the post-graduate level fill a crucial need for U.S. academic institutions from an academic and training perspective. For example, H-1B professional scholars often work on collaborative efforts with U.S. researchers that contribute greatly to a specific field of knowledge, educate U.S. students and scholars, and, in many instances, create significant benefits for all of society. In this manner, H-1B professionals are directly passing on their knowledge to U.S. students and scholars. In some instances, H-1B professionals are the facilitators of learning in particular academic fields....

...The U.S. academic community is strongly committed to expanding the existing talent base of outstanding students and scholars from the U.S. and has actively pursued this mission for many years.... Despite our efforts to expand the U.S. talent base, we must also seek outstanding talent from other parts of the world to contribute to America's technological pre-eminence.

In education, as in business, the flow of human capital and ideas across borders is a key to success in a global society. From an academic perspective, H-1B professionals are essential not only to our mission of helping to create a highly skilled U.S. workforce, but to developing the ideas and training that will help guide U.S. academia and the U.S. workforce into the twenty-first century. An increase in the cap must occur soon, or the teaching and the research that take place on campuses will suffer again.

STATEMENT OF STEPHEN H. LEVEN, SENIOR VICE PRESIDENT, SEMICONDUCTOR GROUP, AND DIRECTOR, WORLDWIDE HUMAN RESOURCES, TEXAS INSTRUMENTS INCORPORATED, ON BEHALF OF THE AMERICAN ELECTRONICS ASSOCIATION, BEFORE THE SUBCOMMITTEE ON IMMIGRATION OF THE SENATE JUDICIARY COMMITTEE, FEBRUARY 25, 1998

...I am testifying today as a representative of Texas Instruments and on behalf of the 3,000 large and small companies that make up the American Electronics Association (AEA)....

...The high-technology industry added some 290,000 new jobs to the U.S. economy in the 1990s. Unfortunately, the future growth of our industry is being threatened by a limited supply of skilled workers.

...One of the questions I frequently hear is whether there really is a shortage of high-tech workers. There are many job classifications that fall under the heading "high tech," but one figure says it all to me. According to a 1996 study by the Engineering Workforce Commission of the American Association of Engineering Societies, National Center for Education Statistics, fewer than 20,000 Bachelor of Science Electrical Engineering degrees are awarded each year. This is about 10,000 fewer than in the 1980s.

Yet the needs of the high technology industry are growing. A 1996 *Forbes* magazine survey found that the top 10 semiconductor companies had more than 12,000 open positions.... [T]he U.S. Department of Commerce projected that one million new computer scientists, engineers, systems analysts, and programmers will be needed between 1994 and 2005. At Texas Instruments alone, we typically have more than 500 job requisitions for skilled talent outstanding at any one time, over 80 percent of which require a technical background.

...We hire foreign nationals not because they are a source of cheap labor—they are not—but because we need engineers to continue to grow in a fast-paced industry. TI needs more engineers than the supply of engineering graduates who are U.S. citizens....

As critical as foreign nationals are to our success, we recognize the vital need to encourage American children to go on in math and science. For some time, TI has been addressing this need through a number of initiatives ranging from Head Start through the university level....

...The solution to the shortage is not, as some have suggested, to cut access to foreign talent and wait while the promise of high wages pulls U.S. students through the pipeline. In an industry in which new and different products are developed every 18 months, we cannot afford to wait for a long-term solution and still remain competitive.

TESTIMONY OF KENNETH M. ALVARES, VICE PRESIDENT, HUMAN RESOURCES CORPORATE EXECUTIVE OFFICER, SUN MICROSYSTEMS, INC., BEFORE THE SUBCOMMITTEE ON IMMIGRATION OF THE SENATE JUDICIARY COMMITTEE, FEBRUARY 25, 1998

...Right now, Sun has 2,300 unfilled positions, 1,200 of which are in core information technology positions.... Sun hired 4,788 people last year, and we anticipate the need to bring on approximately 6,000 more people during this coming year. Unfortunately, with our growing need for skilled information technology workers outstripping the available supply, the numbers simply do not add up.

One source Sun has had to rely upon to make up for the relative shortage of skilled workers at home is the H-1B program. This program allows us to bring in professionals with particular sets of needed skills on a temporary basis. Sun gives employment priority to U.S. workers, but the small part of our total U.S. workforce comprised of foreign-born employees, such as those with temporary H-1B visas, is a critical element of our success....

...There are some who claim that the solution to this problem is simply to step up efforts in the areas of education and training. This is not enough, and, unfortunately, belief to the contrary is little more than an exercise in wishful thinking. Make no mistake, Sun believes strongly in cultivating American talent. We spend approximately $50 million per year on training and education efforts. That sum represents about 3 percent of our total annual payroll....

...But these efforts are inherently long-term approaches. It takes time for the fruits of these labors to develop. Until that time, there has to be a bridge to sustain us.

The answer for the short term is the H-1B worker....

...The information-technology industry is advancing at a whirlwind pace, with product cycles and time-to-market periods shortening and demands for continued innovation and productivity growing with each passing day. The shelf life of a typical product in our industry is only about one year ... and dropping. What we will offer to the world next year has not been invented today. In this environment you either get the RIGHT worker who can do the job and keep you ahead of the rest or you can call it a day....

I earlier referred to H-1B workers as a sort of stop-gap measure to help carry Sun through an interim period while we work to educate and train U.S. workers so they can fill needed positions. However, there is more to it than that. Many H-1B workers fill a particular, time-sensitive need for a very specialized set of skills or knowledge that is in short supply in the U.S. and cannot be covered by simply retraining some other worker

...Other H-1B workers are indispensable because of their unique experience with overseas conditions and markets. Those particular international professionals provide an asset that cannot be replaced by U.S. workers no matter how much extra training they receive....

CHAPTER 8

LEGISLATION TO INCREASE THE H-1B CAP IS NOT NECESSARILY THE ANSWER TO SOLVING THE WORKFORCE NEEDS OF THE INFORMATION TECHNOLOGY INDUSTRY

TESTIMONY OF FRANK BREHM, NORTHWEST REGIONAL COORDINATOR OF THE PROGRAMMER'S GUILD, BEFORE THE SUBCOMMITTEE ON IMMIGRATION AND CLAIMS OF THE HOUSE JUDICIARY COMMITTEE, MAY 25, 2000

Ten years ago the high-tech lobby approached Congress with a request to create a special class of visas for foreign programmers, healthcare workers, and engineers to compensate for what was ostensibly a shortage of suitable American workers. According to the Department of Labor, there is no credible evidence of a shortage of high-technology workers. Congress has, nonetheless, become convinced that it needs to act as America's largest temporary help agency and intervene in the supply and demand mechanisms of the United States labor market. Resulting H-1B legislation has been passed into law without the implementation of adequate safeguards for American high-tech workers.

No other workforce in history has faced the antagonism inherent in congressional attempts to weaken the position of high-tech workers in American society. It is imperative that our representatives avoid any further action on H-1B legislation until such time as the worker protections and information gathering provisions in the American Competitiveness and Workforce Improvement Act of 1998 [Public law 105-277] have been implemented by the [Clinton] Administration.

...Contrary to the promises of high-tech industry, as it becomes increasingly divorced from the realities of the U.S. labor market, it will continue to insist upon ever-larger labor entitlements of foreign high-tech professionals. Unless you, our representatives, gain the courage to wean high-tech CEOs from government dependence, America's software specialists will suffer the same unfortunate fate of U.S. agricultural and manufacturing workers.

Without the Documentation of U.S. Worker Recruitment provision in the American Competitiveness and Workforce Improvement Act of 1998, American high-tech workers will continue to be denied opportunities, which rightfully belong to them.

...Many in the business community say that the Documentation of Non-Displacement of U.S. Workers provision places an unnecessary burden upon employers. This provision, far from being an encompassing worker safeguard, is a diluted substitute for the type of protections which technical workers deserve....

Unfortunately, this provision offers no protection against a more subtle and perhaps larger form of displacement called "offshoring." When a corporation "offshores" workers, the firm brings on site one or more H-1B representatives from a foreign programming business, sometimes referred to as a "job shop." After the foreign programmer achieves competence, he or she begins to channel programming projects to...overseas co-workers at the parent firm. The U.S. corporation is then able to lay off what may be an entire department of American technical specialists....

Congress, in its H-1B haste to provide the private sector with an artificially high number of technical personnel vis-a-vis the market, has been proceeding from the assumption that the dynamics of a knowledge-based industry are similar to that of the commodity producing sector. Complex software is not a commodity, as it requires continuous updates after being sold.

Since 1991, H-1B legislation and its accompanying "offshoring" have led to a significant reduction in the cost to software firms of remedying software defects. Where once every software bug was fixed by a highly paid American programmer, today many of the same defects are handled by low-paid Asian programmers. In the year 2000, software defects in a product are far less injurious to a firm's return on investment (ROI) than was the case 15 years ago. The consumer suffers accordingly. Where once society feared the proverbial four horsemen of pestilence, plague, famine, and war, today we've added a fifth called new software, or the dreaded "dot oh" release. Increasing H-1B quotas are fast taking us from the digital age to the age of unexpected consequences.

At the same time that U.S. high-tech employers allege a shortage of available skilled workers, this country has amassed a surprising surplus of programmers over the age of 40 who are no longer practicing their craft. The requirement of a Report on Older Workers in the Information Technology Field will help to focus congressional attention on the reasons why workers have left what would otherwise appear to be well-paying jobs. As a nation we need to determine where these skilled workers have gone, and whether they left the profession voluntarily, or under the duress of age discrimination. We have available to us many credible studies documenting age discrimination in the software industry. The solution to the problem of age discrimination is fewer, not more, H-1B workers.

Recently, while enrolled in a programming class at a local college, I saw first-hand the difficulties American high-tech college students face when attempting to gain the necessary education for access to information technology careers. Many students were denied admission because a great many seats had been claimed by foreign students who were in our country on student or H-1B visas. The requirement in the American Competitiveness and Workforce Improvement Act for a Report on High Technology Labor Market Needs includes an analysis of the "needs of United States students." It is no secret that American colleges encourage large foreign enrollments in science, engineering, and computer disciplines. Our universities often deny American students admission to computer science study in favor of non-citizens, only to have industry subsequently claim "Americans don't want to work in high-tech!"

It is clear that American high-technology students and workers face a "triple threat" from the H-1B program. First, foreign students, many of whom receive a taxpayer-subsidized education at our finest universities, provide low-paid labor as teaching assistants, and arrive on our shores with the full intention of converting their student visas to H-1B visas upon graduation. Their presence in our universities, regardless of their academic aptitude, adds an extra burden to American students attempting to gain access to high-tech degree programs and classes.

Second, in violation of the intent of Congress, H-1B personnel compete directly with domestic workers for entry-level and advanced positions in high-technology companies.

Third, the process of using H-1B employees as Trojan horses to "offshore" jobs is no different than the process which has devastated American manufacturing industries. "Offshoring" took years to decimate the American manufacturing industry. Thanks to the H-1B program, "offshoring" has the potential to happen with much greater speed in the high-technology field.

Before we unknowingly surrender our prosperity and jobs in the high-tech industry, it is vital that our elected representatives ensure the worker protections in the American Competitiveness and Workforce Improvement Act become implemented as law....

TESTIMONY OF KEITH JACKSON, PHYSICIST, COALITION FOR FAIR EMPLOYMENT IN SILICON VALLEY, BEFORE THE SUBCOMMITTEE ON IMMIGRATION AND CLAIMS OF THE HOUSE JUDICIARY COMMITTEE, MAY 25, 2000

The Stanford Linear Accelerator Center (SLAC), which is managed for the Department of Energy, does not have a single African-American physicist on its technical staff. This would not be so remarkable except for the fact that Stanford University has produced the largest number of African-Americans with Ph.D.s in physics.

The exclusion of universities and non-profit research laboratories from the fees associated with the use of the H-1B workers would provide a financial incentive for these taxpayer-supported institutions to recruit from overseas.

There should be an examination of the impact of H-1B workers in government-supported research and development laboratories, particularly with regard to the inclusion of underrepresented protected classes. The fees generated by the ACWIA [American Competitiveness and Workforce Improvement Act] generated $80 million for scholarship, but government agencies spent close to $1 billion for tuition reimbursements and fellowships.

Compare this to the free higher education provided to students in most European nations. The graduate can then pursue graduate education in the United States in a scientific field and receive tuition, fees, and living expenses from the federal grant that his or her thesis advisor has received. After completing your Ph.D. with this subsidy, you can then be hired by a company who applies for an H-1B visa.

By comparison, the American student, particularly from underrepresented protected classes, must assume a debt approaching $50,000 beginning as an undergraduate. The combination of the end of affirmative action programs and the emphasis on loans instead of grants means that the American student must often work one or more jobs while studying.

The National Action Council for Minorities in Engineering has learned that two-thirds of the underrepresented minority students in engineering drop out of school because of the lack of financial aid.

106   Legislation to Increase the H-1B Cap is Not Necessarily...

Immigration and Illegal Aliens: Burden or Blessing?

You might have seen the section on young entrepreneurs in the Monday *Wall Street Journal*. The African-American entrepreneur on the last page had to start in community college, work, and then get to a four-year institution for a bachelor's degree.

Yet, students from abroad mentioned earlier in the section were able to go all the way to their terminal degree receiving a powerful boost into entrepreneurship....

TESTIMONY OF PAUL J. KOSTEK, PRESIDENT, INSTITUTE OF ELECTRICAL AND ELECTRONICS ENGINEERS-UNITED STATES OF AMERICA (IEEE-USA), BEFORE THE SUBCOMMITTEE ON IMMIGRATION AND CLAIMS OF THE HOUSE JUDICIARY COMMITTEE, AUGUST 5, 1999

IEEE-USA's Interest in the H-1B Specialty Occupation Visa Program

The Institute of Electrical and Electronics Engineers (IEEE) is a transnational technical professional society made up of more than 350,000 electrical, electronics, and computer engineers in 147 countries. IEEE-USA promotes the professional careers and technology policy interests of IEEE's 225,000 U.S. members.

...IEEE-USA's perspectives on high-tech workforce issues and continuing industry demands that Congress relax existing controls on employment-based admissions, both permanent and temporary, are the result of our members' personal experience with booms and busts in domestic engineering labor markets over the past 25 years.

Current Labor Markets for Engineers and Computer Specialists

The answer to the often-debated question of whether or not there is a shortage of core information technology workers (computer engineers and scientists, systems analysts and programmers) depends, in large part, on who you talk to.

Many employers in the public and private sectors—in academia and in industry—contend that the nation faces an endemic IT [information technology] worker shortage of crisis proportions. They point to declining enrollments and degree trends in engineering and computer science in the early 1990s and the failure of our elementary and secondary schools to prepare more students for high tech careers to support their contention that the supply of workers is and will continue to be insufficient to meet increasing world wide demands for trained technical professionals.

Most IT workers, and their professional societies—while acknowledging increasing demand and tight labor markets for workers with very highly specialized knowledge and skills—argue that the existing supply of technically trained personnel is much broader and deeper than is generally assumed.

Economists argue that tight labor markets and spot shortages of workers with very specific knowledge, skills and experience are inevitable short-term results of the information technology revolution that is sweeping the country and the world. Over the longer run, they insist that market forces will work to correct these imbalances.

Research by Carolyn Veneri, an economist at the Bureau of Labor Statistics, suggests that, although no single measure of occupational labor shortages exists, available data on unemployment rates, occupational employment growth, and wage increases can be used to assess the existence of or the potential for shortages.

Writing in the March 1999 issue of the *Monthly Labor Review,* Ms.Veneri hypothesized that if shortages in an occupation were to develop during the current expansion, the occupation's employment growth would be strong; the occupation's wages would increase relative to other occupations, indicating determined efforts by employers to attract more workers; and the unemployment rate for that occupation would decline and remain relatively low.

For the purposes of this research, 68 occupations were evaluated to determine whether, for the 1992–1997 period, the occupation's employment growth rate was at least 50 percent faster than average employment growth; the wage increase was at least 30 percent faster than the average; and the occupation's unemployment rate was at least 30 percent below average.

Despite the remarkable increase in economic growth between 1992 and 1997 (much of which is attributable to advances in information technology), only seven of the 68 occupations met all three of these criteria: management analysts; special education teachers; dental hygienists; marketing, advertising and public relations managers; airplane pilots and navigators; purchasing agents; and mechanical engineers.

Although unemployment rates for core IT occupations, including computer engineers and scientists, systems analysts, and programmers, have been consistently lower than the national rates (for other occupations) over the 1992–1997 period, none exhibited higher than average employment growth or higher than average growth in wages when compared with all other professional specialty occupations.

IEEE-USA doesn't think this kind of evidence supports industry pleadings for another increase in H-1B admissions ceilings!

Responsiveness of Information Technology Labor Markets

None of this is to suggest that demand for core IT workers has not increased significantly in recent years and won't continue to grow in the years immediately ahead. But national labor markets are already responding to increasing demands.

After several years of declines, educational enrollments are increasing in IT-related disciplines. Bachelor's level enrollments in computer engineering and computer science, for example, have more than doubled in the past three years.

Universities and community colleges are responding to employers' needs with specialized IT training programs and proprietary school and company-sponsored IT certification programs are growing in number and popularity.

Many employers are increasing on-the-job training and more IT professionals are taking steps to update their technical, managerial and communications knowledge and skills.

Congressional proposals to extend the expiring income tax exclusion for employer-provided educational assistance and establish an information technology training tax credit will provide additional public support for these important educational activities.

Stakeholders from the public and private sectors are working together to organize innovative, industry-education-community partnerships and skills alliances to expand IT training opportunities for U.S. workers at the state, regional and local levels.

IEEE-USA believes that this robust labor market response mitigates the need for yet another increase in H-1B admissions ceilings!...

Opportunities for Underrepresented Groups

Despite modest gains since the late 1980s, women, certain ethnic minorities, the handicapped and economically disadvantaged Americans are seriously underrepresented in many scientific and engineering fields. And although the proportion of women, blacks, Hispanics and [American Indians] in high school graduating classes is increasing, such individuals continue to be much less likely than white males to pursue careers in these fields.

Among the impediments to greater participation by underrepresented groups include inadequate educational preparation in math and science at the elementary and secondary educational levels, low expectations and non-supportive attitudes on the part of many educators and a lack of opportunities for mentoring relationships in traditionally white male-dominated professions and occupations.

Increasing utilization of talented foreign nationals—to help fill classes and perform teaching and research functions at the nation's colleges and universities, as well as to work in industry—also limits opportunities for traditionally under-represented citizens to obtain the knowl-edge and skills needed for productive employment and advancement in the nation's high tech sector.

Another reason not to support another increase in H-1B admissions ceilings at this time!

The H-1B Program Should be Repaired Rather Than Expanded

Based on findings presented in a 1996 Inspector General's report and at recent hearings before this committee, IEEE-USA strongly recommends that Congress take steps to repair the badly flawed H-1B and other employment-based admissions programs before it even thinks about another increase in visa caps.

In 1996 the Inspector General at the Department of Labor audited the Department's role in the administration of two important employment-based admissions programs: the permanent labor certification (PLC) and the temporary, H-1B labor condition attestation (LCA) programs.

He found that "while the Employment and Training Administration is doing all it can within its authority, the PLC and the LCA programs do not protect U.S. workers' jobs or wages and that neither meets its legislative intent. DOL's role amounts to little more than a paper shuffle for the PLC program and a rubber stamping for LCA applications."

To date, Congress has done little to remedy problems identified in the 1996 report. Earlier this year, the House Judiciary Subcommittee on Immigration and Claims held hearings at which witnesses from the Immigration and Naturalization Service and the Department of State introduced evidence of pervasive fraud by petitioning employers and individual applicants in the H-1B and the L (Intra-Company Transfer) visa programs.

As Subcommittee Chairman Smith put it just last week, "When 45 percent of H-1B visa applications examined at one consulate in India could not be verified and 21 percent were fraudulent, we have a serious problem in the H-1B program."

Conclusions and Recommendations

...In the absence of reliable statistics to support industry's contention that there is a serious national shortage of core information technology workers, ...there is insufficient empirical evidence to justify another increase in H-1B admissions ceilings at this time.

Our concerns are compounded by very credible evidence suggesting that the H-1B visa program and other employment-based admissions programs do not include appropriate, effective, enforceable safeguards for employment opportunities, wages and working conditions for U.S. workers, including citizens, permanent residents and foreign nationals who have been legally admitted to work temporarily in the United States. Until such time as these

108   Legislation to Increase the H-1B Cap is Not Necessarily...

Immigration and Illegal Aliens: Burden or Blessing?

deficiencies have been corrected, there should be no further increase in employment-based admissions....

STATEMENT OF JOHN R. FRASER, DEPUTY WAGE AND HOUR ADMINISTRATOR, EMPLOYMENT STANDARDS ADMINISTRATION, U.S. DEPARTMENT OF LABOR, BEFORE THE SUBCOMMITTEE ON IMMIGRATION AND CLAIMS OF THE HOUSE JUDICIARY COMMITTEE, APRIL 21, 1998

...Our information technology (IT) industry is essential to our continuing strong economic growth and wider prosperity....

...While there is no dispute that there is strong growth in demand for workers in the IT industry, it is much less clear what may be the magnitude of any shortage of skilled U.S. workers to meet this demand, or whether the domestic labor market will be able—as it has over the last decade—to satisfy projected job growth.

...Employment opportunities for computer systems analysts, engineers, and scientists have been growing by 10 percent a year—well above the growth of comparable occupations—and are expected to continue growing at a comparable rate through 2006. The Bureau of Labor Statistics (BLS) predicts that the U.S. will require more than 1.3 million new workers in IT core occupations between 1996 and 2006 to fill job openings projected to occur due to growth and the need to replace workers who leave the labor force or transfer to other occupations.

The IT skills shortage issue is somewhat controversial. Some industry advocates assert that there exist more than 300,000 unfilled jobs within the IT industry, and that these vacancies are raising business costs and hurting U.S. competitiveness....

On the other hand, critics argue that the IT industry (1) overstates the problem by producing inflated job vacancy data and equating it to skills shortages; (2) continues to lay off tens of thousands of workers (e.g., Intel, Netscape, Cypress Semiconductor, and Silicon Graphics recently announced large lay-offs); and (3) fails to tap reservoirs of available talent by insisting on unnecessarily specific job requirements and not providing more training to develop incumbent workers' skills.

One point of contention is the confusion between equating job vacancies and actual skills shortages. While an industry association-sponsored survey indicates that there may be as many as 350,000 job vacancies in the IT industry, as you will hear, the General Accounting Office (GAO) has concluded that this does not necessarily signal an acute shortage of skilled workers. In fact, most industries and firms (particularly those with rapid employment growth and high worker turnover) will have large numbers of job openings that may not indicate skills shortages.

...We strongly urge that any decision to raise the H-1B visa cap carefully consider the possible adverse impact of such a move on the normal process by which labor markets adjust to a growing demand for workers. The labor market should be permitted to adjust to this increased demand without introducing unnecessary factors which could delay, if not prevent, these normal market adjustments. Indeed, the IT labor market has already begun to respond to the signals of increased demand. A survey of U.S. Ph.D. departments of computer science and computer engineering showed bachelor-level enrollments were up 46 percent in 1996 and another 39 percent in 1997—nearly doubling over the two-year period.

It is also important to remember that tight labor markets are good for U.S. workers.... [T]ight labor markets create incentives for employers and workers to react in ways needed to achieve many of the Nation's top priorities: raising wages; providing greater opportunities for lifelong learning; and moving welfare recipients, out-of-school youth, and dislocated workers into jobs.

However, while tight labor markets are good for U.S. workers, labor markets can sometimes be slow to respond to skills shortages. In these circumstances, it is often argued that temporary foreign workers are needed in the short-term to provide necessary skills while the labor market adjusts to provide U.S. workers with the requisite training. Without needed foreign temporary workers, industries experiencing skills shortages may adjust in ways that do not serve the short-term or long-term priorities of the country, either by reducing job creation or by moving jobs overseas. Further, because the IT sector is so critical to our global competitive edge, the U.S. economy could suffer disproportionate harm if skills shortages do become acute.

...We must also be cognizant that raising the H-1B cap may subvert the protection of U.S. workers that is one of the key principles underlying this Administration's strong support of legal immigration. Raising the H-1B cap will almost certainly increase permanent employment-based legal immigration and, perhaps, illegal immigration. Nearly half of those who become permanent employment-based immigrants convert from H-visa nonimmigrant status. Rather than filling a temporary labor shortage, conversion fills permanent jobs that will then not be available to U.S. workers and students who we want to be able and prepared to fill high-tech jobs in our economy.

...The Administration believes that our first response to meeting the workforce needs of the IT industry should be to provide the needed skills to U.S. workers to qualify them for IT jobs....

In sum, ...our assessment of the likely effects of raising the H-1B cap reconfirms our strong conviction that our primary public policy response to skills mismatches due to changing technologies and economic restructuring must be to prepare the U.S. workforce to meet new demands. Yet we recognize that short-term demands for skills may require that we develop a balanced, short-term response to meet urgent needs while we actively adjust to rapidly changing circumstances. However, increased numbers of temporary foreign workers should be the last— not the first—public policy response to skills shortages.... [L]et me now turn to the ...pressing need for reform of the H-1B nonimmigrant program.

...[T]here exist serious structural flaws in the current H-1B program. These flaws are documented in a May 1996 report by the Department's Inspector General (IG)....

...The IG found that, despite the legislative intent, "... the [H-1B] program does not always meet urgent, short-term demand for highly skilled, unique individuals who are not available in the domestic work force. Instead, it serves as a probationary try-out employment program for illegal aliens, foreign students, and foreign visitors to determine if they will be sponsored for permanent status."

The IG also found that "some [H-1B] employers use alien labor to reduce payroll costs either by paying less than the prevailing wage to their own alien employees or treating these aliens as independent contractors, thereby avoiding related payroll and administrative costs." It found, in addition, that "other [H-1B] employers are 'job shops' whose business is to provide H-1B alien contract labor to other employers." The IG concluded that the H-1B program does little to protect the jobs or wages of U.S. workers, and it recommended eliminating the current program and establishing a new program to fulfill Congress's intent.

...Because current law does not require any test for the availability of qualified U.S. workers in the domestic labor market, many of the visas under the current cap of 65,000 can be used by employers to hire foreign workers for purposes other than meeting a skills shortage. In addition, current law does not require a U.S. employer to promise not to lay off U.S. workers and replace them with H-1B workers as a condition for gaining access to these foreign temporary workers, and it allows employers to retain H-1B workers for up to six years to fill a "temporary" need. We simply do not believe this is right.

...[L]et me conclude by restating that the growing workforce needs of the IT industry can only be met—and the strength and growth of the industry secured in the long run—if we take the steps needed to fully develop and utilize the skills of U.S. workers. Increased reliance on temporary foreign workers should, at most, only be a small part of the solution and must be viewed as a minor complement to the development of the U.S. workforce. Further, let me repeat that reform of the H-1B program is essential to eliminating abuses under the program and

providing appropriate protections for U.S. workers. Enactment of these reforms would effectively allocate a greater share of H-1B visas to employers facing actual skills shortages.

PREPARED STATEMENT OF WILLIAM S. PAYSON, PRESIDENT AND CEO OF THE SENIOR STAFF JOB INFORMATION EXCHANGE, INC., BEFORE THE SUBCOMMITTEE ON IMMIGRATION AND CLAIMS OF THE HOUSE JUDICIARY COMMITTEE, APRIL 21, 1998

...I am not a computer technologist. I have been a management and marketing consultant for over 40 years. I started The Senior Staff for one simple reason: At age 70, I couldn't find a job. So I created one. And here's what I have learned in the last five years:

The largest untapped resource of skill and talent in America is the professional workforce over 50 (Payson's italics).

This resource is ignored by many employers, especially high-technology companies who are notoriously youth-oriented and dedicated to the proposition that anyone over 35 is "over the hill." Such attitudes are wholly unwarranted and totally unsupported by facts.

...In my opinion, there are three reasons—in addition to the...simplistic prejudices of ageism—why the high-tech industry prefers foreign workers to America's professional workforce over 50:

1. Foreign workers are cheaper.

2. Foreign workers are easier to hoodwink.

3. Foreign workers are so anxious to come to America that they willingly accept long hours, high pressure, and minimum benefits.

Utilizing the experience, skill, and talent of the professional workforce over 50 will help all Americans meet the challenges of the twenty-first century.

STATEMENT OF DAVID A. SMITH, DIRECTOR OF POLICY OF THE AFL-CIO, BEFORE THE SUBCOMMITTEE ON IMMIGRATION AND CLAIMS OF THE HOUSE JUDICIARY COMMITTEE, APRIL 21, 1998

...The real issue before you today is not whether or not the cap on H-1B immigration should be raised, but whether or not the American employers and the American government consider American workers valuable enough to afford them the opportunity to train for and get well-paying, secure jobs....

The appropriate long-term approach to current and future labor shortages lies in the development of effective, efficient training and education programs that help

American workers to gain new skills. Any temporary guestworker program should be limited to those rare instances where there truly is a demonstrated, urgent, short-term labor shortage that cannot be immediately addressed. We must not overreact to the unproven claim of the IT industry that such a shortage exists today and that we, therefore, must expand a seriously flawed program.

...According to the Immigration and Naturalization Service (INS), over half of all approved H-1B visas were granted last year to information technology firms. In fact, 7 out of the top 10 H-1B employers are not just IT firms, they are IT temporary contractors. These contractors continue to reap millions off of cheap foreign labor while American workers miss opportunities....

...Americans can be easily trained for the skills reasonably necessary for IT jobs. Many American workers rely on computers everyday in their course of work. Contrary to the claims of the IT industry, not every job in this category requires a degree in computer science, or an advanced degree of any kind. In 1993, only one-third of recent college graduates in the field of computer science or programming ...had a degree in computer science. Less than two years of additional training will prepare American workers for many of jobs experiencing a labor shortage.

We believe the Administration should use this opportunity to bring together employers, educators, and labor to develop education and training programs to enhance the skills of U.S. workers to meet the industry's employment needs....

...In closing, I point out to you that the IT industry is fully capable of addressing its labor needs through recruitment and training and, in fact, will do so when they do not have the option of importing foreign labor. I would like to read to you an excerpt from the web page of Mastech Corporation, a firm which, according to the Immigration and Naturalization Service, uses the highest number of H-1B workers in the U.S. In response to a labor shortage, the web page states Mastech took the following action: "In response to this attrition problem, the company increased its U.S. recruiting efforts, enhanced its training programs, and worked with the Department of Labor to revise its filing procedures to resolve the delays. As a result of these initiatives, the company's employee attrition rate returned to normal historical levels in September 1996 and have remained at such levels since that date." Legislation increasing the H-1B cap is not the answer to solving a labor shortage. Utilizing American workers is the long-term solution.

TESTIMONY OF DR. ROBERT I. LERMAN, DIRECTOR, HUMAN RESOURCES POLICY CENTER, URBAN INSTITUTE, AND PROFESSOR OF ECONOMICS, AMERICAN UNIVERSITY, BEFORE THE SUBCOMMITTEE ON IMMIGRATION OF THE SENATE JUDICIARY COMMITTEE, FEBRUARY 25, 1998

I am happy to address the committee about the labor market for information technology workers and immigration policy....

The key points of the testimony are these:

The evidence is far from conclusive about the existence of a serious shortage, especially among some segments of the IT labor market. Employment growth has been rapid among computer engineers, data base administrators, and computer support specialists but not among computer programmers. Most importantly, the trends in real wages do not indicate the rapid growth in compensation that would suggest a market in which employers are attempting to adjust to a labor shortage.

Workers enter the IT field from many fields; only a modest share of IT workers require computer science degrees. Moreover, a very large share of those working in IT fields move to other fields frequently. If the industry could keep more of their incumbent workers, they would [have] a less difficult task filling positions.

The expansion of job opportunities in the IT field should stimulate enhanced public-private initiatives to attract workers to the field through expanded training, the development of clear career pathways and skill standards, and the expansion of youth apprenticeships and career academies. In addition, the public sector should encourage collaboration between employers of IT workers and community colleges and other post-secondary institutions to create a curriculum for use in medium-term and long-term programs that is well-tailored for IT careers.

Government policy makers should be cautious about short-term efforts to expand the supply of workers, especially by increasing the number of immigrant visas. Given the boom and bust cycles often observed in these fields, by the time the government acts to increase supply, the market may have already shifted from an excess demand to excess supply stage. Expanded immigration may have another counterproductive impact. It may deter prospective students from choosing an IT career when they hear that potential immigrants entering the field will gain special access to visas.

MAPS OF THE WORLD

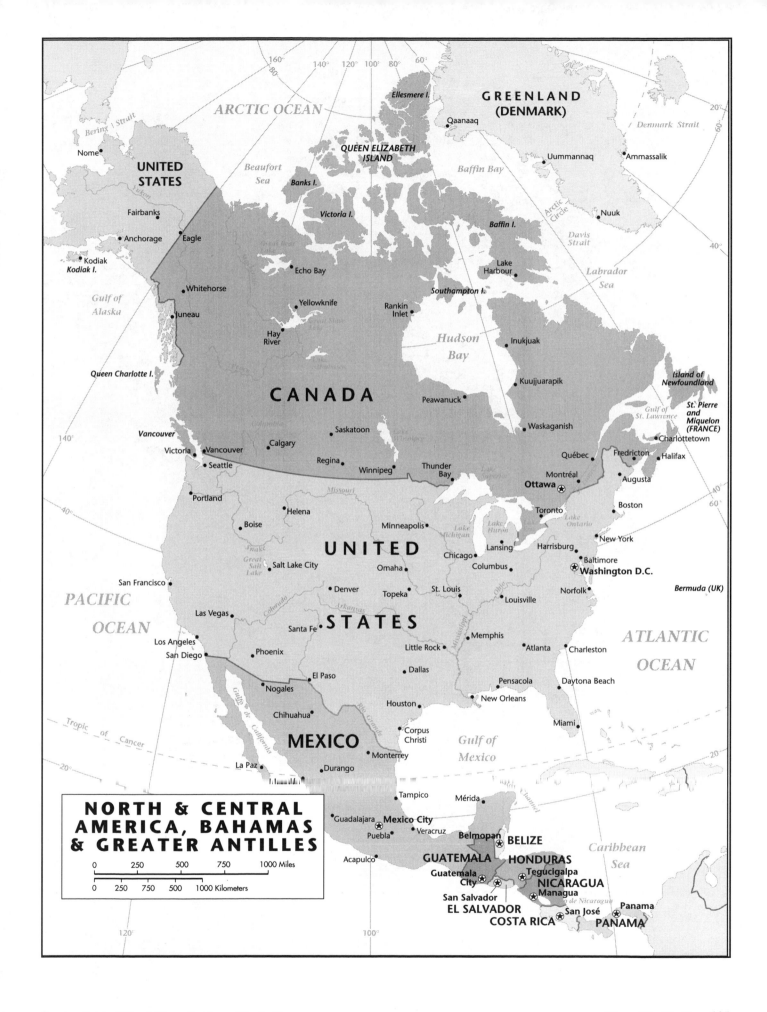

NORTH & CENTRAL AMERICA, BAHAMAS & GREATER ANTILLES

0   250   500   750   1000 Miles

0   250   750   500   1000 Kilometers

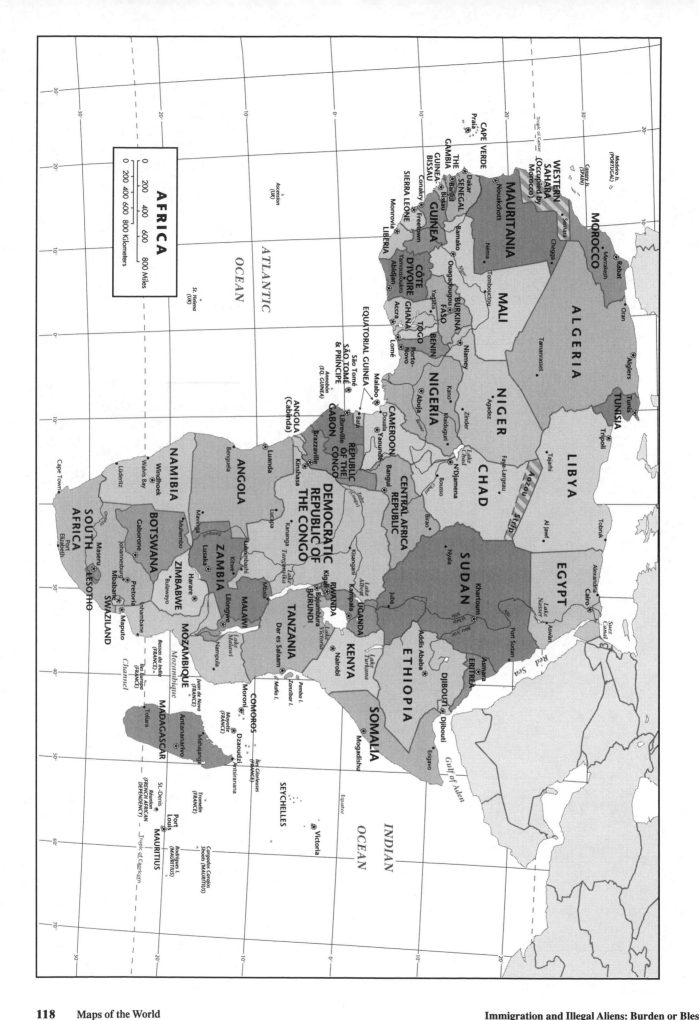

AFRICA

0   200 400 600 800 Kilometers
0   200 400 600 800 Miles

ATLANTIC OCEAN

Madeira Is. (PORTUGAL)

Tropic of Cancer

CAPE VERDE
Praia

THE GAMBIA
GUINEA-BISSAU
SENEGAL
Dakar
Banjul
Bissau
Conakry
Freetown
SIERRA LEONE
Monrovia
LIBERIA
CÔTE D'IVOIRE
GUINEA
Abidjan
Yamoussoukro
Accra
GHANA
Lomé
TOGO
Porto-Novo
BENIN
BURKINA FASO
Ouagadougou
Bamako
Nouakchott
MAURITANIA
Néma
Chegga
Tombouctou
MALI
Niamey
NIGER
Agadez
Zinder
Kano
Maiduguri
NIGERIA
Abuja
Yaoundé
Douala
CAMEROON
Bangui
CENTRAL AFRICA REPUBLIC
N'Djamena
Bousso
Bilma
Faya-Largeau
CHAD
Lake Chad
Tamanrasset
ALGERIA
Oran
Algiers
MOROCCO
Marrakesh
Rabat
WESTERN SAHARA (Occupied by Morocco)
Samara
Ceuta

TUNISIA
Tunis
Tripoli
LIBYA
Tajarhi
Al Jawf
Tobruk
EGYPT
Alexandria
Cairo
Aswan
Lake Nasser
Port Sudan
Red Sea
Suez Canal

Aozou Strip

Ascension (UK)

St. Helena (UK)

EQUATORIAL GUINEA
SÃO TOMÉ & PRÍNCIPE
São Tomé
Annobón (EQ. GUINEA)
Malabo
Bata
GABON
Libreville
REPUBLIC OF THE CONGO
Brazzaville
Kinshasa
DEMOCRATIC REPUBLIC OF THE CONGO
ANGOLA (Cabinda)
Luanda
Benguela
ANGOLA
Lucapa
Kananga
Kisangani
Mbuji-Mayi
Lubumbashi
Kitwe
ZAMBIA
Lusaka
Zaire (Congo)

NAMIBIA
Windhoek
Walvis Bay
Lüderitz
Muhembo
Mavinga
BOTSWANA
Gaborone
SOUTH AFRICA
Cape Town
Port Elizabeth
Johannesburg
Pretoria
Mbabane
SWAZILAND
LESOTHO
Maseru
Orange

ZIMBABWE
Harare
Bulawayo
MOZAMBIQUE
Inhambane
Maputo
MALAWI
Lilongwe
Lake Malawi
Nampula
Juan de Nova (FRANCE)
Bassas da India (FRANCE)
Îles Europa (FRANCE)

SUDAN
Khartoum
Nyala
White Nile
Blue Nile
Nile
Juba
Addis Ababa
ETHIOPIA
ERITREA
Asmara
DJIBOUTI
Djibouti
Erigavo
Gulf of Aden
SOMALIA
Mogadishu
KENYA
Nairobi
Lake Turkana
Lake Victoria
Lake Albert
UGANDA
Kampala
RWANDA
Kigali
BURUNDI
Bujumbura
Lake Tanganyika
TANZANIA
Dar es Salaam
Pemba I.
Zanzibar I.
Mafia I.

INDIAN OCEAN

MADAGASCAR
Toliara
Antananarivo
Mahajanga
Antsiranana
Mozambique Channel
COMOROS
Moroni
Dzaoudzi
Mayotte (FRANCE)
Îles Glorieuses (FRANCE)
Tromelin (FRANCE)

SEYCHELLES
Victoria
Equator

St.-Denis
Réunion (FRENCH AFRICAN DEPENDENCY)
Port Louis
MAURITIUS
Rodrigues I. (MAURITIUS)
Cargados Carajos Shoals (MAURITIUS)
Tropic of Capricorn

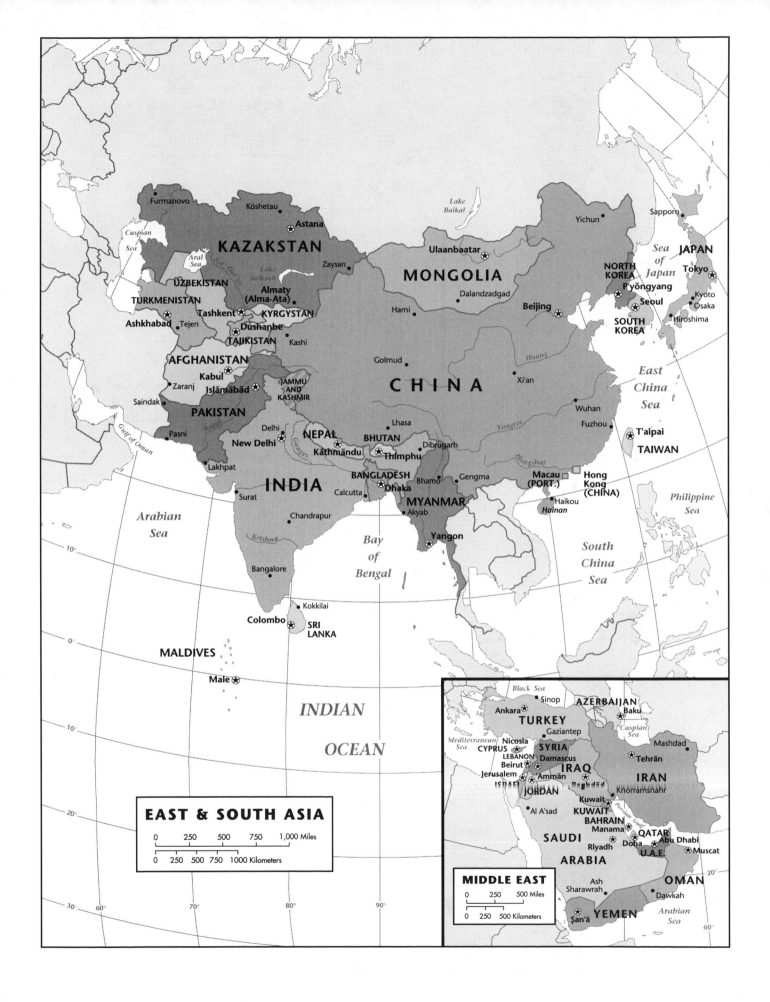

EAST & SOUTH ASIA

0   250   500   750   1,000 Miles

0   250 500 750 1000 Kilometers

MIDDLE EAST

0   250   500 Miles

0   250   500 Kilometers

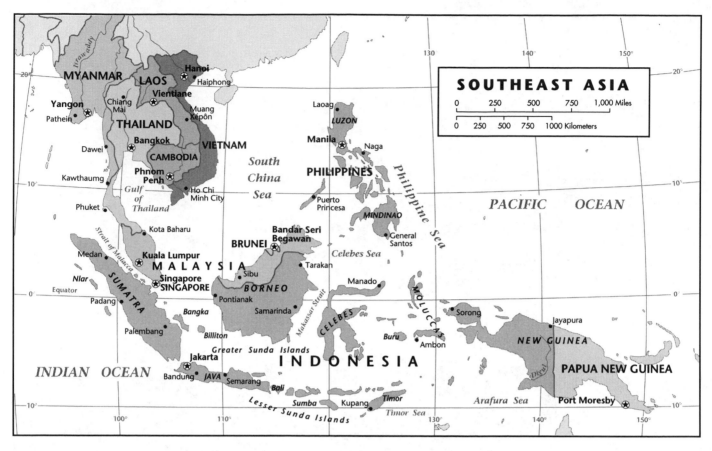

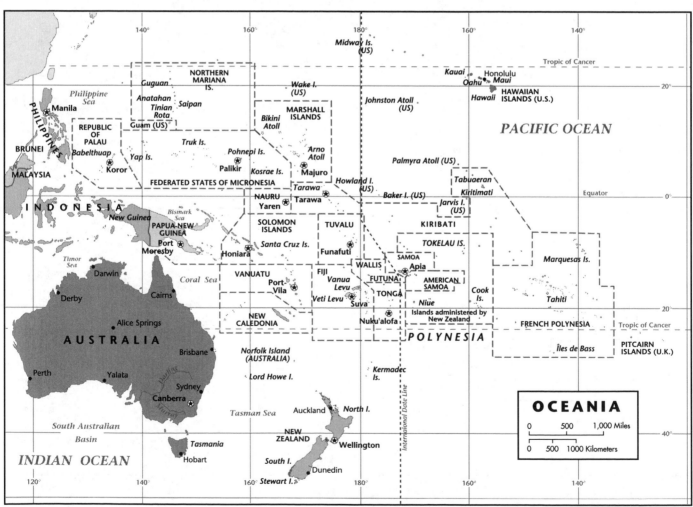

Immigration and Illegal Aliens: Burden or Blessing?

IMPORTANT NAMES AND ADDRESSES

American Civil Liberties Union (ACLU)
125 Broad St., 18th Floor
New York, NY 10004-2400
(212) 549-2500
E-mail: aclu@aclu.org
URL: http://www.aclu.org

American Immigration Lawyers Association (AILA)
918 F St. NW
Washington, D.C. 20004-1400
(202) 216-2400
FAX: (202) 371-9449
E-mail: webmaster@aila.org
URL: http://www.aila.org

American Refugee Committee
430 Oak Grove St., Suite 204
Minneapolis, MN 55403
(612) 872-7060
FAX: (612) 607-6499
E-mail: archq@archq.org
URL: http://www.archq.org/

The Cato Institute
1000 Massachusetts Ave. NW
Washington, D.C. 20001-5403
(202) 842-0200
FAX: (202) 842-3490
E-mail: cato@cato.org
URL: http://www.cato.org

Center for Immigration Studies
1522 K St. NW, #820
Washington, D.C. 20005-1202
(202) 466-8185
FAX: (202) 466-8076
E-mail: center@cis.org
URL: http://www.cis.org

Church World Service
28606 Phillips St.
P.O. Box 968
Elkhart, IN 46515
(800) 297-1516

FAX: (219) 262-0966
E-mail: cws@ncccusa.org
URL: http://www.churchworldservice.org

Episcopal Migration Ministries
Episcopal Church Center
815 Second Ave.
New York, NY 10017
(212) 867-8400
(800) 334-7626
URL: http://www.ecusa.anglican.org/emm

Ethiopian Community Development Council
1038 S. Highland St.
Arlington, VA 22204
(703) 685-0510
FAX: (703) 685-0529
E-mail: ecdc@erols.com
URL: http://www.ecdcinternational.org

The Federation for American Immigration Reform (FAIR)
1666 Connecticut Ave. NW
Washington, D.C. 20009
(202) 328-7004
FAX: (202) 387-3447
E-mail: info@fairus.org
URL: http://www.fairus.org

Hebrew Immigrant Aid Society
333 Seventh Ave.
New York, NY 10001-5004
(212) 967-4100
FAX: (212) 967-4483
E-mail: info@hias.org
URL: http://www.hias.org

Human Rights Watch
350 Fifth Ave., 34th Floor
New York, NY 10118-3299
(212) 290-4700
FAX: (212) 736-1300
E-mail: hrwnyc@hrw.org
URL: http://www.hrw.org

International Committee of the Red Cross
(For U.S.A. and Canada)
2100 Pennsylvania Ave. NW, Suite 545
Washington, D.C. 20037
(202) 293-9430
E-mail: washington.was@icrc.com
URL: http://www.icrc.org

International Immigrants Foundation
1435 Broadway, 2nd Floor
New York, NY 10018-1909
(212)) 302-2222
FAX: (212) 221-7206
E-mail: info@10.org
URL: http://www.10.org

Lutheran Immigration and Refugee Service
700 Light St.
Baltimore, MD 21230
(410) 230-2700
FAX: (410) 230-2890
E-mail: lirs@lirs.org
URL: http://www.lirs.org/

Migration and Refugee Services
United States Catholic Conference
3211 4th St. NE
Washington, D.C. 20017-1194
(202) 541-3352
FAX: (202) 722-8750
E-mail: mrs@nccbuscc.org
URL: http://www.nccbuscc.org/mrs

National Council of La Raza
1111 19th St. NW, #1000
Washington, D.C. 20036
(202) 785-1670
FAX: (202) 776-1792
E-mail: info@nclr.org
URL: http://www.nclr.org

National Immigration Forum
220 I St. NE, #220
Washington, D.C. 20002-4362

(202) 544-0004
FAX: (202) 544-1905
URL: http://www.immigrationforum.org

United Nations High Commissioner for Refugees
1775 K St. NW, Suite 300
Washington, D.C. 20006-1502
(202) 296-5191
FAX: (202) 296-5660
E-mail: usawa@unhcr.ch
URL: http://www.unhcr.ch

Urban Institute
2100 M St. NW
Washington, D.C. 20037
(202) 833-7200
FAX: (202) 223-3043
E-mail: paffairs@ui.urban.org
URL: http://www.urban.org

U.S. Census Bureau
Washington, D.C. 20233
(301) 457-3030

FAX: (301) 457-3620
URL: http://www.census.gov

U.S. Department of Health and Human Services
Office of Refugee Resettlement
370 L'Enfant Promenade SW
Washington, D.C. 20447
(202) 401-9246
FAX: (202) 401-5487
URL: http://www.acf.dhhs.gov/programs/orr

U.S. Department of Justice
Immigration and Naturalization Service
425 I St. NW
Washington, D.C. 20536
(202) 514-1900
FAX: (202) 514-3296
URL: http://ww.ins.usdoj.gov

U.S. Department of Labor
Bureau of International Labor Affairs
200 Constitution Ave. NW
Room S-2235
Washington, D.C. 20210

(202) 693-4770
URL: http://www.dol.gov/dol/ilab

U.S. Department of State
Bureau of Population, Refugees, and Migration
2401 E St. NW, Suite L-505, SA-1
Washington, D.C. 20522-0105
(202) 647-8472
E-mail: askpublicaffairs@state.gov
URL: http://www.state.gov/g/prm

U.S. House Committee on the Judiciary
Subcommittee on Immigration and Claims
B370B Rayburn House Office Bldg.
Washington, D.C. 20515
(202) 225-5727
URL: http://www.house.gov/judiciary

U.S. Senate Committee on the Judiciary
Subcommittee on Immigration
Room SD-323.
Dirksen Senate Office Bldg.
Washington, D.C. 20510
(202)) 224-6098
URL: http://www.senate.gov/~judiciary

RESOURCES

The United States government provides most of the statistical information concerning immigration and naturalization. The primary government source is the Immigration and Naturalization Service (INS), an agency of the U.S. Department of Justice. The annual *Statistical Yearbook of the Immigration and Naturalization Service* (2000) is the most complete statistical compilation available on immigrants, illegal aliens, and refugees who come to the United States. The INS also published the *Annual Estimates of the Unauthorized Immigrant Population Residing in the United States and Components of Change: 1987 to 1997* (a draft report; 2000), *Estimates of the Unauthorized Immigrant Population Residing in the United States: October 1996* (1997), *Border Patrol FY 2000 Recruiting and Hiring Report* (2000), the annual report *Legal Immigration, Fiscal Year 1998* (1999), *Illegal Alien Resident Population* (1999), and the *Estimates of the Unauthorized Immigrant Population Residing in the United States: October 1996* (1997).

Immigration control and administration is primarily the function of the INS; but, because immigration affects so many areas, several other government agencies are also involved. The Office of Refugee Resettlement of the U.S. Department of Health and Human Services (DHHS) monitors the nation's efforts to resettle incoming refugees. *Making a Difference: FY 1998 Annual Report to Congress* (2000) reviews the refugee situation and analyzes the impact and financial cost of refugee admissions. The DHHS also published *Temporary Assistance for Needy Families (TANF) Program: Third Annual Report to Congress* (2000). The Bureau of Consular Affairs of the U.S. Department of State summarizes the availability of immigrant openings in its *Report of the Visa Office 1998* (2000). The Bureau of Population, Refugees, and Migration, an agency of the State Department, administers U.S. refugee assistance and admissions programs. Its data on refugee admissions ceilings and admissions were used in

developing this book. The Department of State, Department of Justice, and the DHHS collaborate annually to determine the number of refugees to be admitted in the coming year. *Proposed Refugee Admissions for Fiscal Year 2001: Report to Congress* (2000) and *U.S. Refugee Admissions for Fiscal Year 2000: Report to Congress* (1999) discuss the U.S. refugee policy and efforts.

The U.S. Department of Labor (DOL) updates the profile of the amnestied population under IRCA in *Effects of the Immigration Reform and Control Act: Characteristics and Labor Market Behavior of the Legalized Population Five Years Following Legalization* (1996). *Developments in International Migration to the United States: 1998* (1999) is an annual update and review of immigration events. *Findings from the National Agricultural Workers Survey (NAWS) 1997–1998* (2000) reports on the demographic and economic profile of the U.S. agricultural labor force, including undocumented farm workers. The Social Security Administration, an agency of the DHHS, provides data on noncitizens receiving Supplemental Security Income in *SSI Annual Statistical Report, 1999* (2000).

The U.S. Bureau of the Census collects and distributes the nation's statistics. Demographic data from the bureau include *The Foreign Born Population in the United States, March 2000* (2001) and projections of the resident population for the nation, published by the Population Projections Program on the Internet (http://www.census.gov/population/www/projections/popproj.html). The Food and Nutrition Service of the U.S. Department of Agriculture provided information on state-funded food programs.

The U.S. General Accounting Office (GAO), the investigative arm of Congress, has studied many aspects of immigration. Some of the reports used in this publication include *Alien Smuggling: Management and Opera-*

tional Improvements Needed to Address Growing Problem (2000), *Illegal Aliens: Opportunities Exist to Improve the Expedited Removal Process* (2000), *H-1B Foreign Workers: Better Controls Needed to Help Employers and Protect Workers* (2000), *Illegal Immigration: Status of Southwest Border Strategy Implementation* (1999), *Welfare Reform: Public Assistance Benefits Provided to Recently Naturalized Citizens* (1999), *Illegal Aliens: Significant Obstacles to Reducing Unauthorized Alien Employment Exist* (1999), and *Welfare Reform: Many States Continued Some Federal or State Benefits for Immigrants* (1998).

The Congressional Research Service (CRS), an arm of The Library of Congress (Washington, D.C.), is a think tank that works exclusively for members and committees of Congress. CRS publications used in the preparation of the book include *Mexico-U.S. Relations: Issues for the 107th Congress* (K. Larry Storrs, updated May 2001) and *Immigration of Agricultural Guest Workers: Policy, Trends, and Legislative Issues* (Ruth Ellen Wasem and Geoffrey K. Collver, 2001). The National Research Council, an agency of both the National Academy of Sciences and the National Academy of Engineering, published *The New Americans: Economic, Demographic, and Fiscal Effects of Immigration* (1997).

Organizations that support and oppose immigration have published extensive information on various immigration issues. Reports used in this book include *A Fiscal Portrait of the Newest Americans* (Stephen Moore, National Immigration Forum and the Cato Institute, Washington, D.C., 1998), *The Costs of Immigration* (Donald Huddle, Carrying Capacity Network, Washington, D.C., 1993), *Immigrants and Taxes: A Reappraisal of Huddle's "The Costs of Immigration"* (Jeffrey S. Passel, Urban Institute, Washington, D.C., 1994), *Immigration in a Changing Economy: California's Experience* (Kevin F. McCarthy and Georges Vernes, RAND, Washington, D.C., 1997), *Measuring the Fallout: The Cost of the IRCA Amnesty After 10 Years* (David Simcox, Center for Immigration Studies, Washington, D.C., 1997), and *The Costs of Immigration* (Federation for American Immigration Reform, Washington, D.C., 2000). The Gale Group thanks all these organizations for permission to reproduce their data and graphics. As always, The Gale Group thanks the Gallup Organization for permission to use its opinion polls.

Illegal Immigrants in U.S.-Mexico Border Counties: The Costs of Law Enforcement, Criminal Justice, and Emergency Medical Services (Institute for Local Government, University of Arizona, Tucson, AZ, 2001) analyzes the costs incurred by all 24 counties on the southwest border relating to illegal aliens who commit crimes. The research, prepared by Tanis J. Salant (principal investigator, University of Arizona), along with Christine Brenner (University of Texas at El Paso), Nadia Rubaii-Barrett (New Mexico State University), and John R. Weeks (San Diego State University), was conducted on behalf of the U.S./Mexico Border Counties Coalition, composed of the county judges, commissioners, and supervisors of the U.S. counties located on the border with Mexico. The Gale Group thanks the coalition and researchers for permission to reproduce their data and graphics.

INDEX

Page references in italics refer to photographs. References with the letter t following them indicate the presence of a table. The letter f indicates a figure. If more than one table or figure appears on a particular page, the exact item number for the table or figure being referenced is provided.

A

Abraham, Spencer, 97
Adjustment of status for aliens in the U.S., 30, 30*f*
Afghanistan, 60
See also Asia
AFL-CIO, 110
Africa
    adoptions by U.S. citizens, 36*t*
    Diversity Immigrant visas to, 22*t*
    immigration to U.S., 4–7*t*
    naturalized U.S. citizens from, 43*t*–46*t*
    percentage of immigrants from, 31*f*
    refugees from, 58*t*, 60
    slaves from, 1
African Americans, 14*t*, 106
Age of immigrants, 37, 41*t*
    compared to native-born, 84*t*
    public assistance in California, 91
Ageism, 110
Agricultural workers, 44–46
    Bracero Program with Mexico, 80–81
    H-2A visas, 40*t*
    and Immigration Reform and Control Act of 1986 (IRCA), 18
    See also H-2A Temporary Agricultural Worker Program
Aguirre-Aguirre, Immigration and Naturalization Service v., 69–70
Aid to Families with Dependent Children (AFDC), 62
AIDS, 51–52
Airlines, 72
Alien and Sedition Acts of 1798, 1, 2
Aliens in U.S.
    denied entry to U.S., 50–52

sanctions against employers hiring, 17–18
    See also Illegal aliens
Alvares, Kenneth M., 103
Amerasian Homecoming Act of 1987, 56
Amerasian refugees, 57*t*, 58
    See also Refugees
American Association of Engineering Societies, 101, 103
American Baptist Churches v. Thornburgh, 69, 70
American Competitiveness and Workforce Improvement Act, 97
    information technology field, 105, 106
    raising the limit for H-1B visas, 47–48
American Competitiveness in the Twenty-First Century Act, 50
American Electronics Association (AEA), 102
American Indians and Alaska natives, non-Hispanic population, 1, 14*t*
American Society for Training and Development (ASTD), 100
American University, 111
Angola, 21
    See also Africa
Annual limits to number of immigrants, 32, 33*t*
Aristide, Jean-Bertrand, 51–52
Arizona, 89
    See also State statistics
Articles of Confederation of 1778, 1
Ashcroft, John, 21
Asia, 30
    adoptions by U.S. citizens, 35*t*
    Diversity Immigrant visas to, 22*t*
    excluded from immigration to U.S., 5–7
    immigration to U.S. by country, 4*t*–7*t*
    naturalization of immigrants from, 38, 44*t*, 47*t*
    number of immigrants from, 11, 12
    percentage of immigrants from, 31*f*, 39
    poverty level of immigrants from, 94*t*
    refugees from, 58*t*, 59*t*
Asians and Pacific Islanders, non-Hispanic population, 14*t*

Asylum, persons seeking, 63–68
    criteria for granting, 67–68
    by nationality, 66*t*–67*t*
    receiving refugee assistance benefits, 63–65
    reform of process, 65

B

Baby Boomer generation, 84
Bach, Robert, 71–72
Bahá'í faith, 60
Battered brides, 20
Black Americans, non-Hispanic population, 14*t*, 106
Black slaves, 1
Border Patrol, U.S., 74–75, 76*f*, 76*t*
    apprehending illegal aliens, 77*t*
    cost of immigration, 87, 89
    creation of, 80
    sectors and statistics, 76*t*
Borjas, George J., 83
Bracero Program with Mexico, 80–81
Brehm, Frank, 105–106
British West Indies, 81
    See also Caribbean
Brooks, Alfreda M., 87*t*
Bureau of Immigration, *Annual Report* (1910), 8
Burma, 60
    See also Asia
Bush, George W., 30, 75
Byrne, Matthew, 92

C

Calcano-Martinez, Deboris, 27
California, 13
    children in, 90*t*
    cost of services to immigrants, 89
    illegal aliens in, 90–92
    legalized aliens in, 17
    number of foreign-born compared with rest of U.S., 92*t*
    public assistance to immigrants, 85, 90*t*
    refugees in, 58
    as residence for immigrants, 35, 36

Guantánamo Bay, Cuba, 67
Guatemala, 69

H

H-1B program, 46–50, 50f
   arguments against raising the limit on,
     105–111
   arguments for raising limit on, 97–103
H-2 Temporary Agricultural Worker
   Program, 44–46
H-2A Temporary Agricultural Worker
   Program, 45–46, 49t
Haiti, 51–52, 56
Henderson v. Mayor of the City of New York,
   4
Hernandez-Montiel, Geovanni, 68
Higher education, information technology
   field, 101, 106
Hispanic American population, 14t
   See also Latin America
Hollman, Frederick W., 13
Home ownership of refugees, 64t
Homosexuals, 68
Hong Kong, 11
   See also Asia
Huddle, Donald, 83
Hungary, 11
   See also Europe

I

IEEE-USA. *See* Institute of Electrical and
   Electronics Engineers—United States of
   America (IEEE-USA)
IIRIRA. *See* Illegal Immigration Reform and
   Immigrant Responsibility Act of 1996
   (IIRIRA)
Illegal aliens, 9–10, 71–82
   adjustment of status, 30
   apprehension of, 77–79, 77t, 78f, 79t
   in California, 90–92
   enforcement of immigration laws, 74–76
   estimates of number in U.S., 71–74
   and the Immigration Reform and Control
     Act of 1986 (IRCA), 15–18, 93–94
   North American Free Trade Agreement
     (NAFTA), 81–82
   number in U.S. by state, 73t
   by region of origin, 74t
   relations between U.S. and Mexico,
     80–82
   smuggling of, 79–80
Illegal Immigration Reform and Immigrant
   Responsibility Act of 1996 (IIRIRA),
   23–26, 50
   adding more Border Patrol agents, 74
   adjusted by the Nicaraguan Adjustment
     and Central American Relief Act
     (NACARA), 70
   deportation of illegal aliens, 79
   mandating an automated tracking system
     for nonimmigrants, 72
Illinois, 13
   public assistance to immigrants, 85
   as residence for immigrants, 36
   See also State statistics
IMMACT. *See* Immigration Act of 1990
   (IMMACT)

Immigration
   foreign-born population, 11–13
   legal, 29f
   persons denied entry, 9
   by region of origin, 4t–7t
   yearly totals to U.S., 3t
Immigration Act of 1917, 9
Immigration Act of 1924, 7, 9, 53
Immigration Act of 1990 (IMMACT), 20–21
   annual limit of immigrants, 32
   H-1B admissions, 47
   naturalization process, 37–38
Immigration Marriage Fraud Amendments
   of 1986, 18, 20
Immigration and Nationality Act of 1952,
   10, 11, 53
Immigration and Nationality Act
   Amendments of 1965, 10, 39, 53
Immigration and Nationality Act
   Amendments of 1976, 10–11
Immigration and Nationality Act
   Amendments of 1978, 11
Immigration and Naturalization Service
   (INS), 10
   adjustment of status procedures, 30
   arresting illegal aliens, 24–25
   automated tracking system for
     nonimmigrants, 72
   and California's illegal aliens, 90–91
   Citizenship USA, 41–42
   in court cases, 68–70
   deporting illegal aliens, 77, 79
   enforcement of immigration laws, 74–75
   estimates of illegal aliens, 71–72
   gender-based persecution, 68
   Green Card Replacement Program,
     40–41
   H-1B visas, 111
   inspections on southwest border, 75
   worksite investigations, 27t
*Immigration and Naturalization Service v.
   Aguirre-Aguirre*, 69–70
*Immigration and Naturalization Service v.
   Cardoza-Fonseca*, 68–69
Immigration Reform and Control Act of
   1986 (IRCA), 15–18, 40
   affecting apprehensions of illegal aliens,
     77
   affecting illegal immigration, 72, 74
   applications for legalization, 16t
   boosting the number of immigrants, 29
   costs of, 93–94, 95t
   electronic verification of employee
     eligibility, 25
   legalized adults by gender, place of
     origin, and age at arrival, 16t
   public assistance given to naturalized
     citizens under, 85–86, 86t
Income, 64t, 93
India, 32
   See also Asia
Information Technology Association of
   America (ITAA), 100
Information technology workers, 49, 97–111
   See also H-1B program
INS. *See* Immigration and Naturalization
   Service (INS)

Institute of Electrical and Electronics
   Engineers—United States of America
   (IEEE-USA), 107
Internal Security Act of 1950, 10
Iran, 60
   See also Asia
Iraq, 60
   See also Asia
IRCA. *See* Immigration Reform and Control
   Act of 1986 (IRCA)
ITAA. *See* Information Technology
   Association of America

J

Jackson, Keith, 106
Jails holding immigrants, 28
Jamaica, 46, 81
   See also Caribbean
Japan, 7, 42, 80
   See also Asia
Jefferson, Thomas, 2
Job opportunities, 92

K

Kasinga, Fauziya, 68
Kennedy, Anthony M., 70
Kennedy, Edward, 20
Kennedy, John F., 10
Know-Nothing political party, 2
Kosovo, refugees from, 61
Kostek, Paul J., 107–109

L

Laos, 60
Lariviere, Richard W., 102
Latin America, 11
   Diversity Immigrant visas to, 22t
   employment status of refugees from, 62
   involvement in multinational anti-
     smuggling efforts, 80
   poverty levels of immigrants from, 94t
   refugees from, 58t, 61
   See also Central America; South America
Lautenberg Amendment, 55, 61
Lazarus, Emma, 1
Lebanon, 11
   See also Asia
Legal Immigration and Family Equity Act
   (LIFE), 28, 30
Legalized adults, 17t
   See also Immigration Reform and
     Control Act of 1986 (IRCA)
Legislation concerning immigration, 4–5,
   15–28
   Amerasian Homecoming Act of 1987, 56
   American Competitiveness in the
     Twenty-First Century Act, 50
   American Competitiveness and
     Workforce Improvement Act, 47–48
   enforcement of, 74–76
   Foreign Operations Appropriations Act of
     1990, 55
   Illegal Immigration Reform and
     Immigrant Responsibility Act of 1996
     (IIRIRA), 23–26
   Immigration Act of 1917, 9